Antwerp

Louvain

RUSSELS

Liège

U

umont

Châlons

Ba
8

Marne

Chaumo
3

Dijo
6

Besançon

Le

ngres

AND

Aix-la-
Chapelle

FAT DIVISION

Meuse

RGON

Ve
Z

château: first headquarters for
Correspondents.

2 Gondrecourt: where the First Division
trained in 1917.

3 Chaumont: Pershing's main headquarters.

4 Arracourt-Einville: where the 1st Div.
went into line in Oct., 1917.

5 Besançon-Le Valdahon: where the
artillery trained (Peggy Hull).

6 Dijon: Hôtel de la Cloche; bake ovens;
Tour.

for St. Mihiel

Hdq. for Meuse-
ct. - Nov, 1918.

q. for Montdidier
v.

q. for the French

Château-Thierry,
ns, June-July, 1918.

ns: where correspon-
night ride from Beauvais.

where correspondents
train for Paris.

is-Morgan-Ashmead
edition in Sept., 1914.

AMERICAN REPORTERS

ON THE WESTERN FRONT, 1914-1918

The morning line-up of automobiles outside American press headquarters in Neufchâteau in early spring, 1918; caravan of correspondents about to take off for Gondrecourt training area, or Le Valdahon artillery camp.

D
632
.C72
1980

AMERICAN REPORTERS

ON THE WESTERN FRONT

1914-1918

by Emmet Crozier

GREENWOOD PRESS, PUBLISHERS
WESTPORT, CONNECTICUT

Library of Congress Cataloging in Publication Data

Crozier, Emmet.
    American reporters on the Western Front, 1914-1918.

    Reprint of the ed. published by Oxford University
Press, New York.
    Bibliography: p.
    Includes index.
    1. European War, 1914-1918--Journalists.
2. Journalists--United States--History. I. Title.
[D632.C72 1980]   940.3'15'097   80-19400
ISBN 0-313-22655-5 (lib. bdg.)

Reprinted with the permission of Oxford University Press, Inc.

Reprinted in 1980 by Greenwood Press
A division of Congressional Information Service, Inc.
88 Post Road West, Westport, Connecticut 06881

Printed in the United States of America

10 9 8 7 6 5 4 3 2 1

To the Five Runaway Correspondents

LINCOLN EYRE
FREDERICK A. SMITH
C. C. LYON
HERBERT COREY
GEORGE SELDES

Whose Resourcefulness and Courage in a Lost Cause
Served the Best Traditions of American Journalism

The author is indebted to a number of publishers and authors for permission to use extracts and other material from copyrighted books bearing on World War I journalism:

BARNARD, Chester Inman: *Paris War Days*, Little, Brown and Company, Boston, 1914. CALDWELL, Major General Sir Charles E.: *Life and Diaries of Field-Marshal Sir Henry Wilson*, Charles Scribner's Sons, New York, 1927. COBB, Irvin S.: *Paths of Glory*, George H. Doran, New York, 1915. Used by permission of Laura Baker Cobb, widow of Irvin S. Cobb, c/o Buhler, King & Buhler, attorneys, 274 Madison Avenue, New York. DAVIS, Richard Harding: *With the Allies*, Charles Scribner's Sons, New York, 1914. FORREST, Wilbur: *Behind the Front Page*, Appleton-Century-Crofts, New York, 1935. FORTESCUE, Granville R.: *Front Line and Deadline*, G. P. Putnam's Sons, New York, 1937. ——— *At The Front with Three Armies*, Andrew Melrose, Ltd., London, 1914. GIBBS, Sir Philip Hamilton: *Now It Can Be Told*, Harper & Brothers, New York and London, 1920. GIBSON, Hugh: *A Journal from Our Legation in Belgium*, copyright 1917 by Doubleday & Co., Inc., New York. Reprinted by permission of the publisher. HARBORD, Lt. Gen. James G.: *Leaves from a War Diary*, Dodd, Mead & Company, New York, 1925. Reprinted by permission of the publisher. IRWIN, Will: *The Making of a Reporter*, G. P. Putnam's Sons, New York, 1942. MILLER, Webb: *I Found No Peace*, Simon and Schuster, New York, 1936. MOWRER, Paul Scott: *The House of Europe*, Houghton, Mifflin Co., Boston, 1945. Used by permission of Mr. Mowrer. PALMER, Frederick: *With My Own Eyes*, Bobbs-Merrill, Indianapolis, 1933. Copyright 1933 by the Bobbs-Merrill Company, Inc. SHEPHARD, William G.: *Confessions of a War Correspondent*, Harper & Brothers, New York, 1917. THOMAS, W. Beach: *A Traveller in News*, Chapman & Hall, Ltd., London, 1925.

FOREWORD

This book owes a certain debt to a man named Edgar M. Moore. He and I worked together years ago on the old *New York Globe*. At that time—late summer and fall of 1918—I wanted very much to go to France as a war correspondent. The struggle was approaching its crisis and other newspapermen were overseas writing of the great American advance in the Meuse-Argonne, but I was tied to a rewrite desk in an untidy New York newspaper office. My only opportunity to write about the war was piecing together the odd fragments Moore brought into the *Globe* city room.

Moore was a leg man, a sort of roving reporter who made his living picking up scraps of news about the war, but he could not write. He used to come to my desk about nine o'clock in the morning with his notes on a folded sheaf of copy paper. If I was busy he would draw up a chair and wait. I see him clearly through the years—a thin, neat, worried man about fifty years old, wearing a blue serge suit and a polka-dot bow tie; always freshly shaved and smelling of soap. There was something uncertain and apologetic about him, as if he didn't quite belong in a newspaper office. But if I had time and would listen, he would unburden himself. He had been a guide, croupier, waiter, performer in a water carnival, itinerant banjo player; now he was a scavenger for war news in hotel lobbies and along the New York waterfront, and he depended on me to pull his stuff together and get it into print.

'Well, Ed,' I would say, 'what have you got for us today?' From his notes on his knee Moore would proceed to tell me what he had picked up on his rounds. It amounted to the backwash of war—adventures of American doughboys in France, human interest stories from hospitals and prison camps, tales of trench life and enemy atrocities. The material came from a variety of sources, all second hand. He claimed he struck up acquaintance with men in uniform back from the war zone and got them talking about what had happened to them and what they had heard—human glimpses and sidelights which the cable news ignored.

Several of Moore's stories dealt with an American soldier called Tennessee Slim. This backwoods character refused to wear shoes and chafed at military discipline, but his aim with a rifle was the wonder of the regiment. He had been known to knock the pipe out a German sentry's mouth at 300 yards. At night he would wander out in no-man's land, bringing back prisoners, a German officer or two, machine guns, souvenirs. When not engaged in these one-man raids he passed his time polishing his rifle or playing his guitar and singing plaintive mountain songs. Moore had picked up half a dozen of Tennessee Slim's backwoods ballads and some of the verses went into each piece I wrote about him.

At the time I must have known some of his tales were contrived but if I had misgivings, conscience was stilled by the thought that Moore was supporting an invalid wife and needed my help to keep his job. Besides, the *Globe*'s city editor liked the stories. Finally, it was my only chance, albeit vicarious, to be a war correspondent.

Five or six years after the war I met Moore in front of a Broadway theater. He borrowed five dollars. I said: 'Tell me honestly, Ed, where did you get all that war stuff you used to bring in to the *Globe?*' He looked at me quizzically for a moment, as if wondering how much I suspected. Then he laughed a dry little laugh.

He told me he used to get on the Ninth Avenue L at Twenty-third Street about 8:30 in the morning, often without any idea for a story. As the local train rolled downtown toward the newspaper office, necessity set his imagination to work. Under the spur of having to deliver a fresh tale of the war to the *Globe,* he would scribble random ideas on paper. Usually, by the time the train reached Chambers Street something had germinated. On two or three occasions, Moore said, he had ridden past his regular stop to Rector Street—once all the way to the Battery—before getting an inspiration for the day's story.

I could not, at that late date, cry fraud and outrage. On the other hand, it was not possible to accept his disclosure with philosophical detachment, for I had been a partner in the questionable business. Together we had played a shabby trick on *Globe* readers and on the integrity of journalism. So the matter lay, a small burr on my conscience, until some months after the publication of *Yankee Reporters: 1861-65* in 1956. Then a letter from Otto P. Higgins brought the affair once more in focus. Higgins, who had been the

Kansas City Star's correspondent in France in 1918, insisted that
the newspapermen of World War I were as varied, resourceful, and
worthy of historical study as the bearded journalists of the Civil
War. This old friend of *Kansas City Star* days volunteered to help
organize such a study, and as the matter hesitated in correspondence between us, suddenly I saw it as an opportunity to straighten
out that old business at the *Globe*. Now I might discover how the
authentic newspaper correspondents worked, what their problems
were, how they lived and squabbled and risked their lives and
fought the censors in France, while Moore and I were spinning our
nonsense in New York.

It seemed impractical to attempt a comprehensive survey of all
World War I newspaper correspondence, covering all theaters of
the great conflict and all phases of journalistic activity in a single
volume. The plan for this book, therefore, (as was that for *Yankee
Reporters: 1861-65*) has been selective rather than all-inclusive.
I have dealt mainly with those personalities and events that interested me as a working journalist rather than the broader aspects
which might engage the professional scholar. The work concentrates
largely on American journalists and some British contemporaries
who followed the struggle on the Western Front. The Russian campaigns, the Dardanelles failure, Alpine warfare between Austria
and Italy, Allenby's campaign against the Turks in Arabia were
remote from the main arena of conflict and imposed special problems of communication and censorship outside the scope of this
work.

The most valuable sources for the study within the limits described were the surviving correspondents, now a diminishing Old
Guard. Without their help the work would have lacked something
in depth, color, and authenticity. Some of them, indeed, made the
project their own, giving unselfishly of their time and memories.

The late Frederick Palmer, in failing health, put aside his own
work in the fall of 1957 to re-examine those events of 1914-18 in
which he played so large a part. Veteran correspondent, sole American journalist to be accredited to the British Expeditionary Force
in 1914, commissioned by General Pershing to organize the Press
Section (G-2-D) of the A.E.F. in 1917 and subsequently attached

to the General Staff, his experience in World War I transcended that of any other newspaper man. From his mellowed perspective and his memories he gave generously to this study.

Special acknowledgment also must be made of the assistance of Thomas M. Johnson. This veteran *New York Sun* correspondent and military historian made available a large file of notes and correspondence relating to the U.S. journalists in France in 1917 and 1918. His friendly co-operation over many months was expressed in letters, notes, and helpful suggestions.

Fred Ferguson took time from his busy desk at N.E.A. (Newspaper Enterprise Association) to recall his journalistic adventures with the A.E.F. in France and recount the circumstances which gave the United Press its scoop at St. Mihiel.

Westbrook Pegler, youngest of all accredited correspondents in 1917, recalled the early days at Neufchâteau, Gondrecourt, and Le Valdahon and with characteristic forthrightness reviewed the circumstances which embroiled him with the Army brass and caused General Pershing to request his replacement.

Reginald Wright Kauffman, only surviving member of a distinguished trio (the others Wythe Williams and Heywood Broun) whose credentials were revoked by the U.S. Army, gave the background of his controversy with the A.E.F. and of the organization formed by the corespondents to fight military control of the news.

Stanley W. Prenosil, Associated Press correspondent who accompanied the first convoy of U.S. troops across the Atlantic, recalled the arrival at St. Nazaire and the lucky break which gave A.P. the first story of that historic voyage.

Otto P. Higgins not only gave the work much of its early impetus but helped continuously to round up stray correspondents and gather material.

George Seldes gave details of the affair of the runaway correspondents, first to enter Germany after the Armistice, an expedition which annoyed G-2-D and pained the less adventurous newspapermen.

The list is long. Among others, Wilbur Forrest, Roy Howard, Paul Scott Mowrer, and the late Percy Noel of the *Chicago Daily News,* Mark Watson, military editor of the *Baltimore Sun,* and Burnet Hershey made significant contributions from their wartime experiences and earned the author's gratitude.

The Army's G-2-D files (1917-18) in the United States Archives in Washington afforded a variety of documentary material—letters, memoranda, reports, miscellaneous records and fragments—dealing with newspaper correspondents, censorship, etc. Much of the general research, covering the published works of World War I journalists, books on censorship and propaganda, war diaries, and historical studies touching the theme, was done at the Yale University Library in New Haven, Connecticut. The Library of Congress and the New York Public Library were explored for related material, and the library of the New-York Historical Society yielded a monumental file of scrapbooks containing newspaper reports and editorials for the entire war period. Representative American newspapers for 1914 through 1918 were scanned at the Yale Library and the New York Public Library's newspaper repository on West Twenty-sixth Street. The British Museum in London yielded some published material and War Office reports not available in America; *The Times* (London) and the *Daily Telegraph* for the World War I years were studied at the British Museum's newspaper library at Colindale, in North London.

A journey through France enabled the writer to discover the principal scenes of the correspondents' activity but the years since 1918 have obliterated most of their traces. In Paris the building which housed the busy press center at 10 rue Ste. Anne had become a hotel. The Hôtel de la Providence at Neufchâteau had been converted into a home furnishing store; only an elderly garage attendant recalled the correspondents' second floor mess and the daily procession of Press cars departing for Gondrecourt. The Hôtel de la Cloche at Dijon and the little Sirène at Meaux are much as they were forty years ago when the newspapermen pounded their typewriters, ate, drank, and made love in their friendly shelter. But the white-haired *grande dame* who owns the Cloche could not remember the occasion when an I.N.S. correspondent disturbed the dining room decorum by hurling bread pellets at his roommate, and no one at the Sirène could recall the dramatic early morning departure of the correspondents for Nancy and St. Mihiel. An elderly lady who presides over the laundry at the Hotel Angleterre recalled the hubbub that stirred the establishment when the Press Corps arrived in Nancy, but no one could be found to point out where the correspondents worked during the assault on St. Mihiel. At Bar-le-Duc, no tablet or plaque marked that dim, untidy store room where the newsmen wrote their tales of the Lost Battalion. This was not so strange, because it all happened forty years ago and since then, mankind had fought another war.

E. C.

Bethel, Connecticut
July, 1959

CONTENTS

AMERICAN REPORTERS

ON THE WESTERN FRONT, 1914-1918

I

PANIC ON THE BOURSE

In midsummer, 1914, when Mme. Henriette Caillaux was brought to trial in Paris for killing Gaston Calmette with a pistol, 142 newspaper correspondents crowded into the courtroom in the Palais de Justice. This concentration of journalists from many countries—perhaps the greatest assemblage of the press since Victoria's Diamond Jubilee eighteen years before—reflected extraordinary public interest in the sensational case. A good part of the civilized world, recently distracted by the assassination of the Archduke Francis Ferdinand of Austria at Sarajevo, now found its attention centered on the stuffy Paris courtroom where the wife of a former Premier of France disclosed the circumstances which led her to shoot the influential editor of *Le Figaro*. The trial involved M. Caillaux's policies as Minister of Finance, his divorce from his first wife, a packet of stolen letters, international intrigue, *l'amour,* and French politics at the cabinet level.

Since that afternoon in March when she had called at M. Calmette's office and fired six shots at close range, with fatal consequences, Mme. Caillaux had been confined in St. Lazare Prison. Awaiting the processes of justice she read Balzac's *Femme de Trente Ans* and, the newspapermen learned, ate a dozen gooseberries the first thing every morning.

In the courtroom, from the special section reserved for the press, the reporters looked quizzically at the crowded benches of spectators, some of whom, the gossips said, paid $200 for their seats. Half a dozen American journalists had been assigned places in the rear row against the wall. Unable to observe the by-play at the counsel's table or catch the subtleties of French justice at close range, they had nevertheless a good view of the whole scene—the dais where the judges looked down, the prisoner in the dock, the rows of standees around the rear walls, and, at one side of the judges' bench behind an iron grille, a flutter of fans and feminine finery where the wives of government officials sat in their summer dresses, bright-eyed, listening.

Only France, with its unique talent for politics, drama, and *l'amour,* could fit so much in one small courtroom. Some of the journalists complained about the closed windows, which, while keeping out street noises, also excluded fresh air. Attendants finally were prevailed on to open two of the seven small windows. The selection of a jury consumed little more than an hour.

By Saturday, July 25, in midsummer heat and tension, the Caillaux case had unraveled most of its tangled skein. Joseph Caillaux had made a number of impassioned speeches defending his fiscal policies and his honor. A duel had narrowly been averted. M. Caillaux's former wife, now Mme. Gueydan, had opened her handbag on the witness stand and produced the stolen letters, offering them not to the prosecution but to Maître Labori, Mme. Caillaux's counsel. Mme. Caillaux, in a simple black dress with white collar and cuffs, fainted.

As the hands of the courtroom clock pointed to 11:30, Wythe Williams, Paris correspondent of the *New York Times,* became aware of a small commotion in the crowded aisle nearby. A court attendant was elbowing a passage through the spectators in the rear, making way for a reporter for *Le Petit Parisien.* The newcomer, a fat, perspiring man, had arrived to replace a colleague, who rubbed his cramped fingers as he departed for lunch. As the new arrival pushed forward to his seat, Williams overheard him remark to an acquaintance in the press section: 'There is a panic on the Bourse.'

The rumor caused a mild stir among the newspapermen. Since the terms of the Austrian ultimatum to Serbia were announced the day before, the crisis growing out of the assassination of the Archduke Francis Ferdinand and his wife, the Duchess of Hohenberg, at Sarajevo in June had assumed grave proportions. Now it entered the Caillaux courtroom in the stage whisper of a perspiring reporter. *A panic on the Bourse.* An English journalist seated next to Williams said: 'The Austrian demands on Serbia have got the bankers scared.' As the report passed from row to row in the press section, the reporters found their attention straying from the court-room maneuvers over Joseph Caillaux's love letters to the larger arena of world affairs. It was as if all the courtroom windows suddenly had been thrown open and the newspapermen could hear above the drone of the advocates' objections and the summer noises from the streets, the beat of a distant drum.

They talked about it at the luncheon recess. The evening editions were already on the streets: PANIC ON THE BOURSE; HARSH TERMS MAKE ULTIMATUM TO SERBS IMPOSSIBLE TO ACCEPT. All through the sultry afternoon, the pencils of the newspaper correspondents followed the court proceedings mechanically, but the Caillaux murder case had been placed in new diminishing perspective.

At the *New York Times* bureau that night, Williams learned from his youthful assistant, Walter Duranty, that the selling wave on the Bourse had been started by a financial house with connections in Vienna. It was the same banking group which two years before had broken the share market and made millions just before the onset of the last Balkan War. Those Austrian financiers must have had confidential information from Vienna that the Serbian reply would be rejected. This could have only one outcome: War.

Williams went over his notes on the Caillaux case and cut the long cable file he had planned to a scant column. The two newspapermen telephoned the American Embassy and friends at the Foreign Office for guidance in evaluating the crisis. While their scraps of information and conjectures were being assembled for the night's cable file to New York, Williams and Duranty heard shouting in the streets. Demonstrations were not uncommon in excitable Paris; recently the night air had been stirred by noisy groups concerned with issues in the Caillaux case. But when they went to the front windows and listened, the newspapermen caught a new and deeper roar. The street outside was thronged with demonstrators and their angry chanting rose until it filled the summer night: '*A Berlin! A Berlin! Alsace! A Berlin!*' Something of that, too, went into the Saturday night cable to the *New York Times*.

At the *Daily Telegraph* office in London Sunday afternoon, Managing Editor John Merry Le Sage read the bulletins from the continental wires and sent for his most experienced war correspondent. Ellis Ashmead-Bartlett had gone to Maidenhead for the week end, but at Mr. Le Sage's telephone summons he quit the boating party on the Thames and hurried back to Fleet Street.

The news bulletins on the managing editor's desk told of the European crisis. From Berlin, Vienna, and Paris the telegraph relayed the tidings: *War!* Mr. Le Sage told Ashmead-Bartlett to pack his bags and catch the nine o'clock express from Charing Cross for Vienna.

His wide experience covering affairs on the Continent had impressed on the *Telegraph* correspondent the importance of a suitable wardrobe. By the time he had finished assembling his effects in his flat in Marlborough Chambers, Ashmead-Bartlett had packed two trunks and five suitcases with clothes, including formal wear (with top hat), riding pants and boots, and suitable accessories. As he climbed aboard the Vienna express at Charing Cross, he may have reflected that not only was he the first correspondent to quit London for the theater of action, but surely the most completely outfitted for war.

The chief European correspondent of the *Chicago Daily News* was a serious young man from the Middle West named Paul Scott Mowrer. His headquarters were Paris, but late in July he went to Liverpool, on instructions from the managing editor, to meet a delegation of aldermen and other distinguished citizens from Chicago. The group was visiting Europe to study the railway terminals in all the great cities with a view to finding a solution for Chicago's haphazard pattern of antiquated stations. Just before embarking the delegation had been commissioned to undertake another civic study for Chicago in European cities—a survey of the regulation and control of prostitution. Mowrer was not happy about leaving his post in Paris but the junket of Chicagoans was important to the Middle West. Dutifully he trailed after the Chicagoans in Liverpool, Manchester, and London, filling his notebook with railway statistics.

With the news of Austrian mobilization, Mowrer quit the Chicago party in London and hurried to Paris. His press colleagues agreed that the signs were ominous. The Associated Press had sent Edward Schuler to Vienna. He reported all Austria clamoring for war.

The Chicago mission crossed the Channel and arrived in Paris.

They inspected the Gare St. Lazare, the Gare du Nord, the Gare de l'Est, and the Gare de Lyon. As they were embarking on a study of Paris brothels, the chairman of the delegation, a prominent Chicago lawyer, consulted Mowrer about the railroad reservations to Vienna. Mowrer, wondering whether the Chicagoans read the newspapers, said they'd better cancel the trip to Vienna; the railroads would be demoralized by mobilization.

The man from Chicago said: 'A local affair; surely the main lines will be running on schedule.'

'Not likely,' Mowrer said. 'It looks like war.'

The Chicagoan dismissed this with a gesture. War? Do not be absurd. There will be no war; it is economically impracticable.

The man from Chicago stalked off to his hotel. Two days later, Mowrer saw him again. He was packing his bags.

Where now? Mowrer asked.

London and home.

Then it *is* war?

Oh, yes, of course. Haven't you seen? The Stock Exchanges in New York and London are both closed.

At 7 A.M. on Tuesday, July 28, Ashmead-Bartlett arrived in Vienna with his trunks and bags and went to the Hotel Bristol. Refreshed by a bath and breakfast, he called on Herr Konreid, Vienna correspondent of the *Daily Telegraph* and editor of a local newspaper. War was inevitable, Konreid said, but it would be futile for Ashmead-Bartlett to try to cover it from the Austrian side. England was almost certain to be involved and the London journalist would likely be interned as an enemy alien. Even if he escaped imprisonment, censorship would make it almost impossible to get his dispatches back to England. Already the telegraph service was interrupted; the money order Mr. Le Sage promised had not arrived, nor was there any message from London. Ashmead-Bartlett persuaded Herr Konreid to advance him fifty pounds gold on a draft on the *Daily Telegraph* and at 4:50 P.M. got his trunks and bags on board a train for Budapest, which seemed a likelier spot from which to cover the war.

That same afternoon in Paris, Mme. Caillaux walked down the steps of the Palais de Justice and smiled wanly for the photographers as she climbed in a taxicab on the Place Dauphine, escorted by her distinguished husband. Of the 142 newspaper correspondents assigned to cover her trial, fewer than 50 were on hand to hear the jury's verdict: not guilty. Her acquittal for the murder of Gaston Calmette did not pass unnoticed, yet it was neither the sensation nor the triumph it might have been, for Russia had mobilized and Austria had formally declared war on Serbia.

At Semlin the next day, Martin H. Donohue, correspondent of the *London Chronicle,* watched the opening of hostilities and sent a brief dispatch from the telegraph office:

Three monitors took up their positions at the confluence of the Danube and the Save, but close to shore, and opened fire. The monitors' guns were directed on the Belgrade barracks and no pains were taken to avoid hitting the public buildings, some of which were seen, even from here, to be damaged. The Serbians made no reply to the Austrian gunfire, but have destroyed the railway bridge between Semlin and Belgrade. The bombardment was bloodless so far as the Imperial forces were concerned.

This was the only news dispatch to reach the outside world. A short time after Donohue's message had cleared the wires, Austrian authorities seized the telegraph office and placed the *Chronicle* correspondent under arrest. He was held for twenty-four hours, and then expelled from the country.

Journalists on holiday in Switzerland hurried to Paris. From Scotland and Scandinavia vacationing editors and reporters came back to Fleet Street like homing pigeons. Groups of newspaper proprietors got together; combinations were formed to share the costs of telegraph tolls and motor hire. War! The news vendors cried extras in the streets and editorial rooms were filled with the clatter of typewriters, telephones ringing, and vast confusion.

Some echoes of all this stirring reached the little seaside village of Knokke, near Ostend, where an American named Granville Fortescue was passing the summer with his family. Fortescue was a soldier of fortune with sufficient income to live abroad and avoid regular employment. Some of his friends were war correspondents.

Seeing an opportunity to join the glamorous profession, he sent off telegrams to the *New York Tribune* and *Collier's Weekly,* offering his services. Neither replied. He put in a telephone call to the *Daily Telegraph* in London and inquired for his friend Ashmead-Bartlett. Ashmead-Bartlett, they told him, had already started for the front and was now at Vienna. (Actually, he was on a train for Bucharest.)

Temporarily baffled, Fortescue decided to send his family across the Channel to London, so that he might pursue his career with more freedom. There were three small daughters, one only a few weeks old, a brother-in-law, and, of course, Mrs. Fortescue. To transport baggage, baby's crib and perambulator, milk bottles, wife, brother-in-law, and other family freight to Ostend, Fortescue hired a trolley car. The journey from Knokke to the Ostend pier was accomplished Saturday afternoon. After putting the family on the Channel boat, Fortescue took a night train for Brussels.

Some caprice of fate brought him at nine o'clock Sunday morning to the doorway of the United States Ministry in the rue de Billiard. At that moment the porter whose duty it was to announce visitors was involved in a discussion with a Walloon peasant. Fortescue could not understand much of what was being said at first but he caught the term '*Allemand*' in the colloquy. The doorkeeper seemed slow to believe what the countryman was telling him; the Walloon persisted. He pointed off to the east and after the fashion of simple folk, embellished his tale with pantomime. Fortescue listened and asked questions. When he entered the ministry a few minutes later, the encounter at the doorstep had given new impetus to his plan. Hugh Gibson, Secretary of the Legation, remembered him from Washington, called him 'Forty,' and seemed glad to see him. Gibson needed help to take care of the sudden inrush of panicky American tourists and asked the newcomer to join the volunteer staff. But Fortescue said 'No' quite firmly and, finding the ministry telephone, put in a call for London.

The name Granville Fortescue might have come from an old playbill. There were overtones of the theater in almost everything he did. Who else would bring his family and goods to the Ostend pier in a privately chartered trolley car? He first disclosed his penchant for the unusual as a sophomore at the University of

Pennsylvania when, at the suggestion of a Hearst newspaperman, he quit his undergraduate studies to deliver a sword to an obscure general leading revolutionaries against the Spanish tyranny in Cuba. This was in 1897 when the Hearst organization clamored for United States intervention against Spain in the Caribbean. Naturally the affair of the sword involved Fortescue in the Spanish-American War. He seems to have played a part in the storming of San Juan Hill and won Theodore Roosevelt's notice, for after some Army service in the Philippines and a course at the Staff College at Fort Leavenworth, he was selected by President Roosevelt as one of his White House military aides. At the outbreak of the Russo-Japanese War in 1904 he went to the Far East as United States military observer. An unfriendly commentator has attributed Fortescue's opportunities to a wealthy and politically influential relative, but the young man must have had some gifts of his own, a certain vital energy and warmth of personality.

In the Orient, young Fortescue, apparently headed for an Army career, got a glimpse of a career he liked better. Sharing the observation posts overlooking Port Arthur were several American war correspondents—Gerald Morgan, Richard Harding Davis (Fortescue had known him casually in Cuba), Willard Straight, Jack London, John Fox, Jr., Guy Scull, John Barry, and Robert Dunn. The English correspondents were Ellis Ashmead-Bartlett, Frederic Villiers, and Bennett Burleigh. He got to know these relaxed, sharp-eyed gentlemen of the press and was struck by their ease of manner and expensive tastes. Occasionally he contributed his own superior military knowledge to their correspondence. Ashmead-Bartlett became one of his special friends, and on one occasion, he got the *Telegraph* man's copy past the Japanese censorship and expedited to London by enclosing it in the U.S. diplomatic pouch, a strategem which did not endear him to the other correspondents when they found out about it.

In 1907 Gerald Morgan, the *New York Tribune* correspondent, invited Fortescue to accompany him on an expedition to explore the headwaters of the Orinoco River. Two years later, during a European sojourn, he got a telegram from Ashmead-Bartlett which led to his first service as a war correspondent.

He was staying with Mrs. Fortescue at the Hotel Splendide in Aix-les-Bains. As he relates the episode in his memoirs, something of Fortescue's lively personality and a good deal of his literary style emerge:

Lying on the bleached table-cloth a blue envelope caught my attention. A telegram. Immediately I felt cold, as if someone had opened a door letting in a chill wind. A premonition? I tore open the telegram:

LONDON, JAN. 8, 1909

CAPT. GRANVILLE FORTESCUE

HOTEL SPLENDIDE, AIX-LES-BAINS, FR.

ARE YOU GAME FOR RIFF WAR IN MOROCCO? STANDARD WANTS CORRESPONDENT, CAN PLACE YOU. IF GAME MEET ME IN MÁLAGA WHERE THE GRAPES COME FROM.

ELLIS ASHMEAD-BARTLETT

I looked about at the luxury of the room. Again I glanced at the newspaper, threw it down. I clipped the top off my egg sharply. I shook in salt, pepper, began eating English fashion. What about Dorothy? I'd promised to motor up in the Alps with her. Heigh-ho! I barked at the valet. Madrid express, wagon-lit, *ce soir*.

From the premonitory chill which seized him at sight of the telegram and the suspense and significance he attached to it one would suppose that Ashmead-Bartlett's message would lead to some extraordinary crisis, perhaps to a tragic denouement. Actually all that happened was that Fortescue got on a train, went off to Morocco, and passed several weeks pleasantly enough with his friend Ashmead-Bartlett, recounting his adventures among the dunes for the *London Standard*. The real significance lay in the fact that for the first time he was able to see some of his own words in print, and, as for many, it was a heady experience. Thereafter, he wanted very much to be a war correspondent.

The call to London connected Fortescue with Harry Lawson, editor of the *Daily Telegraph*. He told Lawson who he was and urged him to listen carefully to what he was about to say. He was calling from the American Ministry in Brussels. A German military force had crossed the Belgian frontier early that morning and was scouting the countryside north of Liége. Mr. Lawson's voice was skeptical. How did Fortescue know this? The American said he had learned about it from a Walloon peasant. Two German staff cars had passed his farm near Visé early Sunday morning. He recognized the officers' uniforms and flags; they asked questions, studied maps. The Walloon was so worried at the encounter that he had hurried by train to Brussels to consult his brother, doorkeeper at the American Ministry. While Fortescue added details, the telephone connection was broken. He jiggled the hook and tried to get the editor again, but the operator told him that service to London had been temporarily suspended.

Fortescue next heard from Lawson Monday night. The London editor's voice was querulous: the *Telegraph's* story about the German's crossing the border had been denied by the Foreign Office. Belgian neutrality had not been violated, British officialdom insisted, and no other newspaper or agency carried the report. The *Telegraph's* Brussels correspondent knew nothing about it.

Fortescue stuck to his story. The Foreign Office, he insisted, might be lying or merely uninformed. The Walloon peasant had neither the imagination nor the motive to make the tale up. Twenty-four hours later Mr. Lawson was on the telephone again, apology in his voice. Britain had just declared war against Germany for *violating the neutrality of Belgium* . . . the German Army was moving across the frontier, and the *Daily Telegraph,* thanks to Fortescue, had beaten the whole world. In this happy mood, Mr. Lawson gave Fortescue a job as war correspondent for the *Daily Telegraph,* and his new career was fairly launched. He would have, for the present at least, an unlimited expense account. Nothing was said about salary.

There was one small catch in it. Mr. Lawson suggested Fortescue call on William Maxwell, the *Daily Telegraph's* regular correspondent in Brussels, and discuss how they might work together. When Fortescue went to see Maxwell at the Grand Hotel, his British colleague greeted him without enthusiasm. There was no friendly reference to the American's story on the Walloon farmer. His only suggestion for co-ordinating their efforts was that Fortescue submit his copy to Maxwell for evaluation and transmission to London. Three men, introduced perfunctorily by Maxwell as members of his staff, shook hands coolly and lapsed into silence. They regarded him not as a new teammate but an intruder. He looked from one to another and saw the indifference in their faces. No matter; he did not need them. As he got to his feet and walked out of the room, he decided that in this new job he would trust nobody and be a lone wolf.

At Budapest, Ashmead-Bartlett transferred his trunks and bags to a train for Brasso, on the Rumanian frontier. The train seemed to stop at every station in Hungary, and at length reached Bucharest at midnight on July 29. This was the day Austria declared war and bombarded Belgrade. Ashmead-Bartlett did not appear to be getting closer to the scene of hostilities, but he had avoided internment and retained a certain freedom of movement. He passed July 30 at Bucharest. Since it was now unlikely that he would deal with diplomatic officials of the Austro-Hungarian empire, the *Telegraph* correspondent decided to unburden himself of the formal attire he had brought from London. The idea of traveling unencumbered seemed so practical that he persuaded Mme. Bertola, manageress of the Palace Hotel, to place all his trunks and bags in the hotel storeroom. Then, with only a kit bag containing fresh socks and toilet articles, he took a train for Sofia.

At the Bulgarian capital he dined with Sir Henry Bax Ironsides at the British Legation, and borrowed one hundred pounds on a *Telegraph* draft from a young Swiss banker. Then he went on to Nis. Germany had declared war on Russia, and Nis was a ferment of refugees, troops, and officials of the Serb government-in-exile. Ashmead-Bartlett took a train for Salonika via Skoplje, reaching the Greek frontier at 1 A.M. August 4, and Salonika three hours later.

At Salonika the morning of August 4 the correspondent boarded the small, decrepit coastwise steamer *Silvie* for Piraeus, hoping to connect there with the Italian liner *Sardinia,* but the dawdling *Silvie* was five hours late and the big liner was gone. However, by hiring a special train for 800 francs, he caught up with the *Sardinia* at Patras. Two and a half days later he walked ashore at Brindisi and caught a train for Milan, transferring there to an express for Lausanne. From Lausanne, he made connections to Geneva and Paris.

Later, when in congenial company at the Savoy bar in London or at the Ritz or Maxim's in Paris, Ashmead-Bartlett would tell of his frantic travels at the outbreak of war. The joke was on him, although Mr. Le Sage had a hand in it and the *Daily Telegraph* had to foot the bill. He was the man who jumped on his horse and galloped off madly in all directions. In the two weeks since that Sunday night when he had left London, he had traversed Belgium, Germany, Austria, Rumania, Bulgaria, Serbia, Macedonia, Greece, Italy, Switzerland, and France. He had changed trains twenty-nine times and sailed in three ships. His travels had cost the *Telegraph* about 500 pounds and he had not yet written a line of copy about the war.

Charles Inman Barnard of the *New York Tribune* watched the posting of the mobilization notices in the Place de la Bourse and then walked to the Place de l'Opéra and the rue de la Paix to see how the crowds behaved. There was little excitement or demonstration; he saw small groups gathered around the bulletin boards, men hurrying into the Métro to get home with the news, waiters looking over the shoulders of their patrons to read the newspaper headlines at the sidewalk cafés.

Mr. Barnard, sixty-four-year-old dean of American correspondents in Paris and president of the Association of the Foreign Press, had planned to retire the previous spring, but at the request of Ogden Reid, the *Tribune's* owner and editor, and because a quiet, uneventful summer was expected, he agreed to continue at his post until the autumn. The 'quiet summer' had started June 28 with the assassination of the Austrian crown prince at Sarajevo. The tragic news had reached Paris that same Sunday afternoon, and many heard it the first time in the cries of the news vendors as they drove back to the city from Longchamps, where they had watched the running of the Grand Prix de Paris. Then came the Caillaux trial. Now this: mobilization; War.

Mr. Barnard sent a cablegram to the *Tribune* in New York, marked 'Private, for Mr. Reid':

SUGGEST SUPREME IMPORTANCE EVENT HOSTILITIES OF BRUSSELS AS CENTER OF ALL WAR NEWS. ALSO THAT HARRY LAWSON, DAILY TELE-GRAPH, LONDON IS OPEN ANY PROPOSITIONS COMING FROM YOU CON-CERNING TRIBUNE SHARING WAR NEWS SERVICE WITH HIS PAPER. ACCORD-ING BEST MILITARY INFORMATION BE USELESS EXPENSE SENDING SPECIAL MEN TO FRONT WITH FRENCH OWING ABSOLUTE RIGID CENSORSHIP.

BARNARD

Mr. Barnard's man-servant, Felicien, was called to the colors and Sophie, the cook who had served his household for thirty-two years, was distressed because as a native of Alsace she was in danger of internment. It would be necessary to appeal to the Ministry of Justice and fill out papers in her behalf.

Meanwhile, taxicabs were becoming scarce as the cab-drivers joined their regiments. Reflecting on the distances between his apartment at 8 rue Théodule-Ribot and the various clubs and ministries and restaurants where he gathered information, Mr. Barnard went to Peugeot's in the Avenue de la Grand Armée and bought a bicycle.

A week had passed since the collapse of the Bourse share market and the posting of the first notices of mobilization. In that brief time, turmoil and military movement had broken the familiar pattern of life all over Europe. Communications had been cut, rail traffic demoralized, more than seven million men called to arms in Austria, Serbia, Russia, Germany, France, England, Belgium.

For the newspapermen it was a period of intense activity and frustration. This was the biggest challenge journalism had known, but it was also a time of confusion, rumors, official secrecy. The impact of war was both a tidal wave and an impenetrable fog. Some of the newspapermen understood what was happening and tried to tell about it. Most of them realized that this was beyond the scale of the Balkan Wars, beyond anything since Napoleon. It could be that the world as they had known it was finished. Meanwhile, they were the historians.

II

THE ADVANCE GUARD SAILS

The *Lusitania* sailed from New York an hour after midnight August 5. A few hours before, America had learned by cable of Britain's declaration of war against Germany for the invasion of Belgium. The big Cunarder moved down the river in darkness and secrecy. Stewards went about the decks extinguishing lights and covering smoking-room portholes. By the time she picked up Ambrose Channel markers below the Narrows, only her running lights were showing.

On board the big steamship five American newspaper correspondents off to report the war took a last look at the shadowy pile of Manhattan and the solitary figure of Liberty. Considering the magnitude of the news, it seems odd there were not more. Until the situation became clearer, most newspapers would depend on the press associations. Meanwhile, these five were an elite corps of the Press.

Richard Harding Davis and his wife, former musical comedy actress Bessie McCoy, occupied a $1,000 suite on the British steamship. He carried a letter from former President Theodore Roosevelt to President Poincaré recommending him as an ardent friend of France. In his luggage was a war correspondent's uniform which had seen service in the Balkans and along the Mexican border. The coat was cut like a British officer's and above the left breast pocket were some campaign ribbons. He had worn it posing for his passport photograph.

At fifty, Davis was still boyishly handsome. He had grown a little tired of getting packed off to wars and writing about them, though. In fact, he had protested to Jack Wheeler when the syndicate manager called him on the telephone at Crossroads Farm a few days before, saying that he had only returned from Mexico in June and needed rest. Maybe the Russian mobilization was only a bluff. But Wheeler had been in touch with editors around the country and had a sheaf of telegrams on his desk. More than a score of the nation's leading newspapers, headed by the *New York Tribune,* were ready to sign up if Davis would cover the European crisis. This was not just another war. Surely, America's leading correspondent, its most popular and successful journalist, would not be content to idle the summer away in a hammock at Mt. Kisco while the most gigantic struggle of modern times was transforming the world. The salary would be $600 a week, plus expenses.

One of Davis's favorite literary figures was the soldier of fortune —handsome adventurer of good background, at home in his Fifth Avenue club yet continually getting involved in South American revolutions, the wars of Riff tribesmen, and quixotic adventures in Burma or Abyssinia. He thought of himself somewhat in this romantic vein, yet he was much more than merely an adventurer. He took his writing seriously and needed money to lead the kind of life his pen had created. He would have ranked himself with Rudyard Kipling rather than Stephen Crane. Six hundred dollars a week would make him the highest paid correspondent in the world.

Two of Davis's companions on the *Lusitania,* Frederick Palmer and Gerald Morgan, likewise were in the front rank of war correspondents. Not in the $600 a week bracket, lacking letters to eminent statesmen, they were nevertheless journalists of integrity and experience. Palmer had covered Victoria's Diamond Jubliee in London eighteen years before. In 1897, he had been under fire in the Greco-Turkish War, and the following year had accompanied a Klondike relief expedition over the Chilkoot Pass. This adventure in the Yukon in 1898 caused him to miss the war against the Spaniards in Cuba. But he went to the Philippines for the *New York World* and *Collier's Weekly,* watched the Boxer Rebellion in China, and was one of the distinguished group that covered the Russo-Japanese War in 1904-1905. Morgan and Palmer and Davis had all been on that one together ten years before and they had worked together again in the last few months in Mexico.

It is not a simple matter to compare the work of top-ranking journalists, each possessed of his own style and personality. In considering the work of Davis and Palmer, this may be noted: Davis usually went home first; Palmer stayed on until the last shot was fired. When the international punitive expedition against the Boxers passed from the stage of hurrying pursuit to military inactivity and boredom, Davis was among the first correspondents to take steamship passage back to the United States. Some weeks later, the conscientious Palmer, who had remained behind, was surprised to receive a parcel in the mail at Shanghai. It was a recent copy of *Collier's Weekly* with his account of the Chinese affair prominently displayed. Davis had sent it by first class mail from New York, a beau geste which required a double row of ten-cent stamps. Palmer never forgot that thoughtful act of a rival journalist. It was a little thing, a double row of ten-cent stamps —and it had happened sixteen years before, yet as they sat together in the *Lusitania's* smoking room, it was one of the ties that made them comrades rather than rivals.

Most people who had worked with him liked Fred Palmer. John T. McCutcheon, *Chicago Tribune* cartoonist, who had shared a tent with him on the Mexican border, described him as having 'nice gray eyes, prominent jaws, an easy joshing manner and striking ability.'

'He was the only man I ever knew,' McCutcheon noted, 'who ordered mashed potatoes all the time. Usually you get them without premeditation.'

McCutcheon had been with Palmer at Monterey on the afternoon of July 27 when a messenger from the telegraph office handed him a message from New York. It was from Trumbull White, editor of *Everybody's Magazine*.

CONDITIONS ARE GRAVE. LEAVE AT ONCE FOR NEW YORK AND EUROPE.

So Palmer and McCutcheon packed their belongings and prepared to wind up the Mexican adventure. They had accompanied the American navy's trip to Veracruz to take a hand in Mexico's affairs. There was a northbound train in two hours and they boarded it, riding together as far as St. Louis.

The cartoonist took a train for Chicago and the next morning, at his drawing board in the *Tribune* building, began to think about the war in pictures. Working against time, he produced five war cartoons, 'The Christian Nations,' 'On Guard,' 'The Sport of

Kings,' 'The Crime of the Ages,' and 'The Colors.' The *Tribune* was greatly stirred by the swiftly developing European crisis and agreed to send McCutcheon abroad. At the last minute, it was decided that he should take a supply of gold—totaling $5,218 and weighing more than nineteen pounds—along to assist friends of the *Tribune* and prominent Chicagoans stranded in London and Paris. McCutcheon missed the *Lusitania,* but sailed three days later on the *St. Paul.*

Gerald Morgan was going over for the *Metropolitan Magazine.* A quiet, scholarly newspaperman, somewhat younger than Davis and Palmer, he had worked with both of them in the Russo-Japanese War and had matched Palmer's adventures in the Klondike with an expedition up the little-known Orinoco River with Granville Fortescue.

Herbert Corey had once driven a hack for a livery stable in a western town. A friendly, casual man given to story-telling and laughter, he was a human interest feature writer rather than a war correspondent. Corey was a forerunner of the roving columnist of a later period whose eye is attracted to the curious and whimsical. The Associated Newspapers syndicate, which employed him, reckoned sensibly that war might have a human interest side worth reporting and so packed Corey off on the *Lusitania.*

Philip Halsey Patchin, fifth of the journalistic group, carried in his pocket a copy of Barnard's confidential cable to Ogden Reid. A trusted member of the *New York Tribune* staff with some experience abroad, Patchin's mission was to reinforce the *Tribune's* London bureau rather than report developments in the field.

It is likely, as the *Lusitania* steamed across the Atlantic, that these first American correspondents looked forward to working in friendly co-operation with the War Offices in Britain and France. The war correspondent's role had been recognized as a quasi-public function since William Howard Russell's dispatches from the Crimea in 1856 upset Lord Aberdeen's cabinet and brought drastic reforms to the military organization. Since then, George Smalley, Alexander Forbes, the Vizetellys, Frederic Villiers, and other able journalists through the last half of the nineteenth century had shown resourcefulness and responsibility in reporting military affairs.

The correspondents knew there would be censorship, but for

those with the necessary experience and qualifications, duly accredited, it was assumed that accommodations would be provided with the armies in the field, where the newspapermen could observe and report military developments as enlightened partners of the Allied arms. If such were their hopes, the American journalists were due for a rude awakening. When they arrived at London on August 11 the American contingent found a baffling impasse. The War Office had established an Information or Press Bureau to issue censored news items to the press, but no newspapermen had yet been accredited to accompany the British Expeditionary Force on the Continent. The newcomers made their headquarters at the Savoy Hotel, convenient to Fleet Street. Discussing the problem with their colleagues, they learned only that Kitchener, Secretary of State for War, seemed indifferent to the press, and no one knew when the War Office would allow correspondents with the Army.

The War Office Press Bureau had been opened August 10 and was too new and confused to find satisfactory answers to newsmen's queries. A member of Parliament, Mr. Frederick E. Smith (later Lord Birkenhead) was its director. Six naval and six army officers were appointed to advise him. His brother, Mr. Harold Smith, was his secretary, and Sir George Riddell represented the newspaper society. The bureau, equipped with half a dozen telephone booths for the accommodation of the newspapermen, adjoined the Admiralty at the top of Whitehall, just below Trafalgar Square. The American correspondents, baffled by the noncommittal response to their questions, turned to the American Embassy. They did not get much help there either.

The prospects in London were so uncertain most of the American correspondents decided to quit the British capital and try their luck in Belgium.

Now that Granville Fortescue was a full-fledged correspondent with an unlimited expense account, he needed transportation befitting his craft. The sound of artillery and machine gun fire had been reported from Liége. To get to the scene from Brussels, he rented a claret-colored limousine with chauffeur. Wearing a golf suit, with a camera slung over his shoulder, Fortescue climbed in his rented vehicle and told the chauffeur: '*A Liége.*'

On the highway just outside Brussels, they encountered a roadblock manned by the Civil Guard. No further, the Guardsmen said, and the claret-colored automobile had to turn back. They tried a more roundabout, southerly route, via Namur. A few miles along the road, they encountered a battalion of Belgian artillery. Again they were turned back.

Returning to the Palace Hotel, Fortescue looked across the Place Charles Rogier at the railroad station. Trains seemed to be running much as usual. Was it possible that the railroad officials were less sensitive about the situation at Liége? He walked up to the ticket window and asked for a round-trip ticket to Liége. To his surprise, the agent sold him one without question and informed him a train was leaving in a few minutes. He got to Liége early in the afternoon and at the Grand Hotel learned that the German Army was indeed on the northeastern outskirts of the town, preparing to attack the defending ring of forts. Another correspondent, an American, Percival Phillips of the *London Post,* had been there but was returning to Brussels.

Late in the afternoon, hearing the boom of a gun, Fortescue walked out through the suburbs of Liége toward the forts. Unfamiliar with the roads, he wandered aimlessly among factory buildings and railway yards, dodging police and soldiery until after dark. The firing continued and grew more intense. It may have been about midnight when, climbing a mountainous slag heap, he saw one of the forts and the flash of its guns returning the German fire. The Belgians seemed to be putting up stout resistance. Occasionally, the correspondent saw infantry squads moving across fields in the foreground, and once spotted what he took to be a clash between German and Belgian foot soldiers, accompanied by the rattle of rifle fire.

It was daylight when he got back to his hotel. The streets were filled with hurrying townspeople, alarmed by the night-long crash of shells.

On his way to the British Consulate, Fortescue was arrested twice on suspicion of being a spy, but he waved his laissez-passer and talked so vociferously that the bewildered police had to believe him. The consul, Mr. Dolphin, gave him breakfast of champagne and sardines and told him what he had learned of the German assault on the forts. Mr. Dolphin appeared relieved when Fortescue said he planned to quit Liége and return to Brussels that same afternoon.

He turned up at the American Ministry in Brussels late that night. There was no room at the Palace Hotel. He needed a place to sleep and write. Hugh Gibson took him in. So Fortescue began to put his night's adventures on paper. Although he had witnessed only an obscure and confused segment of the fighting, his imagination and background of military experience enabled him to construct a long and readable, if somewhat breathless, account of the German attack on Liége and the Belgians' stout resistance. No other newspaperman in Brussels had as fresh or vivid a report on Liége; confidently, he pounded his typewriter, determined to make the most of his advantage and consolidate his position on the *Daily Telegraph.* When he had finished, Fortescue dropped a carbon copy at the post office, addressed to Mr. Lawson in London, and carried the original to Maxwell at the Grand Hotel. The *Telegraph* correspondent questioned Fortescue sharply about some of the details and appeared skeptical about its authenticity but promised to forward it promptly to the *Telegraph.*

Having fulfilled his major responsibility, Fortescue rewrote his story twice, once for the *Metropolitan Magazine* and again for the *New York Tribune.* This was a mistake, for the *Daily Telegraph* had just signed a contract to share its war news with the Hearst newspapers. By making his dispatch available to the *Tribune,* Fortescue had unwittingly violated the *Telegraph*'s contract. But that was a detail. The important thing was that Mr. Lawson called him on the telephone the next night to congratulate him for his enterprise. The Liége story, Mr. Lawson said, was a magnificent piece of work and the *Telegraph* was proud of its new correspondent.

The newspapermen watched what the war did to Paris and each saw something different. In the crowds around the bulletin boards, reading Viviani's solemn mobilization order, they looked at the French faces and tried to learn what they were thinking. The taxicabs drove at a faster pace. One saw a young man running, running; a couple in a doorway locked in desperate embrace. To Paul Mowrer it seemed that all the concierges of all the buildings came up out of their dark cubbyholes to stare at the knots of people and wonder. At the railway stations, the newspapermen watched the conscripts climb aboard the coaches and saw the good-bys and the tears.

Within forty-eight hours, while the mobilization was still draining young men from their ordinary occupations, tourists from all over Europe poured in at the Paris railroad stations or arrived in their limousines. They thronged the hotel lobbies, beseiged the embassies and the banking houses. Mostly Americans, these bewildered visitors clutched folders of travelers' checks and letters of credit, suddenly worthless. They demanded steamships—warships, if passenger liners were not available—and currency that would buy food. All Paris was a wailing wall for their outcries. For a time the tragic involvement of war was relieved by the comic outrage of their small necessities.

It occurred to Wythe Williams that the *New York Times* would like to publish the names of all these indignant and inconvenienced Americans. Anticipating the need for additional help he had, some days before, hired several young men seeking jobs and newspaper experience. Now he put them to work, copying names and home addresses of stranded Americans from the hotel files, checking the lists of those registered at the American Embassy and at the Amercian Express. Within forty-eight hours, the *Times* staff had rounded up a sheaf of 5,000 names and addresses, arranged alphabetically. These were taken to the cable office for dispatch to New York. The censor, newly installed at his desk and conscious of his power, said "No." They might contain a code. The numbers and letters might tell the enemy much.

The censor's arbitrary decision reflected the official mood of the War Ministry. At the outbreak of war, military officials both in England and France regarded newspapers as dangerous instruments of communication with the enemy. At the outset both nations refused to accredit newspaper correspondents to accompany their armies and imposed restrictions which the correspondents viewed as unreasonable on the gathering and publication of war news. The official French attitude was based on what happened to their arms in the Franco-Prussian War of 1870. In that unhappy conflict, according to the military version, war correspondents of France and neutral nations wrote freely about military movements, the condition and morale of the troops, and the plans of the generals. Newspapermen were permitted to circulate freely among the armies. German intelligence scrutinized the press daily and made such effective use of the information that France soon suffered humiliating defeat. Historians have attributed the 1870 catastrophe to French overconfidence, inferior artillery, politics, and ineptitude, but the General Staff in 1914 had an *idée fixe* on the indiscretions of the press.

Apart from using the newspaper correspondent as a whipping boy for 1870, the French General Staff imposed silence on the press to safeguard its grand strategy of defense. French intelligence had become convinced that the affair at Liége was merely a demonstration to draw French forces northwest into Belgium, whereas the main German thrust, they insisted, would come through Alsace and Lorraine. Thus the General Staff wanted no attention paid to the seemingly illogical disposition of its forces east of Paris. Within two weeks, when the German advance through Belgium became a harsh reality, opening a disastrous gash in the French left flank and sending the small British Army reeling back from Mons, the French General Staff had additional reasons for keeping the newspapers quiet.

So, no correspondents with the Army. However, the Ministry of War, realizing the necessity of communicating official intelligence to the public, arranged to issue bulletins three times daily. The newspapermen were summoned to the Ministry and examined by Colonel Commandant Duval, chief of the Press Bureau. Those that had sufficient proof of character, experience, and loyalty were handed a laissez-passer which entitled them not to go with the Army and witness battles, but to enter the Ministry of War at 10 A.M., 3 P.M., and 11 P.M. to receive the official handout.

Mr. Charles Inman Barnard received his laissez-passer along with the others. For a day or two he rode his bicycle to the ministry and stood in line and took the brief meaningless bulletin. He did not bother to send it on to the *Tribune;* there was never any news in it, only vague reassurances that the situation was being dealt with.

On his bicycle, Mr. Barnard made the rounds of the retail district to see what the war had done to familiar American enterprises in Paris. Singer Sewing Machine Company, rue Louis le Grand at the Place de l'Opéra, closed; Hanan's boot and shoe store nearby, closed; at the rue de Pyramides and Place de l'Opéra, Colgate's and the Cheeseborough establishments were closed, too, but further along, Butterick's shop and Brentano's bookstore were open. On the Grand Boulevard, the Remington Typewriter store was closed, and Spalding's shop for athletic supplies was shuttered. The Walk-Over Shoe Shops on the Boulevard des Capucines and Boulevard des Italiens were open.

After lunch at the Cercle Artistique et Littéraire on the rue Volney, Mr. Barnard accepted an invitation from an acquaintance, the Duc de Loubat, to drive out to Versailles. Here the elderly *Tribune* correspondent saw something of the movement and confusion of the Gallic war machine. Versailles was the mobilization center for the Paris district. The drowsy old suburb had been transformed. The wide avenues were packed with men, some in uniform, some carrying their uniforms under their arms:

At first glance, there was nothing but confusion, but the appearance was misleading for, at the Chantiers station, trainload after trainload of troops—men, horses, guns, matériel—have been dispatched, taking the route of the Grande Ceinture railway around Paris to Noisy-le-sec and on to the Est system.

Supplementing this movement of troops, Mr. Barnard noted in his notebook 'lines and lines of guns, hundreds upon hundreds of provision wagons, rows upon rows of light draught horses, many being shod in the street, and in a great pasture, thousands of magnificent cattle.'

Mr. Barnard talked to an American newspaper correspondent at Versailles who at the outbreak of war was living in an apartment in the rue Hardy, the house once occupied by Jacques Louis David, painter of Napoleon. With the sudden influx of troops, housing became scarce and the correspondent was asked to share his domicile with several officers and men. He readily agreed, yielding three rooms to the military, keeping two for himself. The arrangement worked out fine, except that at six o'clock each morning the cavalry officer went to the piano and woke the whole building by playing the 'Pilgrim's Chorus' from *Tannhäuser*.

III

GERMANS ON THE MARCH

At Brussels on Thursday August 13, Hugh Gibson wrote in his diary:

As the tourists and Germans leave, the war correspondents begin to come in. I heard today that there were 200 of them in London and most want to come here.

Barnard had been right in his cabled advice to Ogden Reid; Brussels was the strategic center for war news, the best observation post for the press. Fleet Street reached the same conclusion.

For American newspapermen the Belgian capital possessed additional advantages in the friendly offices of the American Minister, Brand Whitlock, and Hugh Gibson, Secretary of the Legation. Political liberal and reformer, Whitlock also was a writing man of some note. Brussels had been assigned to him with the idea that he would have almost no work to do in that tranquil by-lane of diplomacy and could spend most of his time on his new novel. Gibson, too, had a decent respect for the writing craft. The two diplomatic figures, swamped under tasks imposed by taking over the legations of departing belligerents, and the problems of stranded American tourists, nevertheless realized the significant role of the newspapermen and found time to help them.

Fortescue was the first. Now he was off again, hunting the French and British armies around Namur. James O'Donnell Bennett of the *Chicago Tribune* arrived August 12. Sunday morning August 16 Gibson stepped out of his office and bumped into a familiar figure, tall, broad-shouldered Frederick Palmer, his face still dark from exposure to the Mexican sun. They had met before. In Tegucigalpa, Honduras, on his first assignment from the State

Department, Gibson had put aside other tasks to be friendly and helpful to the journalist who wanted to know about Central American politics. They had taken a liking to each other; both had come up in the world. Gibson expressed amazement that Palmer could have been on the Mexican border watching Villa's ragged guerrillas only two weeks ago; now here he was in the rue de Billiard inquiring how an American journalist could be accredited to the Belgian Army.

That afternoon, Gibson took Palmer to the Gendarmerie Nationale in the Boulevard de Waterloo for laissez-passer and brassard. No foreign correspondents were being accredited to the Belgian Army, but the government laissez-passer and American passport would afford a certain freedom of movement behind the lines.

They had dinner that night on the terrace of the Palace Hotel—Gibson, Palmer, and Daniel Lynds Blount, a young American businessman who had volunteered, with his automobile, to assist the legation staff. As they gave their order to the waiter, a distinguished figure appeared at the doorway, pausing to survey the throng of diners. Richard Harding Davis had arrived from London, had had a bath and changed to formal dinner clothes and fresh white linen. Behind him, as he made his way across the terrace, like an actor coming on the stage, walked Gerald Morgan. The newcomers joined Gibson and presently champagne was cooling in buckets of ice beside the table.

It was such a summer night as Davis liked to put in his romances. When the long twilight faded the diners ate by candlelight. The broad terrace became a sea of soft twinkling candle flames through which the waiters moved with their salvers and trays. From the Place Charles Rogier, where crowds thronged the sidewalks, came scraps of laughter and the voices of young women, appealing for the Red Cross. Presently some of the young women appeared on the terrace, walked among the tables, holding out tin cans for contributions.

Pour les blessés! Pour les blessés!

The Liége forts had held out almost ten days against German artillery. The newspapermen found Belgium's pride reflected in the casual laughter of the terrace diners, the smiles of the young women, the atmosphere of good food, wine, and well-being. The American newspapermen had arrived at a critical time. Even with the German Army poised at Liége, Brussels was calm and cheerful. For a very short while, the newspapermen were to bask in this curious calm before the storm, and make it a frame of reference for their first war dispatches.

Palmer's stay at Brussels was brief. With Gibson and Blount he drove to Louvain the next day. The old university town was ominously quiet. The Americans saw no sign of a German advance: only a British officer and a French colonel with briefcases walked thoughtfully down the steps of the Hôtel de Ville. There had been a conference of war, Palmer surmised, but it was no use trying to find out what had been decided.

Back in Brussels that night Palmer confided to his friends that he must return to London. He could not talk much about it, but a great responsibility was about to be entrusted to him. As a result of negotiations begun a week before, Palmer was to be accredited to the British Expeditionary Forces as official correspondent for the three United States news services—the Associated Press, the United Press and the International News Service. He would be the only journalist so accredited. In effect this would make him the authorized reporter for all the newspapers in America.

Palmer's coup had been accomplished by the prompt, concerted action of the press associations, backed by Ambassador Walter Hines Page and the State Department. His record showed him to be accurate and conscientious as a war reporter. The State Department checked on his dispatches from Mexico and found them more informative and reliable, if not as colorful, as those of his colleagues on the border. Palmer had an added advantage in that he had not recently been connected with any newspaper or press association and thus could not be accused of favoritism. Frederick Roy Martin had just arrived in London to approve the deal for the Associated Press, and Roy Howard would reach Liverpool on the *New York* in a day or two. W. Orton Tewson, European manager for the I.N.S., would be happy to subscribe to the arrangement for the Hearst organization, which was having considerable trouble with British censorship.

Davis congratulated Palmer on his prospective appointment and shook his hand heartily as he left for London, but it rankled a little for the distinguished novelist to see the British accreditation go to another. His own name had been considered. Davis wrote to his brother that the honor would have gone to him except for a grudge borne by the State Department. Secretary Bryan had become incensed at Davis's effort to interview the current political dictator in Mexico City the previous spring, an adventure which took him out of the U.S. Army's lines and landed him in a Mexico City jail. The good offices of the British Ambassador were necessary to get Davis out of the scrape, and the State Department was embarrassed.

Even if the State Department had approved, it is doubtful whether Davis could have accepted the British accreditation. For one thing, he was under contract to Jack Wheeler's syndicate. Moreover, representation for the three press services with the British Army would mean anonymity, and a salary less than half of his syndicate guarantee.

For Palmer, the appointment meant a substantial sacrifice in salary and a long period of frustration. In the end, although deprived of his by-line, it paid off. By the end of 1915, he was undeniably the Number One war correspondent in France.

Meanwhile, in Brussels, Davis and the other newly arrived Americans had gone to the Foreign Office with Brand Whitlock to be presented to Baron von der Elst and to the Gendarmerie Nationale for their laissez-passers. Davis hired the largest and shiniest limousine available to Brussels and started out with Gerald Morgan to see what news could be found:

Those were the happy days. We were given a laissez-passer, which gave us permission to go anywhere; this with a passport was our only credential. Proper credentials to accompany the Army had been formerly refused me by the war offices of England, France and Belgium. So in Brussels each morning, I chartered an automobile and without credentials joined the first Army that happened to be passing.

Namur? Tirlemont? Wavre? The morning newspapers sometimes gave a clew. On a straight tip from their Legation, the English correspondents were going to motor to Diest. From a Belgian officer we had been given inside information that the fight would be pulled off at Gembloux . . . each [correspondent] would depart on his separate errand, at night returning to a perfectly served dinner and a luxurious bed. Over the map of Belgium we threw ourselves (like players at the roulette table) hoping one might rest on the winning number.

Whenever we sighted an army, we lashed the flags of its country to our headlights and at 60 miles an hour bore down upon it. . . . The countryside was beautiful with the colors of the harvest, the small inns had food and wine, the roads were excellent. At night, we raced back to the city through twelve miles of parks to enamelled bath tubs, shaded electric light and iced champagne; while before our table passed all the night life of a great city. And for suffering these hardships of war, our papers paid us large sums.

This glamorous phase of war reporting lasted just two days. Tuesday night, August 18, while they dined on the Palace Hotel terrace, the American journalists became aware of something odd in the sidewalk traffic on the Place Charles Rogier. Their table had been enlarged to accommodate three new arrivals, Irvin S. Cobb, John T. McCutcheon, and Arnot Dosch. As they looked down on the crowded street with these newcomers, Davis and Morgan pointed out country folk in wooden shoes, carrying children and bundles among the city crowds. There seemed to be scores, hundreds of them, as wide-eyed and dazed as immigrants just off the Ellis Island ferry. Some walked beside carts piled with kitchenware and bedding. They were farm families from around Tirlemont. The forts at Liége were smashed at last and the German Army was pouring through. Tirlemont was burning.

Will Irwin arrived in Brussels the next morning. With Cobb and McCutcheon he had crossed on the *St. Paul* three days behind the *Lusitania*. Pausing in London just long enough to discover the futility of calling at the War Office, he had then hurried on across the Channel. With the others, he got his laissez-passer and a letter from the Ministry.

About ten-thirty Wednesday morning, August 19, Cobb, McCutcheon, Dosch, and Irwin climbed in a taxicab in front of their hotel and directed the driver to take them to Louvain. The driver seemed doubtful about the journey, but the Americans produced documents bearing the red seals of the legation, and the prospect of a substantial fee urged him on. A week before, the roads would have been blocked (as Fortescue discovered) by Belgian patrols and military police. With the Liége forts fallen and the German

Army advancing, the Belgians decided sensibly to give the correspondents complete freedom. Nothing they might write could make any difference now. The road to Louvain was open. About noon their taxicab climbed a rise and pulled off at the roadside. The driver said this was as far as he cared to go. The newspapermen could see the towers of Louvain about two miles off. Refugees passing along the road told them the Germans were not far away; the correspondents caught the low boom of a gun and saw an ominous plume of smoke on the horizon. The taxi driver would not risk his vehicle in Louvain, but agreed to wait at the roadside. They went ahead on foot, leaving their topcoats in the vehicle. They never saw taxicab or coats again.

Now it was early afternoon and they were in the outskirts of Louvain. The streets were empty. At the edge of town, they asked a priest where they could find someone who spoke English. He led them through a doorway into a cool monastery garden where they had some bread and cheese, a couple of bottles of wine, and a talk with the priest and his fellows. Thinking back over his war experiences, Cobb liked to remember that hour, cut off from the outside world, listening to the friendly voices of the priests, a peaceful interlude before the storm.

They left the monastery, and as they made their way toward the center of the town they saw two German soldiers, one on a horse, the other on a bicycle. The two gray-clad figures moved along slowly, scanning the upper windows, pausing at intersections to look down cross streets, watchful, methodical, sinister rifles at their sides. After them came a troop of Uhlans, German cavalry, then the German Army.

The four American journalists moved away from the main thoroughfare and found an observation post in front of the Belgian Lion café where, with chairs tilted against the wall, they could watch the stream of horses and men pouring across an intersection a short block away. They were in effect prisoners of the army movement, for the Germans had taken charge of the town and no traffic moved, no pedestrians departed, except by their consent. An officer of the Provost Guard told them to remain quietly where they were until further notice. At night they found lodging in the House of a Thousand Columns by the railroad station. For three days and nights, they watched and waited as the gray-clad troops marched through Louvain.

On the same day that Cobb and his companions rode to Louvain in a taxicab, most of the British correspondents quit Brussels in the opposite direction. A few went to Antwerp, where the Belgian Government and a considerable part of the Army had shifted. Others went home to London. They could not risk being trapped in the German advance. As citizens of an enemy nation, they were liable to internment; if caught taking notes or writing newspaper accounts of what they saw, they might be treated as spies. The Americans had no such fears.

An ominous quiet settled over Brussels that afternoon. Davis and Morgan returned from their motor tour to learn of the departure of the British and the arrival of two more U.S. newspapermen, Harry Hansen of the *Chicago Daily News* and Roger Lewis of the Associated Press. They dined on the terrace as usual and again young women walked among the tables, soliciting money for the wounded, but their entreaties had become tense and a little shrill.

The next morning, Brussels fell silent. Along the route on which the Germans were known to be arriving, houses and shops were shuttered. The wealthy families had left the night before. The streets were empty. There was an hour from 10:00 to 11:00 when almost nothing moved except the special constables Burgomaster Max had appointed to warn citizens against making a demonstration.

Some American correspondents quit the de luxe Palace Hotel on the Place Charles Rogier to move into a small hotel across from the United States Legation. With the eerie sense of doomsday in the air, it was comforting to be able to look out and see an American flag. One newspaperman reserved a leather sofa in the reception room, in case it became necessary to seek the protection of the legation that night.

Shortly after eleven, down the Boulevard Waterloo came three Germans on bicycles. They wore gray uniforms, and they seemed businesslike, but unhurried and at ease as they inquired the way to the Gare du Nord. The captain, slightly ahead, carried side arms; the two privates had rifles slung across their shoulders.

Behind this casual advance guard came a troop of Uhlans, riding their horses in close formation, then long columns of infantry, guns, caissons, field kitchens with fires burning, wagon trains, and more columns of marching men.

Richard Harding Davis watched the marching men and rolling vehicles with interest for two hours; then, bored by the sameness, he went to his hotel for luncheon. In the afternoon, he returned to the spectacle in the streets. Boredom was succeeded by incredulity, curiosity, and awe. He had observed armies before—Japanese and Russians at Port Arthur, the British in South Africa, Americans in Cuba and Mexico, Bulgars, Turks, Greeks in the Balkans—but nothing ever like this. It was unreal, yet it persisted. The human quality in the German Army had disappeared, he thought, with the passing of the three men on bicycles. After them, the gray-clad marching men merged with the wagons and guns in one vast, inhuman juggernaut, a rolling tide of impersonal destructive force.

That night in his hotel room, Davis put together a creditable description of the German Army on the march. He was impressed with the neutral gray of the German uniform:

It was not the blue-gray of our Confederates, but a green-gray. It is the gray of the hour just before daybreak, the gray of unpolished steel, of mist among green trees. I saw it first in the Grand Place in front of the Hôtel de Ville. It was impossible to tell if in that noble square there was a regiment or a brigade. You saw only a fog that melted into the stones, blended with the ancient house fronts, that shifted and drifted but left you nothing at which to point. Later, as the Army passed under the trees of the Botanical Park, it merged and was lost among the green leaves.

This was a challenge, a confrontation; the world's best known war correspondent matching his pen against the greatest military array in history. Davis was middle-aged, softened by good living, a little tired from the day's excitement and the recent aimless dashing about the Belgian countryside. But he had seen something which roused him from fatigue and boredom. The story he wrote in his Brussels hotel room that August night was only twelve or fifteen hundred words. It lacked the tumult and battle of most war literature; but its descriptive power gives it a unique place in history. It served notice on France and Britain that an army was moving like a tidal force across Belgium to confront them. It warned people of all countries what kind of a war soon would engulf Europe. Davis's manuscript was put in the hands of a courier and started on its journey to London Friday afternoon. The messenger, E. A. Dalton, was English, and when he arrived in Fleet Street late Saturday, wearing riding breeches, putties, and a wrinkled jacket, he had a tale of his own to add to Davis's typewritten pages. For the first stage of his journey, Dalton had to follow the main road from Brussels to Ghent, along which the German Army was marching. He ignored the military procession, made friends with refugees along the roadside path and, in exchange for small gold coins, got an occasional ride on a cart or wagon. Beyond Ghent the Army turned south and the roads were closely policed by the military. Dalton was arrested twice. To get away from the Germans, he strolled out in a field, and after hiding for half an hour, began to crawl beside a hedge on his hands and knees. After a mile of this slow progress, he could at last stand upright. Free from the scrutiny of the Germans, he again made common cause with refugees plodding toward the channel, and, traveling most of the night, reached Ostend. He got on a refugee boat there and crossed to Folkestone, reaching London late in the afternoon with Davis's story.

Dalton's adventurous journey from Brussels, his bedraggled appearance and sleepless night were quite a sensation in Fleet Street, and his exploits were cabled to New York. Some weeks later, when he saw the pages of the *New York Tribune* of Monday, August 24, Davis found the messenger's tale sharing the headlines with his own classic prose. It was a little disconcerting; after all, *who* was the distinguished war correspondent?

FAKERS AND ATROCITIES

In London the War Office fended off the newspapermen with one hand; with the other, it set up a War Office Information Bureau. Here in Whitehall would be handed out all that the people needed to know, all that military authorities thought prudent to disclose about events on the Continent. A Member of the Opposition in Parliament, Mr. Frederick E. Smith, was placed in charge. Its first announcement on August 11 stated:

> About two German Cavalry Divisions are in the neighborhood of Tongres, to the North of Liége.

The newspapers printed that, of course, but their editors were indignant, if not contemptuous at the War Office's estimate of news and its indifference to the national temper. All Fleet Street knew that the German Army, hammering at Liége forts, was about to sweep across Belgium; Britain's Army—what there was of it— was being ferried across the Channel to join her ally France in repelling the invader. Historic events were taking shape, and the War Office sought to throw the press a bone about two cavalry divisions at Tongres.

It was hopefully assumed that within a few days, as soon as Kitchener had solved pressing organization problems, he would turn his cool head toward Fleet Street and grant to newspapermen the right to go with the British Army. The days passed, Liége fell, the German host swept down through Belgium, the British Army was desperately engaged, and still the War Office kept the newspapermen waiting. Not now; we cannot at present permit correspondents with the Army; next week, perhaps; no, sorry, come back in September.

The accreditation of Frederick Palmer as official correspondent for the American press associations was a hopeful sign. Palmer was measured for his new uniforms and was seen along Fleet Street wearing the correspondent's brassard on his sleeve. Any day now he would be leaving for British headquarters in France. At the Savoy Bar in the Strand, where the Americans gathered, and at the Wellington in Fleet Street, it was predicted that the long-expected action of the War Office was imminent. Indeed, late in August, the word came from Whitehall that ten or twelve correspondents were about to be selected for accreditation to the British Expeditionary force. All the leading English newspapers and newspaper chains would be represented.

This news caused a stir of activity among the journalistic fraternity. Those with previous experience as war correspondents gave little talks on the organization of a mess, baggage and equipment, uniform, and appropriate insignia. It was generally agreed that the correspondents should have rank corresponding to that of major, and each would be assigned a striker or batman to take care of his laundry and boots and perform other services of a military valet. Methods of dispensing cigars and cigarettes were discussed.

The horse had in the past been necessary to enable a war correspondent to see battles, and the word from Whitehall was: certainly, horses, of course; one horse to a correspondent. The expectant eager newspapermen hurried to the horse barns and stock farms and purchased horses. They practiced climbing on and climbing off, and within a few days some had acquired ease and style in the saddle.

In the important matter of riding boots, correspondents were advised to seek the counsel of Colonel 'Gyppy' Lewis, a veteran of the Egyptian campaign under Kitchener, now writing for *The Times* (London). Lewis had his boots made to order by the most expensive bootmaker in Jermyn Street. Upon delivery they were locked in trees for twelve months, saddle-soaped and polished daily. When at the end of the year they were ready to be worn, they had a patina so rich and brilliant they would serve as a mirror to shave by. The problem in the field, Colonel Lewis warned, was to keep them that way.

One afternoon early in September, a correspondent came into the Savoy taproom and announced to the assembled newspapermen that he had just obtained from the War Office a pass for a horse to go with the Army. This, he said, exhibiting the precious paper, was the real thing.

An Englishman looked at the pass and nodded. 'You are fortunate,' he said, 'that is, if you have a horse that can use a typewriter and is capable of describing his incredible hardships in search of a few oats to sustain him while dashing from point to point amid shot and shell in order that the public may be informed as to his own experiences and emotions and conclusions as to the proper strategy to be employed against the dastardly foe.'

A day or two later, word came from the War Office that horses would not be considered *de rigueur*. In fact, horses were obsolete; accredited correspondents would travel by automobile. The military authorities suggested that the newspapermen dispose of their horses, saddles, and gear, and directed them to remount stations where army buyers would take the steeds off their hands.

During these preliminary negotiations it was stated in confidence that the principal obstacle to favorable action at the War Office was General Joseph Joffre, Commander in Chief of the French armies. Joffre had taken a firm stand against war correspondents. Since the war was being fought on the soil of France, the British were obliged to bow to their ally's wishes. Early in September there were rumors that Joffre's position was changing. Then came the word: Joffre will now permit war correspondents!

The eager newsmen hurried to Whitehall, and a staff colonel at the War Office smilingly assured them that the last obstacle had indeed been removed. Now that Joffre had said 'Yes' for France, only Kitchener's signature was needed to start the correspondents on their way to the embattled continent. The colonel who conveyed this reassuring news also indicated that he expected to go to France as the head of the Army's Press Section, with headquarters in some convenient château behind the lines. He asked the press delegation to excuse him for a moment or two while he conferred with Kitchener and got the signature on the necessary paper. He disappeared in an inner office and the newspapermen waited expectantly. When the colonel reappeared, there was a thoughtful expression on his face. Gentlemen, he said, I regret to inform you General Kitchener says you cannot go.

Kitchener's attitude toward war correspondents may have been inherent in his personality. He was a taciturn, almost shy, man who shunned publicity. Seeking no political advantage, he saw no reason why the British people should be kept informed about what he was doing. Moreover, as the French generals attributed defeat in 1870 to irresponsible newspaper reports, so the British War Office blamed Fleet Street for prolonging the Boer War by publishing military information useful to the enemy. Kitchener's relations with the press got off to a bad start. Within a few days of his appointment as Secretary of State for War, he gave an interview to Lieutenant Colonel Charles à Court Repington, military writer for *The Times,* stating his plans and policies for the Army. Repington was an old friend who could be trusted to quote him accurately. The interview was timely and unobjectionable, but because it appeared exclusively in *The Times,* the other newspapers raised a storm of protest. Was the new Secretary going to play favorites in distributing his news? Annoyed by the vigor and persistence of the editorial denunciation, Kitchener cooled toward Repington and retired into his shell. He would settle the business by having nothing to do with the press whatever.

Austria's policy toward newspaper correspondents was basically the same as England's, yet there were interesting differences in method. The first news from Vienna was that war correspondents would not be tolerated; all news must flow from official sources at the War Office. This was followed in a few days by an announcement that Austria would recognize and accredit journalists representing the press of Germany, Austria, and neutral countries. One hundred and eighteen newspapermen were promptly examined, approved, and equipped with credentials. They included Swiss, Swedes, Danes, and Americans.

To prepare them for service with the Army the government established a *Kriegspresse quartier* in a little town ninety miles behind the nearest battle zone. The correspondents purchased horses, saddles, uniforms, and other equipment and reported at this training camp for a course of instruction, under Colonel John, Curator of the War Museum in Vienna. Lodged in a manor house, they lived in style. The cuisine was Viennese, the wines from

Hungary. Cigars and cigarettes were included in the daily rations and the government footed the bill.

Each morning the newspapermen climbed on their horses and rode in a circle around a riding instructor who criticized their posture and drilled them in correct equestrian procedures. Afternoons in a nearby forest, they practiced revolver shooting. At night they played billiards. It was a pleasant, healthful routine; they got everything but news. Some months passed. The correspondents became restive. The Army needed their horses and took them. Gradually, the newspapermen drifted away, having lost all hope of active service in their profession. The *Kriegspresse quartier* was turned into a rest camp for tired officers.

Through August and September, the newspapers starved for honest news about the war. When it became apparent that neither Britain nor France would permit war correspondents to function in the field, American editors stopped sending correspondents across the Atlantic. Some of them, however, gave credentials as acting correspondents to travelers going abroad on business. This practice created a new figure in wartime journalism—the adventurous amateur who liked to see his name and his handiwork in print. From the newspapers' standpoint, the arrangement seemed to promise interesting letters from the war zone, without any outlay for steamer fare and expenses. The results were doubtful. By mid-October, a score or more of untrained but determined freelances were crossing the English Channel, interviewing refugees, showing their letters to generals and seeking privileges in the name of the press. Most of them were well supplied with funds. Some went about their news gathering travels with a holiday spirit. A gentleman from Massachusetts crossed the Atlantic on the *Lusitania* in October with business cards identifying him as a 'special correspondent' of the Transcript Press, a print shop which published a small weekly in a Boston suburb.

I must confess [he explained] I had no better reason for going abroad than sightseeing, but that seemed to me reason enough. I had wagered a box of cigars with a friend of mine that I could get to England, Germany, Belgium and France and return to New York before Christmas. Hence my determination to smell the smoke of battle in order to puff the cheroot of peace.

The Massachusetts traveler won his cigars and saw more activity than many legitimate correspondents. His adventures—once he was picked up and questioned as a spy—made half a dozen mildly interesting columns.

The bumptious Massachusetts amateur at least was conscientious about the trivia he produced for publication; a few Americans, pretending to be correspondents, were shameless fakers. One wrote:

I was riding on a train near Paris when we suddenly heard shooting. The train stopped and we got off and looking over a hill we saw a battle in full swing. As I looked, I saw one soldier jab another through the head with a bayonet.

It was soon apparent to his editor that he was unreliable, and he was recalled. A favorite of the faker was to exaggerate his own perils in pursuit of war news. One who had been detained briefly by the French near Villers-Cotterêts wrote that he had been arrested as a spy, handcuffed to German prisoners, and led through the village with a crowd of French civilians trying to get at him with knives. Unknown to him, other Americans in the same village witnessed his little adventure. He had been questioned with reasonable courtesy and then escorted by a French officer to the outskirts of the town, where he mounted his bicycle and rode off without molestation.

In the confusion of the early weeks, some of the improbable tales had the dreamlike quality of *The Arabian Nights:*

I was seated here in the hotel lobby [one 'correspondent' related] when a man in uniform came up to me and said, 'Come on, Mr. Newspaperman, and I'll give you a ride.' We got into his car and rode for about three hours. Then he took me into a ditch where a lot of bullets were flying and we had a fine view of the battle.

His fantastic story appeared in 250 American newspapers, yet on the night he wrote about, he had not left his room in the Ritz-Carlton Hotel.

Most freelance efforts dealt with German frightfulness and atrocities. The irresponsible amateurs soon learned that atrocity tales had a news value considerably higher than routine war stuff. Refugees and rumors produced an incredible variety of atrocities from Belgium and northern France during late August and September. It was not necessary to verify these stories; many were improbable and absurd. Yet they were printed, and no censor's blue pencil interfered. One of the leading American journalists in London, commenting on this freelance phase of war reporting, wrote:

The news hungry public was often misled in that period. In the mass of war news, no small amount of fake and lies were fed to it by unscrupulous adventurers who were not trained correspondents and who had no reputation for veracity to sustain ... News, lies, local color, human interest, fakes: all went down the great public gullet in gargantuan gulps.

Everything was believed. Germany had committed the first great atrocity by starting the war. It had committed the atrocity of invading Belgium. It had committed the atrocity of destroying Louvain. Surely, it was capable of standing an innocent priest up against a wall and shooting him, or chopping off the hands of Belgian children.

Germany protested strongly against the publication of such stories in American newspapers. Advocates of the German cause pointed out that Britain's control of the trans-Atlantic cable weighed the scale heavily in the Allies' favor. Germany had only a single and imperfectly functioning communication medium, the wireless, to tell her story to the Western world.

Early in September, the German radio receiving station at Sayville crackled with an official message from Berlin. On Monday morning, September 7, the *New York Times* printed the following dispatch:

The Associated Press has received by wireless from Berlin a message which was sent from Aix-la-Chappelle to Berlin for transmission. The authors, well-known American newspapermen, were originally assigned to Brussels and when that city was taken, they were sent to Aix-la-Chappelle from which city they have been trying to reach London but without success. The telegram is partly mulitated by interference and some words are missing, but the text, here given, is clearly that intended:

'In spirit we unite in rendering the German atrocities groundless, as far as we are able to. After spending two weeks with and accompanying the troops upward of 100 miles we are unable to report a single instance unprovoked.

'We are also unable to confirm rumors of mistreatment of prisoners or of non-combatants with the German columns. This is true of Louvain, Brussels, Luneville and Nantes, while in Prussian hands.

'We visited Chateau Soldre, Sambre and Beaumont without substantiating a single wanton brutality. Numerous investigated rumors proved groundless. Everywhere we have seen Germans paying for purchases and respecting property rights as well as according civilians every consideration.

'After the battle of Blass [possibly Barse, a suburb of Namur] we found Belgian women and children moving comfortably about.

'The day after the Germans had captured the town in [of] Merbes Chateau [possibly Ste. Marie] we found one citizen killed, but were unable to confirm lack of provocation. Refugees with stories of atrocities were unable to supply direct evidence.

'Belgians in the Sambre Valley discounted reports of cruelties in the surrounding countries.

'The discipline of the German soldiers is excellent as we observed.

'To the truth of these statements we pledge our professional and personal word.

> ROGER LEWIS, *Associated Press*
> IRVIN S. COBB, *Saturday Evening Post* and *Philadelphia Public Ledger*
> HARRY HANSEN, *Chicago Daily News*
> JAMES O'DONNELL BENNETT and
> JOHN T. MCCUTCHEON, the *Chicago Tribune*'

Those names were well known to Americans. Irvin S. Cobb was one of the nation's best known humorists with long newspaper training. McCutcheon was one of America's outstanding cartoonists. The others, less widely known, were responsible journalists.

This dispatch was a curious piece of war correspondence. Distributed through the Associated Press, it was published widely and became the subject of considerable editorial comment. Were these reputable American newspapermen being used by the Germans to counteract the growing indictment against the German Army for ruthlessness and brutality? Had they been compelled to sign the statement against their will?

It was generally believed that the five journalists held virtually prisoners at Aix-la-Chapelle had been subjected to such pressure as to cause them to lose their normal judgment and perspective. What kind of statement would they give out when at last they got free of German influence and reached the Allied lines?

V

IN THE WAKE OF THE JUGGERNAUT

The sweep of the German Army across Belgium August 19-26 had caught in its backwash a dozen of America's ablest newspaper correspondents. For the moment they were swallowed up in the dust and immensity of the German advance. Communication with the outside world was cut off. The correspondents at Brussels were temporarily mute but this opportunity was unique. One of the greatest military movements of modern times had taken place before their eyes. With a little luck, they might trail along and witness one of the world's great battles.

Thus far their encounter with the German Army involved neither hardship nor peril. As American citizens they had the protection of the alert and able Brand Whitlock and Hugh Gibson. Moreover, it seemed possible that the Germans would treat the newspapermen considerately to gain a favorable hearing in the American press.

While the dust of the marching columns still hung in the August air over Brussels, the newspapermen went to the Hôtel de Ville to lay their problem before the German official who had taken over affairs at the Belgian capital. Major General Thaddeus von Jarotzky was too occupied to talk to them in person, but his chief of staff, Lieutenant Geyer, looked at their passports and read the letters of identification provided by the American Legation. The newsmen asked for passes authorizing them to accompany the army, but Lieutenant Geyer explained that Herr General's authority extended only to Brussels 'and environs.' Some notations in German script were made on their papers and then the rubber stamps of the German occupation made the recognition official.

How big were 'environs'? Sunday morning, August 23, leaving most of their effects at the legation, eight American correspondents started out to find how far the term 'environs' could be stretched.

Richard Harding Davis paired off as usual with tall, quiet Gerald Morgan, his companion of other campaigns. Their big yellow touring car had been requisitioned by a wealthy family escaping to Antwerp; as the next best thing they hailed a taxicab and told the driver to follow the German Army.

Their route lay through Hal, eleven miles west of Brussels. Passing through that town they brushed a marching German column. An officer jumped on the running board, waving a revolver, and ordered them to pull to the roadside and halt. Unconvinced by their papers that they were on legitimate business, he detailed four soldiers to keep an eye on them. After riding on the running board of the taxicab for half a mile, the four decided to rejoin their regiment and departed. The taxi driver, discouraged by the brief encounter with the men in gray, demanded his money and turned back.

Davis and Morgan took to the roadside and walked on beside the marching Germans 'like small boys following a circus parade.' At Brierges, seated on a stone wall of a roadside bridge, Morgan announced that he, too, must return to Brussels. His papers declared him to be a correspondent for the *London Daily Telegraph*. Although an American citizen, he was afraid his identification with an English newspaper would be held against him. Besides, he argued, they surely had reached the limit of 'environs.' If they were ordered back to Brussels under arrest, their laissez-passers would be canceled and they could no longer move about and function as newspapermen. Finally, he pointed out, there was no fighting, nothing but monotonous marching along the road they were following, and they were taking the risk for nothing.

But Davis was stubborn. He wanted to go on until ordered back by someone high in authority, and he was willing to risk arrest to have another adventure or two with the German Army. So they shook hands and Morgan wished his old friend luck as he took the road back to Hal.

It was noon. The German columns slowed to a halt and the men sprawled in the fields, waiting for their hot stew and coffee. Davis walked a few hundred yards beyond the town and sat down on a grassy bank beside the road. He was eating a sandwich when four young German officers, who had been observing him, slipped up behind and ordered him to put up his hands. Prodding Davis with their automatic pistols, they took him to their colonel, at lunch in a nearby tavern. The colonel looked over his papers, gave him a glass of wine, and then, uncertain what to do with him, scribbled a pass permitting him to proceed to Enghien, two miles further on. Enghien, the colonel suggested, would be a good place to pass the night. It was plain the colonel wanted to get rid of the journalist with the least possible fuss.

At Enghien, a group of German officers scowled at him when he entered the inn. Even after looking at his papers, they held him in suspicion and the inn keeper refused at first to give him a room. But the town burgomaster, M. Delano, was friendly. As an American, M. Delano said, Mr. Davis was free to stay in Enghien as long as he wished. He wrote a note endorsing Davis to the innkeeper and as he handed it to the newspaperman, he winked.

'But I am an American,' Davis insisted.

'Of course, certainly, without a doubt,' the burgomaster said, and again he winked.

After an uneasy night, Davis took to the road to Ath early in the morning. Less than half a mile from town he passed a group of officers at the roadside. He gave them a civil *'Guten Morgen,'* but was not greatly surprised when one galloped after him and demanded his papers. There was a brief colloquy at the roadside. The officer suggested that Davis had better be interviewed by his general. The general was some distance in advance. At last, Davis reflected, he would deal with someone in authority, perhaps someone who would recognize his name and appreciate his standing as a journalist.

It was about seven o'clock in the morning when Davis was taken in custody and thrust into the marching column between a second lieutenant and a sergeant. The troops were moving at the German equivalent of 'double-quick,' something between a fast walk and a trot. With only brief rest periods every hour, Davis was compelled to maintain this brisk pace until noon.

Sometime during the long march his papers were taken from him and sent ahead by messenger to the general's headquarters. About twelve o'clock a staff car arrived from the front and he was taken in charge by an officer wearing a monocle, with many campaign ribbons on his coat. Obviously an officer of high rank, he maintained a correct silence toward the American newspaper-man during the ride to staff headquarters.

The staff was at lunch in a grove of trees. Davis saw a group of elegant, handsomely costumed officers, wearing gloves, capes, and highly polished black boots. Presently, one of these, a slender young officer wearing a uniform of light blue and silver, detached himself from the luncheon group and came to the road where Davis waited. He loked the newspaperman over, noting details of dress and equipment. He bowed, by way of formal greeting, shrugged his shoulders, and gesticulated with his gloved hands. The American thought he resembled a handsome villainous char-acter then familiar to readers of fiction, Anthony Hope's Rupert of Henzau.

'You are an English officer out of uniform,' the elegant young German said. 'You have been taken inside our lines, and you know what *that* means.' He pointed his right forefinger at Davis's heart and wiggled the thumb. As soon as certain formalities were concluded, the young officer indicated, Davis would be executed as a spy; perhaps later that afternoon, surely before daybreak the next morning.

Another group of American newspapermen trailed after the German Army as it marched south toward the French border. On the Sunday morning Davis and Morgan rode to Hal in a taxicab, two ancient carriages shaped like gravy boats pulled by elderly horses carried seven correspondents in a more easterly direction. A Brussels rumor hinted at an impending clash between the Ger-mans and French near Waterloo. Whatever took place on the historic battlefield—even a skirmish—would be newsworthy. The correspondents hopefully directed their coachmen to proceed to the scene of Napoleonic disaster.

Riding in the two carriages were the four who had journeyed to Louvain the previous Wednesday—Irvin S. Cobb, John T. McCutcheon, Arnot Dosch, and Will Irwin—and three others who joined forces with them Sunday morning, James O'Donnell Bennett of the *Chicago Tribune,* Harry Hansen of the *Chicago Daily News* and Roger Lewis of the Associated Press. All had been to the Hôtel de Ville and were authorized by von Jarotzky's rubber stamps to travel freely about Brussels' environs.

There was nothing much at Waterloo. The big lion on his green pedestal looked down on a small camp of German cavalry, and empty beer bottles showed where the infantry had paused the day before. But no battle smoke hung in the air and no blood stained the historic turf. The hired coachmen in their varnished high hats flicked their whips and the ancient carriages rolled on. Late in the afternoon, they came to Nivelles, an odd little convent-church town. In front of L'Aigle Noir on the Grand Place the two livery-men put their heads together and informed the newspaper correspondents they must turn back to Brussels. Will Irwin, troubled all afternoon by a sore throat, and Arnot Dosch decided to return with the carriages. So five were left to pass the night among the anxious refugees at L'Aigle Noir and take the road for Binche the next morning.

All Monday they pushed ahead on foot, spurred by reports of great battles at Maubeuge and Mons, just over the horizon. The day was pleasant and the road level, but they were unused to vigorous walking; by nightfall, at Binche, they were leg-weary and discouraged. The town, as Cobb remembered it, was given over to dullness and lace making; nor did the presence of German supply trains give it distinction. But while they rested their blistered feet at Binche the next day, the American correspondents managed to acquire a dog-cart, a horse to pull it, and two bicycles. The dog-cart would accommodate only three. By mutual agreement those places were assigned to the more sedentary members of the party; McCutcheon, wiry and active, scorned the ease of the dog-cart, but he had never ridden a bicycle before, and two hours' practice under Harry Hansen's tutelage were needed to keep him upright.

Wednesday morning they took to the road again, the two bicyclists riding ahead as scouts, the dog-cart jogging behind. Before they reached Merbes-Ste. Marie, six kilometers from Binche, the sharp-eyed newspapermen discovered in the roadside litter signs of hasty withdrawal by the Belgians or French. Discarded shoes, a new knapsack, a shoulder strap—all of French or Belgian manufacture—testified to the retirement of Allied troops before the German Army. The disciplined Germans left no scrap of equipment behind.

On through Merbes-le-Château, sister village to Merbes-Ste. Marie, and into La Buissière. There had been fighting here; the mill by the river was destroyed and the miller killed by a German bullet. The townspeople seemed dazed but a few were able to tell the newspapermen about the war that had roared around their heads forty-eight hours before. A young German officer took them on a tour of La Buissière, pointing out where the German infantry had advanced across an open field, crossed the Sambre under fire and driven the French from the town. The French outnumbered the Germans, he said, and had the better position, but the Germans swept everything before them.

On a slope at the edge of La Buissière in the litter of what had recently been the French camp, Irvin Cobb discovered a symbol of Belgium's unhappy fate and put it down in his notebook:

Here from the medley and mixture of an indescribable jumble of wreckage certain objects stand out, as I write this, detached and plain in my mind: such things for example as a straw basket of twelve champagne bottles with two bottles full and ten empty; a box of lump sugar, broken open, with a stain of spilled red wine on some of the white cubes; . . . a saber hilt of shining brass with the blade missing; a whole set of pewter knives and forks sown broadcast on the bruised and trampled grass. Farther down, where the sunken road again wound across our path, we passed an old-fashioned family carriage jammed against the bank, with one shaft snapped off short. Lying on the dusty seat cushion was a single silver teaspoon. Almost opposite the carriage against the other bank was a cavalry man's boot, it had been cut off from a wounded limb. The leather had been split all the way down the leg from the top to the ankle and the inside of the boot was full of clotted dried blood. And just as we turned back to return to the town, I saw a child's stuffed cloth doll—rag dolls I think they call them in the States—lying flat on the road, and a wagon wheel or a cannon wheel had passed over the head, squashing it flat.

I am not striving for effect when I tell of this trifle. When you write of such things as a battle field you do not need to strive for effect. The effects are all there waiting to be set down. Nor do I know how a child's doll came to be in that harried, uptorn place. I only know it was there and being there it seemed to me to sum up the fate of little Belgium in this great war. If I had been seeking a visible symbol of Belgium's case, I do not believe I could have found a more fitting one anywhere.

The newspapermen remembered La Buissière. Here they first encountered war. In those August days the correspondents were impressed by everything they saw and experienced. The colors of war were fresh and vivid. Into their notebooks went every ruined building, every dead animal. The roadside groups of refugees with their bundles, the small taverns crowded with Army officers, the trains bulging with frightened travelers, the faces of pedestrians, the street corner talk—all these had martial significance for the eager newspapermen. They tried to relate everything within range of vision and hearing to the war. The results were uneven. There was little time to sort out the material. Much of the writing was as turgid and disorderly as war itself. But even the breathlessness and disorder in their news reports managed to convey to the people at home what war was doing to Europe and its people. As the months passed, the reporters would grow accustomed to the blood and violence and booming guns, and their accounts would become more technical and restrained.

After La Buissière, the ruined and deserted village of Montignies St. Christophe; after Montignies St. Christophe, Beaumont. Here the odd little cavalcade, jogging into the town square at dusk, blundered into the headquarters of a German Army corps. They must have realized they had reached a turning point in their adventure when they saw the long black staff automobiles lined up at the curb, the officers arriving and departing, the air of military significance centered on the most imposing house in town. This was the residence of the Prince de Caraman-Chimay (once married to Clara Ward of Detroit) which the Germans had taken over, together with the prince's huge wine cellar. German officers on the steps of the Chimay house looked with interest and amusement at the dog-cart, with its escort of bicycles. The Americans decided wisely to report themselves at once to staff headquarters.

A puzzled colonel who spoke excellent English looked over their papers in the hallway. In the library they caught a glimpse of an elegant general seated, booted and spurred at a table with maps before him and the big-game trophies of the prince looking down on him from the panelled walls. The colonel shook his head and looked off into space.

'I do not understand how you are here, you gentlemen,' he said. 'We have no correspondents with our army.'

'You have now,' Cobb remarked, thinking to make a little pleasantry. The colonel was not amused. But he was still friendly in a superior, military way. They would most likely be sent back to Brussels but meanwhile they were to remain in Beaumont over night as 'guests' of the Army and report back to headquarters the next day.

Thursday morning, when they returned (after passing the night in a schoolroom) the atmosphere around the princely residence had changed. The general and his staff were moving out, headquarters was being dismissed. Something had happened, some unexpected stiffening of French and British resistance below Maubeuge had thrown the German timetable off. The colonel who was going to send the newsmen back to Brussels took off with the rest of the staff, leaving them in the hands of a Lieutenant Mittendorfer. Some delay had occurred in requesting a car for their journey. The lieutenant apologized. Would the Americans wait?

The newspapermen waited for two days. For a few hours they were locked in with a group of prisoners in a military jail, then freed with apologies and directed to remain in the tavern. Food was scarce. Since they were 'guests,' Lieutenant Mittendorfer felt under no obligation to provide rations, which he would have had to supply had they been prisoners. At length, on Friday night, they were marched to the railroad station and placed on a train with prisoners and wounded, presumably bound for Brussels. They were still hungry, and all five needed baths, but their first adventure with the German Army had ended without mishap, and they had authentic impressions of war in their notebooks.

The elegant young German officer who had taken custody of Richard Harding Davis on the road to Ath did not carry out his threat to have the American shot as a spy. It may be he never had such intention, merely wanting to use his malevolent authority and watch an unhappy victim squirm. Whatever his motive, he was a smiling, sinister figure, something of an actor and much pleased at Davis's evident distress. The Germans did not have Davis searched or ask to see his notebook. The case against him rested on his passport photograph. This showed the correspondent in a white tropical helmet, wearing a military jacket with two rows of decorations on the left breast. The photograph was indeed so British and military that the Germans could scarcely be blamed for inquiring further into Davis's role.

The passport picture, Davis explained, was made eight years before. The military jacket was similar to that worn by the British West African Field Force when the correspondent followed a British campaign on the African coast. Finding the coat cool and comfortable (something like a golf jacket) he had had his tailor copy it. Since then it had been adopted by other British Army units.

The German officer wagged his head with a cynical smile. A likely story. How about the campaign ribbons? Davis said the decorations were clearly in his favor. They represented campaigns he had covered as a war correspondent—Spanish-American War, Boxer Rebellion, Boer War, Russo-Japanese War, War in the Balkans. No British officer, he pointed out, could have participated in all those wars in which his own country was not engaged. Except as a military attaché, the German said. Davis's clothes were obviously from a London tailor; his passport had been issued by the American Embassy in London, and might well be forged. Although his Alpine hat bore the label 'Knox, New York' it could not outweigh the other evidence against him.

At the end of a two-hour roadside interrogation, the German officer ordered Davis taken by automobile to Ligne, where he was imprisoned in a room on the second floor of a house occupied by the German staff. The matter was being referred to the general commanding the Army corps, and as soon as his signature was affixed to the necessary papers, it was indicated, Davis would be led out behind some mill or factory, or at the edge of a clearing, and shot.

The American journalist, in later reports, pictured his plight as he sat that August afternoon in the bare room at Ligne. A fanatic German soldier stood guard at the door. Every time Davis moved, the guard's rifle would shift to cover him. Two bundles of straw on the floor served as a couch. Tired and dusty from his long march, one foot badly cut across the instep, hungry and disheveled, he bore little resemblance to the handsome, debonair correspondent who had covered war's preliminaries with such spirit at Brussels a few days before.

Somehow he managed to get some water in a bowl and shaved and took a sponge bath. His sore foot cleaned and bandaged, in fresh underclothing and a clean shirt, he got out writing materials and composed a note to Brand Whitlock, American Minister at Brussels:

> Dear Brand: I am detained in a house with a garden where the railroad passes through the village of Ligne. Please come quick or send someone in the Legation automobile. Richard.

Another officer, Major Alfred Wurth, looked in on him late in the afternoon and, hearing him talk, decided he was beyond all doubt an American. Davis entrusted his letter to the sympathetic major, who took it to the staff. Soon things began to happen. A passable dinner was served by the cook, supervised by the Belgian gentleman who owned the house. The sentry was withdrawn. Sometime before midnight, while he dozed on the straw, he was aroused and taken by automobile to a château several miles out in the country. Here the young German officer who had conducted his interrogation earlier in the afternoon announced that he was free, provided he would agree to return to Brussels by a stated route (Ath, Enghien, Hal) and report there to the military governor within two days. If found anywhere other than the prescribed route, or after August 26, he was to be treated as a spy. A pass with those conditions, signed by Lieutenant General von Gregor, chief of the General Staff, was put in his hand, and he was ordered to leave his room and start his journey from Ligne at three o'clock in the morning. An elderly German general gave him a lift in his automobile on the fifty-mile journey back to Brussels. When Brand Whitlock heard his story, and saw how shaken he was, he took Davis to the Hôtel de Ville and had officials of von Jarotzky's military government put into writing that Richard Harding Davis was *not* to be treated as a spy, but as an American citizen well known in his own country and highly recommended by the American minister. Thus ended Davis's misadventure in the wake of the German Army. Some of his newspaper associates thought he must have exaggerated the peril of his brief imprisonment. If he had really been in danger, they argued, why did he not confirm his identification by reaching in his pocket for the letter of introduction from Theodore Roosevelt to President Poincaré of France? (Instead, he had torn the letter to pieces and dropped the fragments in the River Sambre on his way back to Brussels, when it was too late to help or harm him.)

The experience left its mark on him. His usefulness as a correspondent in Belgium was ended. On the train to the German frontier August 27-8, Will Irwin found Davis moody and abrupt toward his fellow journalists. 'True, he had been through a shattering experience the day before, and his nerves must have been still shaky. But that hardly excuses the general discourtesy toward us.'

From the train windows the night of August 27, Davis, Irwin, and Gerald Morgan watched the final phase of the destruction of Louvain by the Germans. Before leaving Brussels that morning, they had learned from General von Lutwitz that Louvain was to be made an example for a crime against the German military force. The burgomeister's son had approached a group of German officers at the Hôtel de Ville, so the German version ran, and, drawing a revolver, had killed the chief of staff and two others. The boy's act was a signal to the Civil Guard, the Germans maintianed, for members of that body began firing from rooftops in the neighborhood on German soldiers in the public square.

Forewarned, the American reporters looked out the car windows as the train approached Louvain. Dusk had fallen and the summer twilight was heavy with smoke from burning houses. Their train waited on a siding or was shunted in the yards for two hours. They were forbidden to leave the cars, but enough could be seen from the windows. Squads of soldiers went methodically from house to house, applying the torch. It was a still summer evening without a breeze; the fires burned straight up and the flames illuminated the long processions of Louvain citizens, carrying bundles and children away from the city, and the smaller, more melancholy files being led out to the fields for execution. As their train resumed its slow crawling toward Germany, the newspapermen watched for another hour the reddish glow in the night sky. Irwin was still suffering from his sore throat and Davis had withdrawn into his own moody reflections. But Gerald Morgan quietly made notes on what he had seen from the car windows at Louvain and his pen scratched on after midnight.

Within a day or two, the two groups of American journalists were across the border in Germany. At Aix-la-Chapelle, free from the Army's custody but still under mild surveillance, they bathed, got clean clothing, and caught up on their sleep. They began to write.

About a week later, Lewis, Cobb, Hansen, O'Donnell, and Mc-Cutcheon signed the statement concerning reports of German atrocities. Obviously it was prepared at the request of German authorities, but there is no evidence that pressure was brought to bear on the U.S. newspapermen. They were not prisoners. The statement reflected their own somewhat limited observations and conclusions.

The Belgian chapter was about finished. In mid-August it had begun almost as a lark for the American newspapermen. Motor cars with flags fluttering at the windshields; the excitement of chasing after war by day, then champagne and music on the hotel terrace at night; off to war in a taxicab! The awesome encounter with the German Army at Louvain and Brussels had broken the lighthearted mood and given the newsmen pause. Most of the freshness and early exhilaration had gone. But the Americans realized, as they sat down to write at Aix-la-Chapelle, that what they had encountered was unlike other wars. It was bigger in scale, swifter in movement. It had moved out of the nineteenth century. The pageantry of bright uniforms, horses, and flashing swords had been supplanted, at least on the German side, by grim, mechanized efficiency. The correspondents tried to convey some of this sense of change and awesome power in their reports to American readers.

VI

TIRED MAN ON A BICYCLE

In Paris the American newspapermen appealed to Ambassador Herrick, and the Ambassador made discreet inquiries at the Foreign Office as to how soon American journalists would be permitted to describe the valiant accomplishment of French arms. The Foreign Office conferred with the harassed War Ministry. The language of diplomacy was used to thank Mr. Herrick for his interest and bespeak his patience and understanding. Perhaps a little later when affairs had become stabilized a more favorable view would be taken of the activities of journalists in the war zone. For the present, no correspondents.

Those newspapermen who went direct to the Foreign Office to argue their case were received by a tactful young attaché, Alexis Leger. Guardedly he expressed the view that correspondents would, under certain conditions, be permitted to accompany the French Army. He suggested that the newspapermen establish their qualifications by obtaining a certificate of health from a physician, three photographs, and six letters from French citizens. Paul Scott Mowrer was one who fulfilled these conditions. He went to the Foreign Office daily, with a book under his arm for the long hours of waiting, and took a seat in the reception room.

As he kept his vigil at the Foreign Office the young newspaperman from Chicago may have observed among the journalists seeking recognition a slender, thin-faced Briton, thirty-seven-year-old Philip Gibbs, applying for credentials as a correspondent of the *London Chronicle*. Gibbs had been in Paris at the outbreak of war and passed the early August days in the anterooms of the War

Ministry and the Foreign Office. Later he would make the same futile pilgrimage to the War Office in Whitehall.

The French, like the British, established a bureau for the issuance of official bulletins on the war. Certain correspondents were summoned to the War Ministry, and, after their character and qualifications had been determined by Colonel Commandant Duval of the Bureau de la Presse and they had agreed to abide by certain rules and regulations, laissez-passers were issued to them. These were green cards bearing the insignia of France and the stamp of the War Ministry. They permitted the bearer to enter the ministry three times daily at 10 A.M., 3 P.M., and 11 P.M. to receive the official bulletins. For several days the privileged holders of the green passes reported regularly at the Ministry of War. They were ushered in with ceremony. There was a pressing forward, a polite scramble as the bulletins were distributed and a hurried departure to waiting cabs. After a week or two, when it became apparent that the bulletins contained neither news nor information, the correspondents who called to receive them dwindled to a handful of wire service men. Presently the word was passed at the Bureau de la Presse that rules were being formulated under which newspapermen might accompany the armies of France and write about the war:

All correspondents must be French or citizens of one of the Allied nations (Britain, Russia, Belgium). They must have a perfect knowledge of the French language. A French correspondent will be permitted to represent a newspaper of England or Russia. Each correspondent must submit certificates of character and physical fitness for the field with three photographs to be retained by the military authorities. He must sign a pledge to abide by the regulations. The correspondent will wear a white armlet with his name, nationality and name of newspaper in black letters. He will not be permitted to go about the theatre of war unless accompanied by a specially detailed officer. He must not leave his quarters without a special permit. This permit will not be issued at advance posts.

The censor at stated times each day will give news which the commander thinks is justified in making public. All code messages are, of course, forbidden, and the correspondents must write their dispatches in French.

Correspondents will be lodged and transported at the expense of the government and they will be entitled to medical service free.

British newspapermen hurried to the Bureau de la Presse with photographs, character certificates, letters from the British Embassy, and letters from their editors. They were told it would be necessary to pass a test in the French language. Most of them had a working knowledge of French and some were fluent in it, but when they reported for the written test they were confronted by linguistic problems which would baffle a Sorbonne professor. It was not easy to become a war correspondent; in fact, it was impossible.

Having formulated the rules, the French had communicated with the British War Office, for it was agreed that they should act together. The British said: No, not now; maybe later. The Americans, hopelessly excluded by the French rules, found some satisfaction in the realization that no credentials were being issued to anybody.

The plight of the stranded tourists still engaged the pens of American correspondents in Paris. Relief committees had been organized; widely known bankers and business executives under the chairmanship of Judge Elbert H. Gary, president of the United States Steel Corporation, worked with the American Embassy staff to provide funds and steamship accommodations for the unhappy and indignant travelers. During the last days of August, as the French Government moved to Bordeaux, a few obscure official paragraphs sufficed to deal with the great sweep of the German Army toward Paris and the desperate plight of French and British arms; yet by the irony of military censorship the cables carried scores of thousands of words concerning the small discomforts and confusion of American tourists stranded in Paris and London.

Paris continued to provide wartime oddities for the frustrated newspapermen. Forbidden to write about battles, they described the fences being erected on the lawns in the Bois de Boulogne to enclose sheep and oxen to provision Paris in case of siege. Unable to watch generals in the field, they told how General Victor Constant Michel, Military Governor, hoped to solve the juvenile delinquency problem in Paris by sending teen-age 'apaches' in small gangs to the country to help with the wheat harvest.

The Ministry of War requisitioned all military uniforms in the wardrobes of all Paris theaters; but whether these few hundred were needed to equip troops, or sequestered to prevent them from outfitting spies, the newspapermen did not learn.

The editorial staff of the *Paris Herald* held a meeting and sent an emissary to James Gordon Bennett to learn what measures the publisher proposed to protect his employees in the event of siege or German occupation. Mr. Bennett sent back word that if they were that worried, they could all quit; he would get out the paper himself, with the help of the printer's devil. A few left that night for London.

A new Military Governor, General Joseph Simon Gallieni, was appointed to administer and defend Paris. One of his first decrees was to prohibit newspapers from publishing scare headlines over two columns in width. Type for the headlines must not be of alarming size. News vendors were forbidden to shout the news or the names of the papers on the streets. On the Boulevard des Italiens, one American correspondent noticed a woman news vendor carrying a sleeping child and calling her newspapers gently so as not to wake him. The news that day was that a great battle had been fought along the line of the Sambre and the Meuse and the French armies were falling back.

A few newspapermen dared the wrath of British and French generals and, like the zealous American in Belgium, saw something of the war in the rear of the battle zone. One of those was Granville Fortescue. He quit Brussels ahead of the German Army and traveled by train to Namur, where he thought the first clash between the invaders and the defending British and French was likely to take place.

Fortescue was not one to rest at Liége on his laurels of the week before. He studied a map of Belgium to determine the most probable routes of the German advance. At the French Ministry in Brussels he got a letter attesting his identity as a correspondent and added another laissez-passer from the Belgians.

Railway travel was not as casual as when he had boarded the train for Liége. His papers were scrutinized in the Brussels Station and again at Namur. In the café where he dined that night he made the acquaintance of Captain Paul Gillian of the Belgian Reserves. In civil life, M. Gillian conducted a wholesale delicatessen business, but the military had appropriated his smoked fish, preserves, and cheeses, and his business was now war. He turned out to be a useful acquaintance. Captain Gillian told Fortescue that a German column was advancing toward Dinant, where several French regiments awaited the attack. Dinant was thirty miles away. When Fortescue expressed a desire to go there, the captain said: 'By all means, I have nothing to do tomorrow and I will be happy to drive you to Dinant.' M. Gillian had the password for the day. Their car was stopped at every hamlet and crossroad along the way, but Gillian's magic waved them on.

There was fighting at Dinant. The newspaperman watched the German attack on the citadel, saw French soldiers killed as they stumbled down the hill, and watched German shells explode in the streets of the town. The French had only a couple of regiments there; an officer told Fortescue the German attack was only a bluff; the real fighting would take place in Alsace.

But there was real fighting in Dinant and Fortescue's notebook was filled with eyewitness observations of the struggle. Late in the afternoon a battery of French 75's arrived and began shelling the German position, but it was too late. The German flag flew over the citadel, the bridges could no longer be defended and Dinant was doomed.

During the early fighting Fortescue sent off a fifty-word bulletin to his paper in London. Now, eager to get a complete story on the wire, he started his retreat from Dinant at dusk along the Florennes highway. His goal was the telegraph office at Charleroi. He passed the first night in a roadside inn, thronged with French officers, most of them asleep with their heads pillowed in their arms on the tables, or, like Fortescue, burrowing in straw on the floor. When he attempted to leave early the next morning, a cynical French colonel questioned him, demanded his papers, and ordered him to report to staff headquarters at Athenée.

Athenée was on the road to Charleroi. Fortescue found the house where the French colors waved over the door and presented his papers to a captain seated at a desk. The captain scowled at his correspondent's credentials and informed him that newspapermen were not permitted to accompany the armies of France. After a brief colloquy, Fortescue gathered up his envelopes and told the captain that since the French refused to accommodate him, he would return to the zone of the Belgian army, where more civil treatment could be had. A few hundred yards along the road, he was overtaken by a cyclist in uniform who ordered him to return. The general wanted to see him.

General Percin turned out to be an elderly fat man with white hair and dyed black mustache. When he had finished informing Fortescue that correspondents were not permitted with the Army, the newspaperman bowed and repeated his intention of returning to the Belgians.

The general said 'no' again, replying that Fortescue was aware of military matters of great importance, and that under the circumstances he could not be allowed to send accounts to his newspaper.

Fortescue explained that as a former Army officer he could distinguish information of military importance; he promised that nothing useful to the enemy would appear in his dispatches.

'How do I know you will keep that promise?' the general asked testily.

'I give my word, Monsieur.'

'Bah! The word of a newspaper correspondent!'

Fortescue had been a newspaperman only two or three weeks, but the honor of the craft already was something to be defended. He had a quick temper.

'My word,' he said, 'I consider as honorable as that of even a French general.'

General Percin glared at him, pushed back his chair and stood upright. His voice took on an unpleasant edge.

'*Les gendarmes!*' he called.

Fortescue did not succeed in sending his dispatch about Dinant from Charleroi. He was taken under arrest, protesting, to Givet, riding on a farm wagon. There he declined to occupy a cell in the military fortress and presented his case so vigorously to the commandant (threatening international complications) that he was permitted to lodge at the local inn, Le Cheval Blanc, under guard. The food was good and Fortescue's dinner—onion soup, roast pigeon, rum omelette—was served in his room by an attractive waitress named Guinevère. The four days of his imprisonment passed quickly. One morning he was taken to Rheims and put on the train for Paris with instructions to report to the police. The detective assigned to conduct him got off the train at the start of the journey, so he was alone when he arrived in Paris.

At the police station, where he showed his papers and recited his grievances, he was received with polite lack of interest. The police lieutenant listened to his tale but seemed disinclined to take sides. When Fortescue demanded to be taken to the American Embassy, the official shook his head and said the embassy would be closed at that hour. Why not just go to a hotel?

At that moment it dawned on Fortescue that he was no longer under arrest. He thanked the lieutenant, walked out, and took a cab to the Hotel Edward VII. The next morning, by bribing a hotel porter and a railway attendant, he managed to squeeze his way aboard an overcrowded train for Calais and by nightfall was in London. Mr. Lawson greeted him with enthusiasm, and once again he was a romantic hero in the *Daily Telegraph* office.

Ellis Ashmead-Bartlett arrived in Paris with his hilarious story of tortuous journeys through the Balkans in search of a war that was being fought in Belgium. He replenished his wardrobe, got a small suite at the Ritz and registered for a laissez-passer at the Bureau de la Presse. To his astonishment, because of censorship and the restrictions placed on correspondents, he seemed no nearer the battle line than he had been in Salonika.

Robert Dunn of the *New York Evening Post,* one of the veterans of the Russo-Japanese War, became disgusted with the daily hand-outs and the frustrations of Paris. He bought a bicycle and got on a train.

Wythe Williams, Mowrer, Elmer Roberts of the Associated Press, and Barnard of the *Tribune* stayed on. The French government had moved to Bordeaux. Nearly all the stranded tourists were gone. Paris was almost deserted, but the roads from the south were dusty and crowded from the droves of cattle and sheep being driven in for the siege. The *Paris Herald* cut down its daily edition to a single page and raised the price from 15 to 25 centimes.

On those still afternoons in late August, the American news-papermen gathered at a shady sidewalk café near the embassy.

Ambassador Herrick was still in town carrying on his duties, although the new ambassador, John Sharp Williams, had arrived and was expected soon to take over. It was a convenient rendezvous for the Americans—this sidewalk bistro—for their offices knew where to reach them and they could observe the activity at the embassy entrance.

The afternoon of Thursday, August 27, a man on a bicycle rode slowly along the street to the sidewalk café. As he dismounted and leaned his cycle against a tree, the newspapermen recognized Robert Dunn of the *New York Evening Post*. He was covered with dirt and very tired. At the table with the other reporters he drank his whiskey slowly and said he needed sleep. Dunn did not talk much about where he had been or what he had seen, except that he had been a prisoner of the British for a couple of days. He was moody and thoughtful, and after a while he got up and went down the street, walking his bicycle. The correspondents saw him turn in at the American Embassy.

Williams waited a decent interval, then paid his recokoning with the waiter and strolled along the avenue to the embassy. Making sure that Dunn had gone, he sent in his card to Ambassador Herrick.

Yes, the Ambassador said, Dunn had brought news from the British front. Naturally, he could not betray the confidence of the *Post* correspondent by disclosing his news to the *New York Times*. But Mr. Herrick could pass on to Williams certain information from other sources. The situation was grave. By the time he left Ambassador Herrick's office that afternoon, Williams knew that the British Army had been thrown back in disorder from Mons and the French beaten at Charleroi. The Germans had opened a gap in the Allied line and the British and French armies were in full retreat.

'The news is such,' Ambassador Herrick said, 'that of course the censor will not let you send it.'

The next day, August 28, rumors of disaster were supplemented by the arrival of refugees from the north. Dunn remained in his hotel room writing the long, dramatic story of his adventures with the British at Mons. He knew it would be futile to submit it to the censor. No part of it could go on the cable, but he might get it back to New York by mail, perhaps within ten or twelve days.

Williams, lacking first-hand knowledge of the battle scene, nevertheless was determined to get some hint of the disaster through to the *New York Times.* On the night of August 28 he began his cable dispatch to the *Times* with routine news, harmless items about war charities and benefits, activities of the Red Cross, unrelated trivia. Then buried halfway down the page, a short paragraph:

Refugees crowding Gare du Nord tonight from points South of Lille.

It was his hope, if the censor passed it, some editor in the *New York Times* office would discover that cryptic paragraph and find on the map the significance of the refugee exodus from 'points South of Lille.' The censor did pass it. But when he got a copy of next morning's *Times* some weeks later, Williams found the dispatch on an inside page, and the reference to the refugees remained buried and obscure.

Paul Scott Mowrer managed to send to the *Chicago Daily News* on August 29 a bulletin stating that the Germans had turned the Allied left flank. Two days later he confirmed the fact, adding that the British and French forces were in retreat, but intact.

Mowrer had a brother, Edgar Ansel Mowrer, who had come to Paris to study and was living on the Left Bank absorbed in a long, critical essay on the plays of François de Curel. Now Paul appealed to his younger brother to take over the routine at the *Daily News* Bureau. If Ansel would sidetrack his scholarly pursuits, Paul offered to teach him the rudiments of journalism and also pay him a salary.

The younger Mowrer was interested to learn that a war was going on. He needed little newspaper instruction. His first few dispatches to Chicago were prefaced by classical quotations and occasionally enhanced by Greek poetry. However, he soon learned that cable tolls were 25 cents a word and became a sound reporter.

September 1, carrying a raincoat and a small black satchel, Paul Mowrer booked passage to London via Le Havre and boarded a train at Gare St. Lazare. He had no intention at the time of going on to London, but it was impossible to purchase a ticket to any French town in the war zone without a police permit. From his study of the war maps, he knew Rouen was a likely center of observation, and when his train stopped at Rouen, Mowrer got off. The city was well behind the battle line. Nevertheless, its streets echoed with the traffic of war and the hotels were jammed with officers, walking wounded, military stragglers. Mowrer, arriving at night, slept on the floor in the dining room of an old hotel by the railway station. In the morning he got a room at the Hôtel des Postes. He went to call on the American consul, Lucien Memminger, who told him what he had learned about the military situation. Memminger gave him a note attesting his U.S. citizenship and directed him to the British camp outside the town.

The British were breaking camp, but some of them found time to smoke a cigarette with the earnest young newspaperman and tell him about Mons. They were regulars, tough and experienced. They had been through hell the week before and blamed the French for pulling back and leaving the British right exposed. Mowrer talked to half a dozen officers and some enlisted men. At a hospital in Rouen he talked to a few of the wounded.

At last he had shaken off the feverish hothouse of Paris and got somewhere close to the war. By nightfall, piecing together the accounts of a dozen embittered Britons, he had a comprehensive story of the defeat at Mons. This was one of the first great clashes of the war, but the world outside knew almost nothing about it. He knew it would be useless to file his dispatch from Rouen; the French censor would kill it. The same fate awaited it in Paris. Mowrer's best chance was to get to London, but that too presented difficulties. He had no pass to accompany the British Army, no police permit to travel behind the lines in France. The distance from Rouen to Le Havre was short, but whether he tried to go by rail or highway, he was certain to be stopped and searched.

Mowrer postponed making a decision. Reasonably safe at Rouen, he got a night's sleep at the Hôtel des Postes. He was at work on his story in the hotel garden at noon the next day when he saw a large limousine drive up. He recognized the occupants—Judge Gary, recently head of the relief committee in Paris, and Mrs. Gary. With them was a traveling companion, James Deering of Chicago. Equipped with papers from Ambassador Herrick and the French Foreign Office, they were on their way to Le Havre to catch a steamship.

The judge remembered Mowrer. The Chicago newsman had worked closely and intelligently with him on the problem of the stranded Americans. When he learned Mowrer wanted to get to London, Judge Gary invited him to ride with them to Le Havre.

After luncheon at the hotel, Mowrer climbed in the front seat of the Gary limousine with the chauffeur. Leaving Rouen, the car was stopped by French and British sentries. The papers of the distinguished passengers in the tonneau were impressive; the sentries saluted and waved the car on. Three times on the short journey to Le Havre the limousine was flagged down by military guards, who never bothered to ask the chauffeur or the young man beside him for credentials. At Le Havre Mowrer got a channel steamer and was in London that night.

He found Fleet Street still seething from an incident which was to have important consequences for the newspaper profession. Five days before, *The Times* (London) had startled the nation with pessimistic reports about what was happening to the British Army in France. The *Morning Post's* denunciation of *The Times'* 'panic journalism' had run well over two columns, and the matter was still under discussion in Parliament. But the British public still had little idea what had happened to the B.E.F. Mowrer got his story cleared through censorship and within a day or two the people of Chicago knew more about what had happened to the British at Mons than the English who lived almost within earshot of the heavy guns.

Lord Northcliffe, walking along Fleet Street, ran into W. Beach Thomas, garden editor of the *Daily Mail*.

'It's no good being in England, is it?' Northcliffe asked. 'Why not go to Paris?'

Since Northcliffe owned the *Mail* (also *The Times*), his casual suggestions were taken seriously by the staff. That was how Thomas stopped writing about petunias and mulch and went to France to become a war correspondent for the *Daily Mail*.

These were strange days for British newspapermen who wanted to cover the war. Philip Gibbs recalled:

We went in civilian clothes without military passports—the War Office was not giving any—with bags of money which might be necessary for the hire of motor cars, hotel life and the bribery of door keepers in the ante chambers of war. The Old Guard of War Correspondents besieged the War Office for official recognition and were insulted day after day by junior staff officers who knew that 'K' hated these men and thought the Press ought to be throttled in time of war; or they were beguiled into false hopes by officials who hoped to go in charge.

Gibbs, a slender, frail man in his thirties, traveled along the edge of the fighting zone with H. M. Tomlinson and W. M. Massey. They joined forces, hired an automobile, shared lodgings and tins of potted beef. Gibbs called his companions the Strategist and the Philosopher; the three made an amiable team. Talking to officers, stragglers, and walking wounded they managed to keep in touch with affairs as the enemy swept down from Lille and Mons. At Amiens they learned of the French withdrawal on the right, the German breakthrough and Smith-Dorrien's valiant stand at Le Cateau. At Beauvais two days later, they learned of the German sweep to the east. That night the frail Gibbs collapsed from fatigue, and the Strategist and the Philosopher carried him up the steps of their hotel to bed.

At first Gibbs carried his dispatches back to the *Chronicle* office, returning across the Channel every few days. Later he saved time by dispatching some by an accommodating King's messenger who carried them to the War Office, where they were forwarded promptly and without question to Fleet Street. Early in September his luck ran out. Arrested by Scotland Yard men at Le Havre, he was taken before General Bruce Williams. The general, sharing Kitchener's distrust of correspondents, said he had a mind to have Gibbs 'shot against the white wall.' Instead, he put him under house arrest at a hotel in Le Havre, where the correspondent languished for a week. Gibbs managed to smuggle a note out to Robert Donald at the *Chronicle*. Donald caused a rumpus at the Foreign Office, and General Williams was ordered to return Gibbs to London. There he rested awhile, returning eventually to France and an outstanding correspondent's career.

BAD NEWS FROM AMIENS

On Saturday afternoon, August 29, a courier arrived at *The Times* in Printing House Square, London, with two news dispatches from the Continent. One was from W. Arthur Moore, a *Times* staff correspondent, and the other from Hamilton Fyffe of the *Daily Mail*. They had been sent that morning from the vicinity of Amiens, via Dieppe and New Haven. The news in their penciled pages was gloom and doom. Something very like disaster had overtaken the British Expeditionary Force.

I would plead with the English censor, [Moore wrote] to let my message pass.... Our losses are very great. I have seen the broken bits of many regiments ...

Fyffe was no less moved:

This is a pitiful story I have to write. Would to God it did not fall to me to write it. But the time for secrecy is past. Only by realizing what has happened can we nerve ourselves for the effort we must make to retrieve it....

Those *Times* editors who remained at Printing House Square to cope with the Sunday War Edition were called into conference. Moore and Fyffe were experienced, responsible newspapermen, not given to drink or exaggeration. Yet their accounts, which seemed to verify each other, were so unusual as to plunge *The Times* editors in a quandary. Should the dismal reports be held up, awaiting official corroboration from the War Office? Should the more gloomy passages be crossed out and the hints of disaster toned down before submitting the pages to censorship? The editorial conference reached no satisfactory conclusion. The two dispatches were sent to Whitehall Saturday evening after painful editorial soul searching. Pencil brackets indicated where cuts might be made. *The Times* editors believed it more than likely that censorship would seize the two dispatches in its maw and nothing would be heard from them again.

The editors reckoned without Mr. F. E. Smith of the War Office Information Bureau, who was patriotic and unpredictable. The doubtful dispatches were returned to *The Times* after being held three hours in Whitehall. They were approved substantially as Moore and Fyffe had written them. A censor's pencil had fussed over them; there were signs of things crossed out and restored, passages temporarily deleted and then marked 'stet.' A confidential note signed 'F. E. S.' stated:

Passed—far more than the War Office would sanction but I think we should realize the truth.

Mr. Smith had also penciled at the end of Fyffe's dispatch an admonitory postscript:

England should realize and realize at once that she must send reinforcements and still send them. Is an army of exhaustless valor to be borne down by the sheer weight of numbers while young Englishmen at home play golf and cricket? We want men and we want them now.

Since the outbreak of war some three and a half weeks before, England had grown accustomed to the silences, the vague and evasive bulletins from the War Office Information Bureau which purported to record the progress of British arms. A certain reticence was understood. Kitchener was a quiet man. The enemy must not be informed about the army's plan. The whole British Expeditionary Force had been moved to the coast and ferried over to France without premature mention in the press. Since the official announcement August 18 of its safe arrival on the Continent, the lack of news had been accepted as prudent concealment of the blow about to be dealt the enemy. So it was that on Sunday morning, August 30, *The Times* of London's front page spoke to a nation uninformed, a little anxious, hoping for the best.

Along Fleet Street, rival editors read the shocking news in *The Times* with understandably mixed emotions. Where were their own correspondents when the British regiments were being broken to bits? If disaster had overtaken the Army, why had the War Office not issued a bulletin? If *The Times* and *Daily Mail* reporters were permitted to follow the Army's misfortunes at Amiens, why were the same privileges not extended to all the press? The day being Sunday, no one at the War Office could be found to answer those questions. The Information Bureau had no information; at the censorship office, discreet silence.

By Sunday night the opinion in Fleet Street was that *The Times* had gone overboard. The news from France still was vague, but no subsequent dispatches received since Saturday from other sources confirmed a major disaster. It seemed to newspaper rivals that someone at *The Times* had given undue prominence to exaggerated and unverified reports. Furthermore, it appeared incredible that censorship would approve such dispatches, so (it was assumed) *The Times* must have published them without official permission. All this was the more regrettable, for *The Times* had always been regarded as safe, conservative, dependable. In their indignation the other newspapers did what they could to minimize the gloomy reports and scold *The Times*.

On Monday, probably aroused by the outcries in Fleet Street, members of Parliament laid aside other business to denounce *The Times* in the House of Commons. Prime Minister Asquith joined the attack. The Government's wisdom in placing censorship under a member of the Opposition was now appreciated. The influential *Morning Post* devoted more than two columns to the affair, denouncing its rival in Printing House Square for what it called 'panic journalism.'

The Times expected Mr. Smith to come forward and assume a reasonable share of responsibility for the doleful dispatches. But Mr. Smith was a politician and the occasion called for equivocation. The censors, he declared, had acted without complete information on the situation in France. They had been misled but their motives were patriotic.

At length, *The Times* got around to issuing a statement which was read in Commons. The *Daily Mail* swung a cudgel in defense of its elder brother by printing Mr. Smith's confidential note, virtually recommending publication of the dispatches. The air cleared a bit. Mr. Smith resigned to enter active service with the Army. (As Lord Birkenhead, he was to go on to a useful career as Lord Chancellor.) Reports from the Continent verified the fact of a full-scale British retreat. For a few days, at least, it had been more disorderly rout than withdrawal. Moore and Fyffe had encountered one of the worst phases around Amiens. Yet the British Expeditionary Force had not been destroyed. What was left of it—a very sizable and battered remainder—was now refitting and pulling itself together just southeast of Paris. The dispatches of Moore and Fyffe were borne out by the facts, although breathlessness and for-God's-sake were not in the best tradition of British journalism.

Kitchener remained aloof from the fracas, but as he read *The Times'* special War Edition that Sunday morning it may have occurred to him that his own knowledge of the Army's whereabouts and condition was incomplete. While the uproar still echoed in the House of Commons and Fleet Street, Kitchener crossed the Channel and took the train for Paris. He met Sir John French at the British Embassy on September 1. No newspapermen were present to record their conversation on this historic occasion, but it is probable that Kitchener wanted to know the Army's condition and why it had not turned and fought the German. Sir John reported the main course of events since the encounter with the enemy at Mons, but refused to be hurried into battle. He would fight, he told Kitchener, in his own good time. At one point when the question of military jurisdiction arose, Sir John suggested that the Secretary of State for War return to London and get on with recruiting and munitions, which was his business, and leave fighting, which was Sir John's, to the field commander.

What concerns us chiefly about this journey of Kitchener's is the decision he reached upon his return to Whitehall. Sometime during his brief sojourn in France, perhaps as he stared out the train window, his mind went back to the shock and uncertainty caused by the Amiens report in the Sunday *Times*. These newspapers! What could be done about them? He had ordered all pressmen barred from the Army's lines, yet they managed to get their untidy dispatches back to London. Undoubtedly the newspapers had a function in wartime; perhaps the War Office should provide more material about the Army than the formal bulletins.

Back in Whitehall, Kitchener discussed the problem with his associates, then suggested that an Army officer be appointed to supply information to the press. Something more was needed than the official bulletins now being issued by the War Office Information Bureau. The newspapers wanted fresh and timely reports, such stuff as might be jotted down by an eyewitness. Very well, the Army would provide the eyewitness.

Some years before, the attention of Winston Churchill had been caught by a small brochure on Boer War tactics called 'The Defense of Duffer's Drift.' The author, Major Ernest D. Swinton, had originality, Mr. Churchill told the War Council, lively style, and a sound knowledge of the mechanics of war. The Churchill recommendation was sufficient for the War Office. On Monday, September 7, Major Swinton, then serving as Deputy Director of Railways for the British Expeditionary Force, was detached from duty and ordered to report to Whitehall. Sir Reginald Brade, War Office Secretary, outlined his new assignment. Lord Kitchener, Sir Reginald explained, had definitely come to the conclusion the nation ought to háve more news about the war than it was getting. Swinton had been selected to go to France as official correspondent, to write for the press. The next day Kitchener, busy at his desk, shook Swinton's hand, and in a brief interview told him what he wanted. He was to report to the Commander-in-Chief at General Headquarters on the Continent and write daily articles on the operations of the Army—not in the style of official reports but more informal, something like the diary of a trained, discreet observer— an eyewitness.

That afternoon Swinton started for France. He carried in his kit a packet of foolscap, some pencils, and India rubber. As he took his seat with the King's messenger, Major Cadogan, in a staff car destined for Southampton, it did not occur to him that Kitchener was using him as a device to keep newspapermen from doing their job. He could not know as he rode down to Southampton that Sir John French would receive him with suspicion, or that Fleet Street would come to ridicule his eyewitnessing. Least of all could he foresee that during those months while he was fussing with his foolscap and India rubber in the by-lanes of France, his mind would be at work developing a revolutionary new weapon, one which would have a profound effect on the outcome of the war.

VIII

IN DURANCE VILE

On the terrace of the Café Napolitain, just around the corner from the Place de l'Opéra, the newspapermen gathered early in the afternoon of Friday, September 4 to discuss the strangeness of a Paris drained of tourists, government clerks, and vehicles. The exodus had begun early in August but in the last ten days with the doomsday approach of the Germans it had become a great mass migration, a Niagara of human movement. The Government was gone to Bordeaux with all its bureaus and secretaries; the gold of the Bank of France was removed to Rennes. Wealthy families had departed with their cooks and nursemaids and chauffeurs. Shopkeepers and waiters long since had joined their regiments. Signs on shops declared *'Personnel mobilisé.'* The last of the tourists were on trains for the channel ports. A great stillness had settled over the city; no children were left to play in the empty streets.

Most of the correspondents had been following the German advance on their maps. Namur and Dinan thad fallen; German siege guns had smashed the border fortress at Maubeuge. After Mons and Charleroi, the armies of the Kaiser had swept down across northern France—Lille, Lens, Arras, Le Cateau, St. Quentin, Douai, Aulnoye, Cambrai. Another gray-clad army poured through Luxembourg. By the end of August, the invaders were across the Somme, across the Oise, across the Meuse, across the Aisne. It seemed inevitable that they would soon be at the gates of Paris.

Over their glasses, the newspapermen talked about the eerie emptiness of the city. Paradoxically, their own ranks had been reduced by the war. Little more than a month before, 142 journalists had assembled for the Caillaux trial. Now with a story of far greater importance—the impending fall of Paris to the Germans—

fewer than a score remained. Most of those were Americans. Nearly all French journalists had joined the colors. Many of the British, fearing imprisonment if Paris fell, had accompanied the French Government to Bordeaux, or had gone back to London. That morning—September 4—the military government of Paris had advised the remaining correspondents to quit the city; but they had stayed on. Frederick Palmer and William G. Shepherd arrived from Le Havre. The only correspondent officially accredited by Britain, Palmer wore his officer's uniform and carried a rare civilian pass, but he could get no nearer the war than the others. The newcomers were particularly struck by the deserted streets and the silence. Palmer, checking in at the hotel where he always stayed, found himself one of half a dozen guests among 500 empty rooms. There was something ghostly about the big hotel, Palmer said, for in each of the rooms a clock ticked on in correct time and the elderly man whose task it was to wind them with a key made his rounds faithfully every day to keep them going. Yet there were no guests to consult the dials, and the city was so quiet one could almost hear the 500 clocks ticking on in the empty rooms.

Bill Shepherd told of walking with another correspondent from their hotel to the Place de l'Opéra. Standing in the middle of the avenue, they looked for blocks in every direction without seeing a vehicle or a human being. The prairies of Texas, he observed, were never more silent.

All afternoon the newspapermen listened for the sound of German guns. Uhlans had been reported that morning in the forest of Montmorency, ten miles away. The question seemed to be, would the Germans attack the city's outlying defenses that night, or wait until Sunday morning? Few among the American correspondents believed the French could stem the German advance.

One who had gone to the Bureau de la Presse for the afternoon communiqué reported an unusual concentration of taxicabs in the streets off the Boulevard des Invalides. There was some speculation about this. Some thought they had been summoned to haul the War Ministry—its desks, files, and minor bureaucrats—off to the south. But no, more likely they were being used to transport some of General Manoury's army, charged with the defense of Paris, toward the front. At the time the news had little significance, but some of the correspondents, having nothing better to do, wandered off to watch the procession of taxicabs roll across the Seine bridges and note that they carried soldiers with rifles. Most of them left the city by the Porte de la Chapelle. What did it matter? They, too, would be swallowed up in the maw of the German advance. Later, when they thought about it, the American newspapermen saw the role of the taxicabs as unique. Whoever heard of sending an Army off to battle in nondescript autos of the city pavements, with meters clicking? They could not learn how many regiments were thus transported, or how vital this troop movement was to the turning of the tide along the Marne. But at least it was something they knew about and could write about, and soon it became a legend: The Taxicab Army had won the Battle of the Marne!

The correspondents heard no guns Friday night or Saturday. But Sunday morning the rumble of artillery drifted down on the still September air. They were not German guns, but French 75's; the Battle of the Marne had begun. No newspaperman was present at the Battle of the Marne. Few were closer to it than the terrasse of the Café Napolitain. (One correspondent was taken prisoner by the French and dragged along at the Army's rear for four days.) But when it was over, they realized something historic had happened.

The official communique issued at Bordeaux on incomplete information and transmitted to Paris Monday was a curiosity of understatement. Given out at the Bureau de la Presse, it stated merely:

> Our advance troops defending Paris have come in contact with the forces of the right wing of the Germans. *The small engagement has resulted to our advantage.*

It was no longer possible for the newspapermen to sit on the terrasse of the Café Napolitain and wait for something to turn up. By Wednesday, September 9, it was clear that the German advance had been checked at last and Paris saved. Now surely the correspondents must go over the ground where the historic battle had been fought. Some renewed their entreaties at the Foreign Office, others tried again at the War Ministry. They did not consult together or discuss their plans; rivalry had succeeded apathy, and it was every man for himself.

First to benefit from the favorable turn in France's military fortunes were the veteran Associated Press correspondent Elmer Roberts, and Palmer, representing in theory all three American press associations. They were included in a select party of six, the others being M. Paul Doumer, former president of the Chamber of Deputies, now acting as *chef de cabinet* to General Gallieni, commandant of Paris; General Fevrier of the French Medical Service; and two other officers of Gallieni's staff. They drove out the Porte de Pantin and were saluted by reservists as their handsome big automobile took the road toward Meaux. At a little hamlet called Claye, fifteen miles from Paris, they saw the high-water mark of the German advance from the northeast. There the gray-clad skirmishes had been turned back. Beyond, from Meaux to Château-Thierry, then north to Soissons, they passed through battleground cut and slashed by shellfire, marked with new graves. East of Soissons, toward Compiègne and Noyon, they saw a horizon overlaid with smoke and shaken by artillery fire, as the battle raged twelve miles away. Turning southwest in late afternoon they came back through Senlis to Paris. Theirs had been a historic journey. For the first time, two American newspapermen had been conducted through France's military lines and permitted to look at a battlefield.

Richard Harding Davis and Gerald Morgan, newest American correspondents to arrive in Paris, took advantage of the relaxed atmosphere to ride across much the same terrain. But they were unaccompanied by officers and equipped only with passes authorizing them to call at the War Ministry for the daily communiqué. Riding in a hired limousine with liveried chauffeur, they proceeded along the road to Meaux, examined the first evidences of fighting along the highway north of the town, and followed the course of the week-old battle to Soissons. Returning to Paris that night, Davis almost convinced himself that he had witnessed, in an artillery duel across the Aisne, the culminating stage of the Battle of Soissons.

Wythe Williams enlisted the aid of Ambassador Herrick and

obtained a formidable laissez-passer. It was signed by General Gallieni and authorized the bearer to proceed to the scene of the recent battle to view the damage inflicted by the Germans on unfortified villages. With two others similarly equipped, he loaded a motor car with tinned food, wine, biscuits, cocoa, sausage, bottled water, and bread. An alcohol lamp for roadside cooking was added, plus aluminum plates and collapsible drinking cups. Prepared for a more extended stay in the battle zone, they took a northerly road out of Paris. After two days of adventures behind the lines they were arrested and imprisoned at Senlis. Their car and the passes were confiscated.

Granville Fortescue was in town with a pocketful of gold and a fresh assignment from the *Daily Telegraph*. Editor Lawson wanted him to discover what part the German Crown Prince had played in the Battle of the Marne, and whether it was true that the German battle orders for the first week in September had been drawn up with the idea of having the Crown Prince personally lead his troops into Paris.

Fortescue told an odd tale of his departure from the newspaper office in Fleet Street. Lawson told him to draw what funds he needed from the *Telegraph*'s business office. Descending the stairs, he turned in at the small, musty counting room where the money was handled!

> The kindly gentleman who alone presided over the cash in the office asked me how much I needed.
> 'Two hundred pounds,' I ventured.
> On a nearby desk was a grocer's scale. The cashier dropped two weights on one end of the balance. He proceeded to open the ancient safe. He pulled out one of the lower drawers, took a grocer's scoop, scooped up a pile of glittering sovereigns and dropped them gingerly onto the scales. When the gold coins balanced the weights, he poured them out on the table.

Fortescue went to the *New York American* office in Paris. Asking the Hearst correspondent C. F. Bertelli how best to get to the battlefront in the neighborhood of Châlons, he was met with a shake of the head. Impossible. The French wouldn't even let their own pet journalists go that far from Paris. No newspaperman could hope to see any of the battleground, much less the actual fighting, without a pass, and no one had a pass.

Nevertheless, Fortescue took a train the next morning for Sézanne, 100 kilometers east of Paris and a little more than half way to Châlons. In the Hôtel du Boule d'Or, where he managed to get lodging, he heard a good deal about the fighting ten days before and some mention of a high German officer who might have been the Crown Prince. This German officer made his headquarters at the Château de Mondemont, about ten miles northeast of Sézanne. Fortescue hired an automobile, driven by a French reservist, and, arriving at the château, talked to the gardener, some peasants, and a priest who had witnessed much of the fighting. When the concierge was showing him the untidy rooms of the château, left by the hurriedly retreating Germans, he told him, 'Every night the Crown Prince makes a fête.' How did the concierge know it was the Crown Prince? Because he had the nose of the Crown Prince; he had seen his portrait in the Paris comic paper. That was enough for Fortescue. He made a quick survey of the terrain, questioned some local folk and a restaurant proprietor and then, back in Sézanne, reconstructed a whole battle in which the Crown Prince was defeated and his dream of marching into Paris at the head of the German armies shattered.

This made interesting reading in the *Daily Telegraph*. Again Editor Lawson complimented Fortescue on his enterprise; no other newspaper had the detailed story of the fighting below Châlons and the sensational rebuff of the Crown Prince.

It turned out to be a fairly accurate account of one segment of the Marne battle, but Fortescue was mistaken about the high command. It wasn't the Crown Prince but the Duke of Wurttemberg. Since his whole sensational story was built around the defeat of the Kaiser's own son and heir, the journalistic lapse was a major error, but Fortescue took it in stride. So what?

'This error enormously enhanced the value of my story. It was lifted from the *Daily Telegraph* and spread over the front pages of almost every newspaper in France.'

Flushed with early successes at Liége and Dinant, praised by his editor, his name on the front pages of a dozen great newspapers in Britain and America, Fortescue had not yet learned in his four weeks' experience as a correspondent that accuracy and integrity —and sometimes humility—are more important in journalism than expediency.

At dinner at Maxim's one night in mid-September, Richard Harding Davis, Gerald Morgan, Granville Fortescue, and Ellis Ashmead-Bartlett reviewed the plight of the war correspondent and the evil time that had fallen on their craft. These distinguished journeymen, all veterans of earlier campaigns, were distressed at the continued obstinacy of the French High Command in refusing to allow correspondents with the Army. They were made to wait endlessly in the anterooms of military bureaucrats, and when they ventured to take the field, they were harassed, insulted, arrested, treated as spies.

A few hopeful signs were noted. Since the German Army had been turned back at the Marne, a few correspondents had ventured beyond the confines of Paris. General Gallieni was said to have issued a few special passes. The recent experience of Fortescue in the neighborhood of Sézanne, and Morgan up toward Soissons, indicated that the military police were relaxing their vigilance.

Warmed by comradeship, stirred by the recital of their grievances, fortified by champagne, teased by the unspent expense funds in their pockets, they decided again to challenge military restrictions in an expedition to the front. It was agreed that Davis would provide the transportation. The Wheeler syndicate had put at his disposal a large, chauffeur-driven limousine, its trunk already stocked with tinned meats, cheese, paté, and table wines. For credentials, the four would depend on the laissez-passers issued by the War Ministry for admission to the Bureau de la Presse. Before they left Maxim's for a few hours' sleep, they had decided on their destination. This, too, was Davis's contribution. Instead of war correspondents seeking battle, they would go to Rheims in the guise of tourists, to see what the Germans had done to the historic cathedral. As they stumbled across the Place de la Concorde on the way to their hotel, it seemed like a wonderful idea.

A sentry stopped their automobile at the Porte de Pantin the next morning. He scrutinized the pass which Ashmead-Bartlett extended from his seat beside the chauffeur, and waved them on. Fortescue and Ashmead-Bartlett considered this a good omen.

They had escaped from Paris, the road ahead was open, and luck was with them. But Morgan warned that other sentries and military guards waited in the zone of battle. They were not out of the woods. Besides, he said, the sentry at Pantin was impressed more by the size and magnificence of their automobile and chauffeur in livery than by the slip of paper. They would encounter others who would read the paper more closely and pay less attention to the car.

They passed through Meaux without incident and turned northeast. Beyond, the landscape was littered with the pockmarks and debris of war. For two hours along a road that flanked the Marne, they passed ruined hamlets, farmhouses blackened by fire, rubble, and new-made graves. Most of the bridges had been destroyed. The 56-mile journey took most of the day. Late in the afternoon, their car climbed a low hill beside the river, and there was Rheims.

Thin plumes of smoke rose from the town where recent fires from German shells had burned, and smoke wisps drifted around the towers of the great cathedral. As their car moved through suburban streets choked with refugees and their carts, the correspondents learned that the city was still under occasional fire from enemy artillery, and the population was demoralized. The demoralization soon overtook their chauffeur. After they had crossed the canal bridge, he jammed on his brakes and announced the end of the line.

The correspondents proceeded on foot. The streets swarmed with military activity. Officers with long capes on horseback, couriers on bicycles, and small squads of infantry wearing blue blouses and red pantaloons scurried about on their martial errands. Nobody stopped the correspondents or questioned their right to be there. The Germans had occupied Rheims from September 4 to September 12, then pulled back across the Vesle. On the 18th, when it became known that French forces had entered the town, the Germans began a systematic bombardment with field guns and howitzers.

The four newspapermen went directly to the cathedral, for this was their story. In the square beneath the historic church they looked up at the great towers, blackened by smoke, and walking around saw beneath their feet fragments of glass from the great rose window shattered by exploding shells. This was the place.

Gerald Morgan recalled, where Joan of Arc had helped place the French crown on Charles VII. Morgan knew much of its history. All but six of the Kings of France had been crowned there. It was considered one of the most beautiful structures produced in the Middle Ages. Now it was a shambles. Many of the statues on the west façade had been broken off, much of the rose window shattered. The interior was scarred by fire and shell blasts. Fortescue got out his camera and began to focus on the wrecked masonry; the others talked to the curé, M. Frezet, and to the Abbé Chinot, and made notes.

While they climbed the stone stairway to the bell tower, the abbé explained what had happened since the Germans occupied Rheims September 4. When they pulled back across the Vesle on the 12th, they left behind about fifty of their seriously wounded. The priests tended the wounded as best they could, turning a portion of the nave into a hospital by covering the stone floor with thick layers of straw. When the French forces returned to Rheims on the 18th, the Germans began to bombard the city. One of the shells had struck a wooden scaffold erected several months before to repair the walls. When this caught fire, the flames spread to the roof, and soon blazing oak beams and molten lead were falling among the wounded. The straw caught fire and the helpless Germans were threatened with death by smoke suffocation, flame, and falling timbers. When the priests, at the risk of their own lives, helped the wounded out on the cathedral steps, enraged citizens of Rheims threatened to bludgeon the helpless men to death. Only the intervention of the Archbishop Landreux held the crowd at bay.

In the cathedral tower, Abbé Chinot pointed out the French and German artillery positions. Two French aviators, on leave, joined the party and scrutinized the landscape across the Vesle. While they watched, the rumble of German guns was heard again and loud explosions marked where shells fell near the cathedral walls. Fortescue said the German artillery observers might have seen uniformed men in the tower, surveying the countryside through binoculars. Ashmead-Bartlett wore a British officer's tunic and carried glasses. Whatever the provocation, it was unmistakable that the Germans were still directing their fire at the old church.

The four correspondents stayed two days at Rheims, finding

lodging at the Hotel du Nord. Davis, Morgan and Ashmead-Bartlett worked late over their stories, reconstructing the tales told by the abbé, describing the terrible ordeal of the German wounded and the ruinous effects of the enemy's shells on the beautiful Gothic structure.

Again the following morning, the four correspondents went to the Cathedral Plaza. In the morning light, they made another survey of its broken statues and shattered windows. Again they questioned the Abbé Chinot. Davis and the abbé walked through the dim interior, and the priest pointed out the altars and statues of the Virgin which had been miraculously spared by the flames. Fortescue took more pictures, and he and Ashmead-Bartlett got down on their knees and picked up fragments of glass, blue, green, crimson, and yellow-gold beneath the great shattered windows. The glass was nearly five hundred years old, Morgan said, and the secret of its rich coloring was lost in the Middle Ages.

Davis was now anxious to get back to Paris with his somber story, but one errand remained. While the others made a rendez-vous with their chauffeur, Davis called on William Bardel, the American consul. He rejoined the others a short time later, bringing three bottles of champagne of a good year which Mr. Bardel had contributed from his cellar.

It was 10 A.M. when they made a last survey of battered Rheims and climbed in their limousine for the return journey. There was a difference of opinion about the route they should take to Paris. Morgan wanted to get away from military activities as quickly as possible and urged the others to direct the automobile south through Epernay. But Fortescue and Ashmead-Bartlett had heard that there was fighting ten or twelve miles west of Rheims. Why not press their luck a little? They might see something of a real battle by taking the road to Fismes. Over Morgan's protest, they took the road to Fismes.

On the outskirts of Rheims, they picked up a hitchhiker, a farmer who verified the reports of fighting and said that his farm overlooked the battle area. If they would give him a ride to Fismes, he would be their guide and host. It seemed a reasonable bargain. But a few miles further west, their progress toward Fismes was slowed by the military traffic on the road. Supply wagons and artillery batteries, marching infantry columns, troops of cavalry moved in a steady stream along the highway. Frequently they were required to pull off the road and stop to accommodate the military flow. Several miles short of Fismes, about noon, they were directed to quit the highway at a crossroads hamlet, Ravigny; their limousine paused before a house from which hung staff colors—a military headquarters. A young staff lieutenant emerged, stared at the automobile and its civilian occupants, quickly crossed to confront them.

Ashmead-Bartlett extended his War Ministry pass and explained that they were English correspondents.

The lieutenant was not impressed. He noticed that their pass gave them permission to visit the headquarters of the General Staff in Paris—at certain hours of the day. There was no permission to come with the armies in the field.

Davis explained they had been at Rheims and were returning to Paris with accounts of the outrage committed by the Germans on the historic cathedral. The lieutenant shook his head.

Davis appealed to Gerald Morgan, who spoke better French, to explain their mission, and Ashmead-Bartlett also joined the discussion, but the lieutenant was not impressed. He ordered them out of the car and led them across the road to the house with the flags. The chief of staff and his adjutant were summoned. These officers examined the papers, letters, and passports produced by the four correspondents. Again, at Davis's urging, Morgan explained that their stories of the shelling of Rheims Cathedral by the Germans would be read by many millions of readers in the United States. Sympathy for France would be aroused and the American Republic would become a spiritual ally. Davis and Ashmead-Bartlett were such widely known journalists, Morgan said, that their work commanded attention throughout the English-speaking world.

The chief of staff was unmoved by Morgan's earnest pleas. He shuffled the credentials in his hands and conferred with his associates. The newspapermen overheard the word: *'des espions.'* They were reconciled to being disciplined for venturing too far without proper passes, but until then it had not occurred to them that the logical, reasonable French would mistake them for spies. The adjutant advanced the view that their credentials might have been stolen or forged.

Morgan remarked that if the four of them were German spies it was unlikely that they would be riding so conspicuously in the French lines in a big limousine.

Why not? replied the chief of staff. German spies were capable of any arrogance. The matter had come to an uncomfortable impasse when a newly arrived line officer recognized Ashmead-Bartlett as the newspaper correspondent who had been with the French Army in Morocco five years before. They shook hands, and the newcomer explained to the chief of staff that these assuredly were not spies but newspapermen and he would vouch for them.

The recognition relieved the tension, but it did not release them. The chief of staff said they had seen too much on their unauthorized jaunt. He would have to consult his general before deciding what to do with them. Meanwhile, they would be good enough to accompany the gendarmes to a place where they could relax while awaiting word from the general. The place of relaxation was a barnyard compound in the rear of the house, surrounded by a stone wall. Like all French barnyards, it harbored a manure pile. When they realized that the French proposed to detain them in a cattlepen, Fortescue and Davis made a noisy protest.

The French Army, startled by the vigor of this protest, compromised by allowing the four correspondents to eat their luncheon on a bench outside the barnyard. As the newcomers unpacked their sandwiches and opened cans of canned meat, they were greeted by raucous laughter from the barnyard gate. A group of newspaper colleagues from Paris, taken in custody two days before, gave them a sarcastic welcome.

Fortescue recognized the leading spirit of the barnyard group— Wythe Williams of the *New York Times*. The two were not friendly. Williams's sarcastic greeting had not endeared him to the others. Fortescue suggested that they pay no attention to the barnyard rabble. In meekly accepting disgraceful imprisonment they had dishonored journalism. Besides, they were unwashed and their clothing was disheveled.

So Davis, Ashmead-Bartlett, Morgan, and Fortescue ate their sandwiches and drank their wine apart from the others and replied to their hilarious taunts with only hauteur and indifference.

In the afternoon there was another anxious moment when the chief of staff returned with General Asebert to consider the disposition of the correspondents. From unofficial sources members of the Davis party had heard that they were to be confined in the farmyard for eight days. They were ready to make another vigorous and prolonged protest to the General when the chief of staff, after a conference with his superior, announced that they were to be returned to Paris. The matter would be turned over to staff headquarters for disposition.

The two groups of correspondents, traveling in separate automobiles, began the journey back to Paris at 3 P.M. Although still under guard, with gendarmes riding beside the chauffeurs, they had no doubt that once back in the city their troubles would be over. It was almost midnight when the two automobiles entered the courtyard of the military government headquarters on the Boulevard des Invalides. The captain in charge of their party entered the building to report, and, while they waited, Davis and Morgan, Ashmead-Bartlett and Fortescue stretched their legs in the yard. Williams and his companions were not permitted to leave their car. Half an hour passed. The captain emerged with Major Henri Bernstein, the French playwright, whose military duties involved censorship and the press. These two brought the news that the correspondents were to be sent to a military prison and held under arrest.

Fortescue had controlled his temper during most of their difficulties, but now, with Bernstein's announcement, he broke into a violent rage. He had been an Army officer, he shouted, and he did not propose to be dishonored by imprisonment. This did not please his newspaper colleagues, unable to claim military standing. He mentioned the name of an influential relative in the United States who would be offended, and reminded his captors that he had fought at San Juan Hill and been a military aide to President Roosevelt.

Major Bernstein's only answer was to order him to get into the automobile. He was going to jail.

Fortescue faced the officer and shaking his fist under his nose, called him a pompous ninny. He demanded that Ambassador Herrick be notified, that Colonel Cosby be sent for, that the *New York American* office be called.

Bernstein once more ordered Fortescue into the automobile, saying that he was holding up the others, who were all seated quietly in the cars. When Fortescue said 'No' again, Bernstein called for a gendarme to assist him into the car.

The gendarme advanced and lowered his bayonet until its blade pressed the correspondent's waistcoat. He was prodded, still protesting, against the running board and fell backward across the knees of his companions.

A few minutes sufficed to carry them through the quiet streets to the gloomy pile of Cherche-Midi off the Boulevard Raspail. Iron gates creaked and again they found themselves in a stone courtyard. This was the military prison where the unhappy Dreyfuss awaited his trial. It was musty and damp and the jailer waiting to escort the seven newspapermen to their cells carried an oil lantern. The kitchen had long been closed and there was nothing to eat. This was a crowning indignity.

The Davis car had made several stops during the afternoon, taking advantage of those pauses when the chauffeur asked directions to seek refreshment at the nearest tavern. But none of the party had eaten dinner, saving their appetites for Paris food and wine. Those who had accepted the situation philosophically now raised their voices at the prospect of going hungry to a cold bed.

When the head jailer had listed the names, he considered the matter and decided they might send out for supper. Ashmead-Bartlett took a roll of large bills from his pocket and financed the operation with a 1,000-franc note. While they waited for food and wine, the newspapermen renewed their protests with such vigor that the prison authorities began to listen. Nothing quite like this had ever disturbed the routine of the old prison before. It was something like the last act of *Die Fledermaus*. The noisiest demonstrator, Fortescue, was permitted to go under escort to seek aid at the American Embassy. Meanwhile, the warden telephoned to a high official of the French Military Government.

Food came presently, accompanied by a dozen bottles of table wine and another dozen of champagne. The hungry newspapermen sat at a table in the prison reception hall, and for a time their expressions of indignation gave way to more agreeable comments on the roast duck, cold smoked salmon, baked chicken pie with vegetables, salad, and assorted cheese. The jailer accepted a glass of wine and expressed the opinion that they were surely not ordinary prisoners. To this they agreed. Fortescue returned to find they had saved a bottle of champagne and half a roast *poulet*. Although he had reached one of the secretaries, his mission at the embassy had failed. Williams attributed his failure to an old row Fortescue had had with the military attaché.

The wine had made them mellow, if a little noisy, and they were in good spirits as they studied the caterer's *addition*. Instead of letting Ashmead-Bartlett settle the bill with his 1,000-franc note, the newspapermen decided to share the cost and insisted on written receipts, dated inside Cherche-Midi Prison, showing that they had paid for their suppers.

While they were involved with the caterer's arithmetic, the military official summoned by the warden's telephone call arrived. He recognized Wythe Williams, Davis, Morgan, and Ashmead-Bartlett, and realized at once the importance of the material Davis and his companions had brought back from Rheims. Seizing the caterer's bill, he tore it up; these gentlemen are guests of France. He had no doubt that the whole affair could be settled amicably in the morning. Meanwhile, he suggested that instead of passing the rest of the night in Cherche-Midi's cells, the newspapermen return with him to the Boulevard des Invalides. The Military Government had taken over a girl's school adjoining staff headquarters, and comfortable lodging could be had in the dormitory. The offer was accepted readily by all except Richard Harding Davis, who declared he must pass the night at Cherche-Midi. Earlier in the evening, taking advantage of Davis's boyish enthusiasm and credulity, Ashmead-Bartlett had remarked what a wonderful story Davis could write if the prison authorities would only lock him up for the night in the cell once occupied by Marie Antoinette. His imagination roused by champagne, which likewise dulled his sense of history, Davis fell for the hoax. The others, he said, could go to the schoolgirls' beds if they liked, but for him he wanted to share the cell of the tragic queen. He had been inconvenienced and treated ungraciously by the military; now by way of amends they could humor his journalistic whim.

It was after 3 A.M. and the hour for comedy had passed. Everyone was tired after the long day of travel and wrangling. Those few who were in on the hoax were embarrassed by Davis's gaucherie, the others irritated and bored. The military official said that Marie Antoinette's tomb was not here.

But her spirit must return, Davis argued, to the cell where she passed her last hours on earth.

That cell, the official explaned, was in the Conciergerie on the Ile de la Cité, not in Cherche-Midi. There was an awkward silence. Davis turned on Ashmead-Bartlett, who said gravely, I am a cad, and then everybody laughed.

Ambassador Herrick interceded for the American newspapermen at the Foreign Office the next day and obtained parole, which provided they must not leave Paris for eight days. Ashmead-Bartlett was included in the general amnesty.

Davis's story on the German bombardment of Rheims Cathedral was passed by the censor and appeared two days later on the front pages of scores of American newspapers. Gerald Morgan wrote a fine account of Rheims, too, but Davis said it read like an essay on Gothic architecture.

Fortescue's photographs made a double-page spread in the *London Daily Telegraph,* and were published widely in America. The rambunctious amateur had scored again.

THE SPLENDID STORY

Newspapermen always linked Will Irwin to San Francisco. He had broken in there on the *Chronicle,* a youngster just out of Stanford University, before going East to work for the *Sun* in New York. It was not just his California background and Western manner which stamped 'San Francisco' on his personality along Park Row, but an extraordinary story he had written in the *Sun*—'The City That Was.' This was a reconstruction in print of San Francisco, almost block by block with all its famous landmarks, and something of its spirit, the day after the great earthquake and fire of 1906 reportedly had reduced the city to ruins and ashes.

By 1914, Irwin ranked among the first ten American journalists, not far behind Richard Harding Davis and Irvin S. Cobb. He had gone to Europe with his Park Row reputation and Western zest, $500 in gold in a money belt around his waist, war commissions from *Collier's Weekly* and the *American Magazine.* In the early months of the war he accomplished little. The great stories seemed to elude him; he could not get his teeth into anything significant. With Cobb and McCutcheon he watched the German Army pour through Louvain, but by the time he got the story on paper for *Collier's,* Davis's fine account of the German host at Brussels had appeared in scores of American newspapers and the war had moved on. A sore throat turned him back from the party of American correspondents trailing after the German advance. Returning to Brussels, he had tossed feverishly two days in a hotel bed. When his throat was improved, he joined Gerald Morgan to follow the German right wing; Maubeuge had fallen, the historic encounter between the Germans and British at Mons had taken place, and only the refuse and litter of battle remained. He and Morgan returned empty-handed. Back in Brussels again, Irwin accompanied Morgan, Davis, Dosch, and Mary Boyle O'Reilly by train to Aix-la-Chapelle. That journey enabled them to see something of the burning of Louvain, but by the time he reached London, Louvain's fate was an old story, and there was little he could add to it, except 'I watched the affair from a train window.'

Some crisis in Irwin's personal affairs made it necessary for him to return to the United States. He had accomplished nothing outstanding; now the frustrated correspondent must lose more valuable time crossing the Atlantic again. But the September voyage was not a total loss, because westbound he was able to write a couple of acceptable magazine pieces, and on the return journey he met a man named George Gordon Moore.

Irwin stayed in New York only three days, time enough to transact his personal business, signing papers in a lawyer's office; then, anxious to get back to Europe, he booked passage on the *St. Louis,* sister ship of the *St. Paul.* One of his fellow passengers was James Hopper, another magazine writer, going over for *Collier's.* In the smoking room of the *St. Louis,* Irwin and Hopper met an affable, well-tailored traveler who showed much interest in their profession and indicated he might be in a position to help them. This was George Gordon Moore, handsome, well informed, somewhat mysterious, wealthy, debonair. Although an American, he seemed to have important connections in England and knew a great deal about Britain's military affairs. Before the voyage was over, Moore showed Irwin cable messages from Sir John French indicating he was a trusted friend and confidant of the British general then in command of the British Expeditionary Force. This was an important connection for the American journalist, something that might lift him into an inner circle, give him a glimpse of personalities and events above the reach of ordinary newspapermen.

For a time, nothing came of it. Irwin took his chances with the other correspondents in France, dodging behind the fighting lines, which were slowly becoming stabilized, and shuttling between the Channel and Paris. In late October, he stayed at the Grand Hotel in Calais. The Germans had shifted their attack to the British front and Irwin tried, by carriage and on foot, to reach some vantage point where he might see some fighting. He was arrested and sent to the rear. For two or three days, he worked as a stretcher bearer.

Once on the dock at Calais he ran into Moore, who had just come from Sir John French's headquarters near Ypres—a friendly exchange, casual hello and good-by.

Calais was declared out of bounds for correspondents early in November, and Irwin went back to London. He became involved with a group organizing food and relief for Belgium, headed by an American mining engineer, Herbert C. Hoover, who had been an upperclassman at Stanford when Irwin was a rambunctious freshman. The Hoovers had a house in Hornton Street, Kensington, and Irwin moved in with them. A great battle was being fought in northwest France, but only fragmentary accounts came through censorship, and most of the newspapermen, like Irwin, had given up. Irwin worked out some magazine pieces in London, threw himself into the Belgian relief problem—which was largely a matter of rousing the United States—and in December sailed for home again, to organize publicity for the Hoover project. Frustrated, sidetracked, unable to point to a single outstanding piece of work after four months of war reporting, Irwin went on a monumental drunk in New York New Year's Eve and emerged from a monumental hangover feeling somewhat better.

Nineteen fifteen brought a change in his fortunes. At the end of January he got a long cablegram from George Gordon Moore. The debonair American wanted him to return to England; he would be given an opportunity to see something of the war and learn what was going on. The cable was discreetly worded but there was enough in it to raise Irwin's hopes, and he confided enough to the *Tribune* to arouse the newspaper's interest in what he might discover. So, back to England in February he went with a newspaper contract in his pocket. A surprise was in store for him at Euston Station. When the boat train arrived from Liverpool, Walter Hines Page, the American Ambassador to the Court of St. James's, was on the platform to shake his hand and wish him well. This was unusual for a newspaperman—to be treated with such deference.

Moore took him to dinner at Lancaster Gate, the London residence which the wealthy American shared with Sir John French. The talk was about censorship, the munitions shortage, Kitchener, the War Office. There was some mention of the battle of Ypres. Moore gave the American newspaperman to understand, confidentially, that his friend Sir John had just about saved the day for

Britain at Ypres. Of course it was an old story. Strangely enough, it had not been told.

As the evening wore on, Irwin learned that Moore had consulted Ambassador Page, Herbert Hoover, and others concerned over Anglo-American relations. The problem was to find an outstanding American journalist, help him gather essential facts, and through his pen tell the story of British military achievement to the world. That story had been lost, fumbled, obscured in bureaucratic fog. Kitchener was sitting on it. A vigorous editorial stroke was needed to pierce the censorship shrouding affairs in France and jolt Kitchener's monolithic complacency. Irwin's record showed him to be able and trustworthy. His writing had color and gusto. He was the man for the job.

Several days later Irwin had a private meeting with Lord North-cliffe. The British publisher knew enough of Irwin's background to put him at ease. He also knew Irwin was putting together some hitherto undisclosed facts about the war. Northcliffe wanted to be in on it. Whatever Irwin wrote, he would publish in the *Daily Mail.* When Irwin explained his contract with the *Tribune,* the publisher cabled New York and bought the English rights to the *Tribune*'s war news. It was agreed that Irwin's story would be sent to New York by mail or courier, circumventing War Office censorship. The *Daily Mail* would publish it in London, acknowledging its American origin, the same day it appeared in New York.

'We may face a jolly row, you and I,' Northcliffe told Irwin as they shook hands over the deal.

A few days later—about the middle of February—Irwin sat down at a desk in Lancaster Gate and began to write 'The Splendid Story of the Battle of Ypres.'

The Battle of Ypres had lasted 16 days, beginning late in October and continuing through the first two weeks of November. Irwin had seen a small segment of it and had helped carry some of the wounded at Calais, but at the time no one except the officers in command knew much about it. William S. Shepherd of the United Press probably saw more of it than any other American correspondent. Philip Gibbs described some of the fighting in dispatches to the *Chronicle.* Colonel Ernest D. Swinton, official 'Eye Witness' attached to Sir John French's headquarters, sent back some guarded accounts of the fighting for release by the War Office Information Bureau, but his dispatches were ten days late. The action was so continuous and confused that Swinton, even with his superior facilities for gathering news, was unable to learn the approximate truth about the situation until long afterward.

Thus, although it was more than three months in the past, few in England or America knew what had happened on those autumn days in Flanders when the thunder of German guns could be heard along the Channel.

Irwin's desk at Lancaster Gate held Sir John's official reports, maps, memoranda from the War Office, and confidential information gathered by George Gordon Moore. A coal fire glowed in the library grate. Moore came in at discreet intervals to answer questions, verify dates, fit pieces together. In a glass cabinet nearby was the gold baton of a British Field Marshal, proud symbol of French's command.

This was quite a journey from the hubbub and litter of the old *Sun* office, but Irwin threw himself into the Battle of Ypres with the same gusto and feverish concentration which had recreated San Francisco on Park Row eight years before. He took the British Expeditionary Force on its valiant retreat from Mons to the Paris suburbs, put it into the line at Soissons to help the French win the Battle of the Marne, and moved it back to Flanders in October in time to meet the German's thrust toward the Channel. Through the closing days of October and early November he traced the shifting phases of the long, terrible battle as Sir John maneuvered his meager forces and inspired them to beat back the onslaughts of the determined Hun.

The morning 'The Splendid Story of the Battle of Ypres' appeared in the *Daily Mail,* Irwin, released from his arduous task, strolled along the Strand and dropped in at a haberdasher's to buy some shirts. He told the proprietor to send his purchases to the Savoy Hotel, giving his name. The haberdasher dropped his pencil. 'Mr. Irwin! Mr. Will Irwin! Oh, I want to tell you how I was moved by your splendid story of Ypres! Magnificent! Everyone is talking about it!'

When he got back to the Savoy, the hotel clerks were beaming too. There were a dozen telephone calls. A duchess wanted him for tea; a Pall Mall club sent a guest card. During the afternoon messengers arrived with invitations to dinner. For the next two weeks, Irwin was the social lion of London. Mayfair opened its exclusive doors; dinner invitations piled up, most of them bearing crests of the British nobility; societies and clubs invited him to come and say a few words.

This was a giddy experience for the spectacled newspaperman. He attributed it, sensibly, to the fact that the British had for the first time been given a graphic connected narrative of historic events, hitherto obscured by censorship. But at the same time that he was enjoying the praise and attention unusual for a journalist, Irwin became aware of a slight coolness at the War Office and in Fleet Street. The resentment of British newspapermen toward the ebullient American was natural enough: he had beaten them on their home grounds and he had evaded censorship by a device. But in Whitehall, the resentment had a different source. Kitchener and Sir John did not see eye to eye on the conduct of the war. Irwin's splendid Ypres gave all the credit and glory to the British commander in the field, and the War Office could not overlook the extravagant praise lavished on a general whose ambitions appeared to outrun his ability.

Viewed more calmly later, 'The Splendid Story of the Battle of Ypres' disclosed two serious flaws. It overemphasized Sir John's role, and it ignored the substantial contribution made by the French Army on the British right. The War Office bided its time. Early in the spring, orders were issued quietly to arrest Mr. Irwin if he attempted again to cross the Channel. His credentials were canceled. He was blacklisted both by the British and the French. No longer a social lion, discredited by the war lords on both sides of the Channel, Irwin scraped together some magazine pieces out of war's backwash in London and turned once more to the Belgian relief work of his friend Herbert Hoover. He had gone up like a skyrocket and come down like a stick. Nearly two years would pass before he could resume his career as a war correspondent.

X

FOOLSCAP AND INDIA RUBBER

Kitchener's attempt to bar all newspaper correspondents from the Army's lines and provide the reading public with glimpses of the war through an official eyewitness was, of course, doomed to failure. The official mouthpiece sometimes stutters; often it is too smooth. Inevitably it lacks freshness and candor and variety. Under the circumstances Major Ernest D. Swinton of 'Duffer's Drift' made a straightforward, courageous try. He arrived in France with his bundle of foolscap and India rubber just a few days after the Germans had been thrown back in the First Battle of the Marne. After the long motor ride with the King's messenger from Le Havre, followed by a sleepless night, he finally located Sir John French's headquarters at Coulommiers, due east of Paris. The British Commander-in-Chief was busy and his nerves were on edge. Suspicious of Swinton's mission, he imagined at first that Swinton had been sent by Kitchener to keep a watch on the general's actions. When Swinton convinced Sir John of his role as 'eye witness' for the press, the Commander wanted his reports to present Sir John's views on the proper conduct of the war. Swinton declined. He had been appointed to give the British public any news that could be divulged without disclosing military information to the enemy; he could not use his position to challenge the policy of the Government.

Sir John accepted the situation. He told Swinton he was greatly disturbed by the failure of the War Office to send him the Sixth Division, then embarking for France. With the Sixth, he intimated, he could have driven the Germans back in a rout—with some help from the French, of course. But Kitchener had let him down.

The Commander called in General Lambton, who had been collecting reports and making notes on current operations, and instructed him to make his information available to the newcomer. Henceforward, Swinton would be a member of Sir John's official family. After a talk with Major General Henry Wilson, second in command—who shared General French's dim view of Kitchener—Swinton looked around for a place to work. He found a packing case in a corner of a room where the intelligence staff was working, got out his foolscap, and started to write 'Dispatch from an Officer at the Front.' The date, September 11, 1914.

From Coulommiers, French's headquarters were moved to Fère-en-Tardenois. Two newcomers arrived from London to assist 'Eye Witness' Swinton, Colonel J. E. Edmonds and Captain Lord Percy. Later at Abbeville, Swinton got another addition, G. S. Oxburgh, Superintendent-Clerk, who brought a typewriter and a black deed box, with more foolscap and India rubber.

With opportunities to listen and observe, Swinton picked up some odd scraps of news behind the British lines. In rear areas he watched groups of soldiers punting a football and trotting about the village *place* in a pick-up game of soccer. Commenting on this typical British sport, he wrote that, according to rumor, a low-flying German aviator who observed those activities reported back to his command that the British forces were thoroughly disorganized and running about their post in blind panic.

Another item concerned a transaction between a British cavalry division and a division of Turcos (French Algerian) infantry in an adjoining sector. The cavalry force lacked artillery support because of an ammunition shortage; the Turcos were low on rations. Two thousand tins of bully beef went from the British cavalry stores in exchange for the support of two of the Turcos' heavy guns.

The affair seemed harmless enough when Swinton's pen scratched it out on September 29. Censors passed it, London editors printed it. The War Office, on the other hand, found it indiscreet, and Swinton was reprimanded. 'Eye Witness' had disclosed to the enemy an embarrassing shortage of artillery ammunition and also revealed the proximity in the line of British cavalry and French colonials. It is possible Swinton's lapse, if it was a lapse, was called to the attention of the War Office by newspaper editors. Chafing under Kitchener's restrictions, impatient to send their own correspondents to France, they were inclined to be critical of the official 'Eye Witness,' conscientiously as he might fill his role.

Turning from military concerns, Swinton tried his hand at human interest color and atmosphere. Early in October he described scenes in the rear areas:

In the presentation of striking contrasts this war is no exception to the rule. Within sight of the spot where these words are being penned the chauffeur of a general staff motor car is completing his morning toilette in the open. After washing hands and face in a saucepan minus handle, which he has balanced on an empty petrol can, he carefully brushes his hair with an old nail brush, using the window of the car, in which he has slept, as a looking glass. From the backward sweep he gives his somewhat long locks, and judging by his clean, but dull brogue shoes it is clear that he has once been a 'knut' [dude, Beau Brummel] in spite of his oil stained khaki service jacket and trousers. He is, in fact, an ex-public school boy who enlisted for the war to do his bit for his country and a right useful part he is playing.

The resignation with which many of the inhabitants accept whatever happens is a remarkable feature of the situation. They seem in no way perturbed by the incursion of strange officers and men billeted on them, whose presence, even if they appear in the shape of deliverers, must be at least a great inconvenience. At the dinner hour yesterday in a house which at ordinary times is a second class café in a small country town this trait was exhibited to a curious degree. The main entrance of the café opens onto a combined entrance-hall and kitchen containing a long, zinc-covered table and furnished with a large cooking range. Whilst the officers billeted in the house were eating lunch and smoking in the salon next door, a continuous stream of orderlies, motorcycle dispatch riders, intelligence agents, telegraph operators and staff officers were passing through the hall, one soldier servant was frying something at the range and others were slicing tomatoes and onions at one end of the table.

Quite unperturbed amidst a cloud of flies the patron, his wife and family were discussing their own dejeuner with gusto, immersed in their own affairs and also in a shower of grease, for they were eating artichokes, each petal of which was first dipped in a bowl of melted butter and conveyed to the mouth with a flourish. There was so much noise that it was impossible from inside the house to hear the incessant booming of the guns.

Nothing here offended the War Office or gave the censor pause. But in Fleet Street editorial rooms and taverns, the dispatch was greeted with ridicule. The chauffeur's morning toilette, the inn-keeper's family at lunch seemed to the newspapermen superficial and trivial at a time when the greatest war of all history was approaching a crisis. It was about this time, when the essential futility of his task became apparent, that Swinton's alert mind began to turn in another direction.

Sometime early in October, after a number of British counter-attacks had been stopped by German machine gun fire and when it was apparent that the enemy's vastly superior machine gun equipment was taking heavy toll of British lives, Swinton began to wonder whether it would be possible to manufacture a heavy, armored vehicle capable of traveling over rough terrain and of attacking gun positions with impunity. He had watched an American tractor with caterpillar treads in an English field some months before, and the basic design seemed admirably suited for rough going. Since his duties as 'Eye Witness' were not arduous, and gave him time for reflection as well as observation, he was able to develop his idea with rough sketches. He prepared a memorandum on the proposed vehicle. On October 20, he returned to London on leave and submitted his idea at the War Office. It was turned down.

He got back to British headquarters at St. Omer in time to eye-witness the long, desperate battle around Ypres. This occupied him and his staff until late in November; yet they never were able to get a comprehensive account of the affair back to London; the scale of operations was too big. In December, fighting slowed down all along the front from Belgium to Lorraine. The Armies burrowed like moles in the ground and waited for spring. Swinton continued to send his reports back to Whitehall. Now he had time to resume work on his armored vehicle; he made a new set of sketches. He would present the idea for a tank to half a dozen officers, in the field and at the War Office, before it would finally be found acceptable and put into production. Except for the time and opportunity afforded by his post as eyewitness, it is likely the development of this revolutionary new weapon would have been long deferred, or would have waited for another inventor.

The winter of 1914-15 was the beginning of the Dark Age of war correspondence. Many of the newspapermen gave up. Richard Harding Davis, Irvin S. Cobb, John T. McCutcheon, Bill Shepherd, and others returned to the United States. Wythe Williams, Philip Gibbs, Ellis Ashmead-Bartlett, and Percy Noel joined the Red Cross, carried stretchers, acted as ambulance attendants and hospital orderlies to catch some glimpses of what was going on.

The publication of Irwin's 'Splendid Story of the Battle of Ypres' spurred London newspapers to build up fragments of news received from France into major battle pieces. For a time, undoubtedly, they overdid it, provoking Sir Stanley Buckmaster, Government Press Bureau Director, to protest:

> The magnitude of the British task in this great war runs serious risks of being overlooked by reason of exaggerated accounts of successes printed daily in the Press and especially by exhibiting posters framed to catch the eye and magnify comparatively unimportant actions into great victories. Reported reverses to the enemy are proclaimed as crushing defeats, Germany is represented as within measurable distance of starvation, bankruptcy and revolution and only yesterday a poster was issued in London declaring that half the Hungarian Army had been annihilated.
>
> All sense of just proportion is thus lost, and with these daily and often hourly statements of great Allied gains and immense enemy losses, the public can have no true appreciation of the facts or of the gigantic task and heavy sacrifices before them.
>
> The director appeals to all those who are responsible for the Press to use their influence to bring about a better knowledge of the real situation and rather to emphasize the efforts that will be necessary before the country can afford to regard the end for which we are striving as anything like assured. The posters, more especially those of the evening papers, are very often preposterous as well as misleading and, at such a time those responsible may fairly be asked to exercise a reasonable restraint and help the nation to a just appreciation of the task it has undertaken and the necessity for unremitting effort to secure the only end that can be accepted.

There was some justification for that reasonable protest to the British newspaper proprietors. Yet Sir Stanley's communication left an opening for a valid counterstroke. If the newspapers were oversensationalizing the news, was it not because the War Office had suppressed information which the public was entitled to know? The publishers met, considered their problem and formulated their reply.

March 26, 1915

To the Director of the Press Bureau

Dear Sir:

My council have had under consideration your memorandum of March 12, 1915, Serial No. D 183, for which in their opinion there is no adequate justification. The Press has dealt faithfully with the news furnished by the Naval and Military authorities, but it may well be that the public misunderstand the situation and that this misconception is producing serious results. If, however, the people are being unduly soothed and elated the responsibility lies with the Government and not with the Press. In this connection my council desire to direct your attention to the optimistic statements of the Prime Minister, Sir John French, 'Eye Witness' and other persons possessing official information. The Press acts upon the news supplied. If this is inaccurate or incomplete, the Government cannot blame the newspapers. My council desire to represent that the methods now being adopted are fraught with grave public danger. Ministers are continually referring to the importance of energy and self-sacrifice on the part of the industrial population, who cannot be expected to display these qualities unless, generally speaking, they are acquainted with the facts. In dealing with the news, the Naval and Military authorities should consider not only our enemies and the armies in the field, but the commercial and industrial classes at home, upon whom so much depends. It is futile to endeavor to disregard the long-established habits and customs of the people. Yours faithfully,

George A. Riddell

This exchange cleared the air. Late in March and in April, three parties of newspaper correspondents were permitted by the War Office to make short tours behind the lines in France. They were accompanied by Army officers, and their movements were closely restricted, but they saw how the troops lived, they waded in muddy trenches, and they took back to London a first-hand glimpse of the front.

Shortly after those first tentative excursions by selected groups of correspondents the static front in Flanders erupted in the Second Battle of Ypres. This was not intended as a major offensive by the Germans, but it achieved historic significance through the introduction of poison gas to the fighting on the Western Front.

The gas attack was launched against the Forty-fifth (French)

Division at Langemark, north of Ypres, about 5 P.M. April 22. No newspapermen were there to watch the brownish-yellow vapor as it drifted from the German lines to the trenches manned by French colonials. Within a few minutes, as the deadly chlorine fumes inundated the trench system, panic seized the African troops, and those that survived fled gasping to the rear. Unable to cope with this fearful new weapon, the Forty-fifth Division abandoned its guns and gave up the entire sector on a two-mile front, leaving the Canadian division on the right with its left flank in the air.

Cautiously, as the gas waves subsided, the Germans advanced into the French position, but they failed to realize the opportunity in their grasp. The gas had been discharged late in the afternoon; soon darkness cloaked the area, concealing the great gap in the French lines and the extent of their demoralization. By morning the British and the French had begun to reinforce the line and close the gap, thus preventing a large-scale breakthrough. Another gas attack April 24 forced the adjoining Canadians to give ground, but within a few days the advantage of surprise had been lost, and improvized masks and respirators restored confidence to the defending Allied troops.

An American was among the first of the newspapermen to learn about the gas attack. Through the good offices of the same George Gordon Moore who had helped Will Irwin gather material for his 'Splendid Story of the Battle of Ypres,' Bill Shepherd was invited to Sir John French's headquarters in France. The United Press man arrived at St. Omer just as the Germans were about to launch the Second Battle of Ypres and was the only correspondent on the British front (except Eye Witness Swinton) when the gas attack was launched at Langemark. Shepherd did not actually witness the twilight spectacle which introduced a new element to modern warfare—Langemark was 30 miles from St. Omer—but he learned about it that night. He tried to tell something about the gas attack in his first story from the British front, but censorship precluded anyhing but vague and obscure references which failed to convey its real significance.

Eye Witness Swinton approached the story warily. Five days after the event, he announced the gas attack with circumlocution and restraint.

27th April

Since the last summary there has been a sudden development in the situation on our front and very heavy fighting has taken place to the north and northeast of Ypres, which can be said to have assumed the importance of a second battle for that town. With the aid of a method of warfare up to now never employed by nations sufficiently civilized to consider themselves bound by international agreements solemnly ratified by themselves, and favored by the atmospheric conditions, the Germans have put into effect an attack which they had evidently contemplated and prepared for some time.

At this point Swinton paused to trace the location of the battle line on the British front as it stood just prior to April 22. This required some 12 lines; then:

An effort on the part of the Germans in this direction was not unexpected, since movements of troops and transports behind their front line had been detected for some days. Its peculiar and novel nature, however, was a surprise which was largely responsible for the measure of success achieved.

Major Swinton's pencil now disclosed, at long last, that the German surprise was a cloud of chlorine gas. In contrast to his casual approach to the extraordinary event, another British 'eye witness' gave a more dramatic and graphic description of the scene.

Utterly unprepared for what was to come, the [French] Division gazed for a short while spell bound at the strange phenomenon they saw coming slowly toward them. Like some liquid, the heavy colored vapor poured relentlessly into the trenches, filled them and passed on. For a few seconds nothing happened; the sweet smelling stuff merely tickled their nostrils; they failed to realize the danger. Then, with inconceivable rapidity, the gas worked and blind panic spread. Hundreds, after a dreadful fight for air, became unconscious and died where they lay—a death of hideous torture with the frothing bubbles gurgling in their throats and the foul liquid welling up in their lungs. With blackened faces and twisted limbs, one by one they drowned— only that which drowned them came from inside and not from out. Others, staggering, falling, lurching on, and in their ignorance keeping pace with the gas, went back. A hail of rifle fire and shrapnel mowed them down and the line was broken. There was nothing on the British (Canadian) left—their flank was up in the air. The northeast corner of the salient around Ypres had been pierced. From in front of

St. Julien away up North toward Boesinghe there was no one in front of the Germans.

The new method of warfare produced loud outcries against Germany in Britain and France, and eventually its impact weighed heavily in the neutral countries. Indeed it may be said, considering the limited gains and surprise attack won in Flanders, that the political advantage to the Allies greatly outweighed the temporary military advantage to Germany.

The British and French were slow to capitalize on the propaganda weapon the Germans had placed in their hands. Under stringent censorship regulations, with correspondents barred, the confusion and terror of the first gas attack could not immediately be disclosed in the press. While the military situation remained in doubt, nothing could be published. Twenty-four hours later. Sir John French sent to the War Office a reference to the 'irritating smoke' as a footnote to the day's battle report. Eventually, when correspondents had an opportunity to talk to gassed victims in hospitals and interview those who had witnessed the scene as the gas engulfed the trenches, the story assumed sensational prominence in the war news. (Sir John French did not get around to writing his official report on the gas attack until June 15.)

While the fumes and strangeness of the first gas attack still hung in the air over Flanders, a distinguished London journalist visited the British front. Charles à Court Repington, military correspondent of *The Times,* had served in the Army with Kitchener in Egypt and South Africa and later as military attaché in Brussels. He had turned to journalism in 1904, when an unfortunate domestic complication interrupted his military career. In ten years with *The Times* his forthrightness and assurance in military affairs had given him a special place in British journalism.

Repington, with special credentials from the War Office, passed several days at Sir John French's headquarters at St. Omer. The Second Battle of Ypres (April 22-May 25) was in its middle phase. *The Times* correspondent talked long to the British Commander-in-Chief, dined at the headquarters mess, and watched the inconclusive fighting around Hill 60.

Back in London Colonel Repington wrote in *The Times* (May 14) that victory was being denied the British Army in Flanders because of a lack of high explosive shells. He criticized the War Office policy, which still placed main reliance in old-fashioned shrapnel and ignored progress in high explosive ammunition which had revolutionized artillery's role in trench warfare. It was apparent from tone and context that *The Times* man spoke for Sir John French, or at least reflected his views. In his role as an independent journalist, Colonel Repington could bring into the open matters forbidden to Eye Witness Swinton. In Army circles it was known that sharp differences existed between Sir John French and Kitchener over the munitions supply, but until the publication of Repington's article the field commander had no way to make his protests effective.

Sixty years before, the Crimean War dispatches of another *Times* (London) correspondent, William Howard Russell, had similarly criticized military policy, shocking the nation and contributing to the downfall of the Aberdeen cabinet. Now, within a few days of Repington's disclosures, the nation was aroused, and Commons was angrily debating the lack of high-explosive shells. As a direct result of Repington's article in *The Times,* a coalition government was formed May 25, and David Lloyd George became director of a newly created department—the Ministry of Munitions. Britain's war effort, thereupon, took a great stride forward.

Meanwhile, the French War Ministry had begun to accredit a few newspaper correspondents for regular service at the front. Now the British, as spring advanced, finally arranged for a group of permanent newspaper correspondents with the Army. Swinton had learned early in May that a change was contemplated in the function of the official military correspondent; on June 1 word came from Whitehall that the post of Eye Witness was to be abolished.

Early in June, six accredited journalists crossed the Channel with their portable typewriters and kit bags and traveled by motor car to the village of Tatinghem, near general headquarters at St. Omer. Their press center was a small old house, called by courtesy a château, the summer home of a French dry goods merchant. With their own mess, and specially assigned cars with drivers, they began the routine of covering the war nearly eleven months after its onset. The British officer in charge of their movements was amiable. He provided maps, arranged for the daily communiqué, suggested tours along the front. The correspondents would not learn until more than a year later that as he left the War Office, the officer in charge had been given a last confidential instruction: 'Waste their time.' Kitchener was still fighting a rear guard action against the press.

Philip Gibbs recalled the scene as the first group of correspondents settled down to work. It was only a short ride over Cassel Hill to the edge of the Ypres salient. In the mornings they divided up the front, each going forth in a separate car.

When they had returned to their château in the afternoon, they would sit around a table in the library going over their notes and exchanging information on what they had gathered on their separate missions. They shared all the significant news. Then to work. W. Beach Thomas, the *Mail*'s garden editor, put into his stories little glimpses of nature among trenches and shell holes, some wild flowers growing in the ravaged earth, a bird's nest in a wrecked caisson. Phillips 'turned pink and white under the hideous strain of nervous control, with an hour and a half for two columns in the *Morning Post*. A little pulse throbbed in his forehead.' Philip Gibbs worked over his copy with a critic's detachment, striving to embellish the military news with his own reflections, and lightening the paragraphs with pictures wrought from his imagination. Frederick Palmer, the American, drew upon his long military experience to make the battle developments intelligible for American readers. Through the long summer of 1915 they worked and worried over their writing as men on trial. For the first time the outside world began to understand what was happening on the Western Front.

XI

SURVIVORS AT QUEENSTOWN

About the time the first group of correspondents began their work behind the British front in France, the *London Evening News* published a story telling of the vision of a wounded British soldier during the early retreat from Mons. This was 'The Bowmen,' by Arthur Machen. It was presented as fiction, but newspapers do not always make the distinction clear.

In 'The Bowmen' the wounded man, lying at the edge of a field, saw an extraordinary spectacle. As the German hordes advanced toward the outnumbered British forces, the soldier saw in the clouds a troop of old English archers, such as fought at Agincourt. As he watched, the ghostly company in the sky fitted arrows to their longbows and drew on the oncoming Germans. A strange thing happened. The Germans stumbled, suddenly stricken, and pitched forward, row after row falling to the ground. They were unmarked, according to the story, but nevertheless quite dead. The enemy fell back in confusion before the unseen bolts from the heavens. The German advance checked, the little army of British 'Contemptibles' made good its escape.

Most readers realized 'The Bowmen' was fantasy, but some believed it and passed it along. A short time later a letter from the front appeared in one of the London newspapers. A soldier had seen an angel in the sky over Mons.

Another letter, from a convalescent hospital, confirmed the apparition; he, too, had seen the angel. More letters poured in on the Miracle of Mons, Angels, Bowmen, King Arthur and his Knights, Sir Nigel and the White Company—the heavens were peopled by a great legendary host hovering over the retreating British as they stumbled away from Mons. Many believed the supernatural stories. Without news, the public didn't know what to believe. It was small wonder fantasy found such wide acceptance when honest, straightforward battle news had so long been suppressed.

The year 1915, as the newspaper correspondents soon realized, was a time of stalemate on the Western Front. Some attempts were made, beginning in March at Neuve-Chapelle, to break the German trench positions after heavy bombardment, but the gains were small. In September the French launched an attack in the Champagne, co-ordinated with a British assault at Loos, which for several weeks engaged the pens of the eager correspondents. As the year wore on, their task became not so much battle reporting as a continuing attempt to reconcile casualties reckoned in tens of thousands with gains measured in yards.

Elsewhere—except for the loss of ships and prestige in the Dardanelles—a series of events in this dark year laid the foundation for eventual Allied victory. Beginning with the introduction of chlorine gas by the Germans at Langemark April 22, the events followed in rapid order:

May 7: The S.S. *Lusitania* sunk by a German submarine;

May 23: Italy joined the Allies, declared war on Austria;

May 25: Britain reorganized its war cabinet, creating a Ministry of Munitions under Lloyd George;

September 8: A Zeppelin dropped bombs on London;

October 12: Germans executed British nurse Edith Cavell for helping English and French soldiers to escape from Belgium.

Although the effect of those events was not immediately apparent, their cumulative result was to win support for the Allied cause from neutral nations and to strengthen the purpose of those opposing German militarism.

In the early months of the war the belligerent governments organized special bureaus to create and disseminate information favorable to their cause. By the end of 1915, propaganda had come to be recognized as an important and frequently overworked weapon of modern warfare. In retrospect it now appears that the efforts of government propaganda bureaus were largely self-defeating; nothing could influence world opinion as persuasively as facts

—facts presented, as objectively as the time permitted, in the press.

Late in the afternoon of May 7, 1915, an office boy walked into the United Press office in London with a rumor he had picked up in Fleet Street. Trying to be casual about it, he remarked to Wilbur Forrest that the *Lusitania* had been sunk in the Irish Sea. Forrest, a newcomer to the United Press staff, passed the report along to Ed Keen, head of the bureau. Together they scanned the city news ticker and the late afternoon papers. Not a line about the *Lusitania*.

The Cunard steamship's voyage had been a matter of news concern for nearly a week. On May 1 a brief cable dispatch from New York told of an advertisement in the morning newspapers, warning prospective steamship passengers of the hazard of trans-Atlantic travel on ships of a belligerent nation. The advertisement, signed by the 'Imperial German Embassy,' was clearly directed at the *Lusitania,* but the notice was dismissed as German impudence by Cunard officials, and passengers embarked at New York in cheerful disregard of the warning.

Turning all this over in his mind, Forrest called Admiralty Intelligence in Whitehall and asked for Captain Reginald Hall. The press associations had a confidential understanding with the Admiralty; they would not bother Intelligence with routine inquiries; but Hall would confirm or deny promptly any report of major news importance. Forrest put the question in his calm, matter-of-fact Midwestern speech:

'We hear the *Lusitania* has been sunk; is it true?'

'Yes, it's true.'

'What can you tell us about it?' Hall was not supposed to supply details of news to the press; that was the function of the War Office Information Bureau. But the *Lusitania* story was too big to wait on protocol. Sensibly, Hall told what he knew. Within sixty seconds an urgent cable to New York was relaying the tragic facts which Forrest gleaned over the telephone: the *Lusitania* sunk off Old Kinsale Head; two torpedoes from a German submarine had struck the ship on the starboard side, and she had gone down in twenty minutes; survivors were being landed at Queenstown (Cóbh), Ireland.

From the United Press bureau in Temple Chambers to the Cunard Line office in Regent Street was a 15-minute taxi ride. By the time Forrest got there, so fast had the news spread along Fleet Street and mid-town London that a crowd of more than a hundred thronged the sidewalk in front of the building. Some were London newspapermen; others were relatives of *Lusitania* passengers. The doors were locked and the bolder ones in the crowd pounded on the glass in vain. The steamship line officials had no answers to the anxious queries; frightened clerks shook their heads. On the way back to Temple Chambers, Forrest stopped at the War Office Information Bureau in Whitehall. Sir Stanley Buckmaster confirmed the sinking and indicated many lives had been lost, but the official announcement was vague, lacking in detail. The obvious place, the only place to cover the story, was Queenstown, Ireland.

From London two night trains provided service by different routes to Ireland. The best known and most generally traveled left Euston Station for Holyhead, Wales, connecting with the Irish Mail steamer for Kingstown (Dun Laoghaire) and Dublin. The other train, from Paddington Station, went to Fishguard, Wales, connecting with a ferry service across the Irish Sea to Rosslare. Both pulled out of London at the same hour, 8:30 P.M. Keen and Forrest decided the Fishguard-Rosslare route was the most direct to Queenstown. With £10 expense money pooled by the staff, Forrest took a taxi for Paddington, arriving at the ticket window four minutes before train time.

He asked for a ticket to Rosslare, but the agent explained the railway booking ended at Fishguard; separate arrangements would have to be made for the ferry crossing to Ireland.

'All right,' Forrest said, 'make it Fishguard.' The agent's ear caught the newspaperman's American accent and recognized him as another correspondent hurrying to the scene of the *Lusitania* disaster. He was sympathetic, but rules were rules. Fishguard was the center of the British Navy's fleet patrolling the Irish Sea and all its antisubmarine activity centered there. The place was forbidden to aliens; only British citizens were allowed in the town. By the time the ticket man had explained that, it was 8:28. From the platform outside came the warning blast of a guard's whistle.

'But I've got to get to Ireland,' Forrest cried. 'What can I do?'

'I'll sell you a ticket to Landore,' the agent said. 'That's the last station this side of Fishguard. Maybe they'll pass you through.'

The United Press man climbed abroad as the train began to move along the platform. One other American journalist, Fred Pitney of the *New York Tribune,* was among the half a dozen correspondents he found on board. Comparing notes, Forrest learned that he, too, had only identity cards, minimum of wartime credentials. Although aliens, they would have powerful arguments to use on the Admiralty watchdogs at Fishguard. The sinking of the *Lusitania* was a matter of tremendous interest to America. Many prominent Americans were on the passenger list. Surely the British could waive the rules to let them through.

Forrest wrote a telegram to Keen as the train gathered speed through the London suburbs and dispatched it by a trainman at the first stop. He urged Keen to get Admiralty clearance for him and Pitney, asking a reply at Landore. It was after midnight when the train arrived at the Welsh town. Military and naval police came on board and began to move through the cars, screening passengers for the last stage of the journey. Forrest and Pitney got out their cards, preparing to argue their way through British red tape. Just then the Landore station master arrived on the scene, calling 'Mr. Forrest, Mr. Forrest!' and brandishing a telegram. All was well; the Admiralty had cleared the way for their passage through Fishguard. Naval officers greeted them at the quayside, and with the Admiralty's blessing, they sped through the night across the Irish Sea to Rosslare. A morning train carried them down the Irish countryside to Cork and Queenstown, where they arrived an hour before noon.

Forrest, a native of Peoria, Illinois, and little more than a cub reporter, had arrived in England with his bride only three months before. In London most of his work had been office routine and small rewrite jobs, scanning the London newspapers, putting minor items into cabelese for the file to New York. Now at Queenstown he was thrust headlong into one of the great stories of the war.

It was a strange setting for a war story, remote from the crash of heavy guns and the din of battle. No squads of hurrying men, no stretcher bearers, bloodshed or smoke. Only a quiet seaport town on an Irish hillside, numbed by catastrophe, suddenly peopled by dazed men and women who a few hours before had walked the decks of the world's greatest steamship. A silent fringe of townspeople and survivors waited on the docks. They watched the harbor mouth for the trawlers and Navy vessels which were bringing in the last of those on the life rafts and the bodies of the drowned.

Hurrying to the telegraph office with a ten-word bulletin, Forrest was surprised to discover that he was the first press association man to get on the wire. In a public house across the street from the telegraph office, the United Press man found a small room off the lobby with a writing table and chair. He paid the proprietor ten shillings and spread out pencils and a pad of telegraph blanks in his improvised 'headquarters.'

It was a simple matter to distinguish the survivors from the townsfolk; their disheveled clothing and the shock and bewilderment in their faces set them apart. Most of them talked readily to the newspapermen. Each had had his own unique experience on the stricken steamship, whether on the canted decks, in the lifeboats, or floundering in the water. A few sobbed and cried, recalling the faces of those struggling in the water as the doomed ship went down.

Early in the afternoon the train from Dublin brought two Associated Press men, Frank Elser and Ben Allen, and ten or twelve more Fleet Street newsmen who had taken the northern route via Holyhead and Kingstown. Soon they, too, were going among the survivors with their notebooks and pencils, adding to the mounting file in the telegraph office.

After the eyewitness stories, the most important task for the newsmen was to compile lists of the survivors, the missing, and the dead. Service messages from London made repeated inquiries about widely known United States citizens on the passenger list, particularly Alfred G. Vanderbilt; Charles Frohman, leading theatrical producer; author Elbert Hubbard; and Frank Stone, son of Melville E. Stone, general manager of the Associated Press. Forrest and the Associated Press correspondents questioned the survivors for the fate of those four; no one could recall seeing any of them in the lifeboats; one thought he had seen Vanderbilt, Frohman, and Stone standing together on an upper deck shortly before the last lifeboat was launched.

A warehouse at the quayside had been requisitioned as a temporary morgue. More than two hundred bodies recovered during the morning lay in rows on the floor. Forrest got permission to go inside from one of the Queenstown police guarding the warehouse door, but when the United Press man asked the guard to accompany him, so that they might identify some of the victims, the policeman said: 'I wouldn't go in there and touch them for a thousand pounds!'

Alone in the dim warehouse, Forrest walked between the rows of covered figures, pausing at length beside one whose face and proportions corresponded to the description of one of the missing Americans. From an inside coat pocket the reporter extracted a wallet and found damp cards in it, inscribed with the name Charles Frohman. Checking over his names in his hotel cubbyhole that night, Forrest found that, of 124 Americans on the passenger list, only 35 had come ashore at Queenstown.

The telegraph office was swamped with messages. Besides the thirty or forty newspapermen, all the survivors wanted to communicate with the outside world. From his room across the street, Forrest watched the procession of men and women filing into the telegraph building and worried about getting his own dispatches through the jam. He noticed that the clerk at the front desk would take the messages as they were submitted and impale them on a spindle. When the spindle was full, he would hand it back to an operator seated at a table behind him, who would begin to transmit the messages from the top of the spindle, in the reverse order in which they had been received. The observant newspaperman decided to take advantage of this careless routine. Writing his dispatches to the United Press in brief bulletin form in the public house, he would wait until the current spindle of accumulating messages was nearing the top; then he would dash across the street with enough copy to fill the remaining space, whereupon the clerk would pass the full spindle back to the operator and Forrest's copy would go out first.

Some time early the next morning Forrest fell asleep with his head on the table, but for the three days it took to clean up the *Lusitania* story at Queenstown he never went to bed. Hard work, the responsibility of his task, and the excitement kept him going, with an occasional dish of soup and glass of Irish whiskey. The

United Press was pleased with his work. When he got back to London, a messenger met him at the train, saying he was to go to the Carlton Hotel in Haymarket. A friend of A. G. Vanderbilt, anxious for the latest word about the missing millionaire, had made an urgent appeal to Ed Keen, who arranged for Forrest to give him a personal report.

At the Carlton, in the suite of Vanderbilt's friend, Forrest got a bite of supper while he told what he knew about Vanderbilt's chances and who had last seen him alive. As he finished the recital he yawned and his eyes began to droop. His host suggested he stretch out on the sofa, and covered him with a fur coat. Forrest slept on the sofa for eighteen hours.

There was a great outcry in the press over the *Lusitania*. In America some considered the affair sufficient to bring the United States into the war, and Theodore Roosevelt called for aggressive action, deriding President Wilson's efforts to deal with the situation by notes of protest to the German Government. Yet the second U.S. note was so strongly worded that Secretary of State Bryan refused to sign it, and, alarmed that its vigorous phrases might involve the United States in war, resigned.

Germany's submarine policy was still a matter of controversy and diplomatic exchange when, four months after the *Lusitania* disaster, bombs fell from the night sky over London, and more defenseless civilians were killed. Women and children were among the victims.

Earlier in the year a Zeppelin had crossed the Channel and dropped bombs on coastal areas southeast of London. But on the night of September 8, in favorable weather conditions, one of the huge airships hovered over the English capital. From Fleet Street rooftops, editors watched the play of searchlights and the glare of the flames; reporters hurried by cab, bus, and underground to the explosion scenes. All London was aroused by Zeppelin attack. The War Office Information Bureau decided, however, to keep the matter quiet.

Within a few minutes after the last bomb explosion, while London fire engines were still dealing with the flames and ambulances carrying the wounded to hospitals, the Press Bureau sent word to all newspaper offices and press association correspondents. No mention must be made of the Zeppelin attack. Not only were the newspapers forbidden to publish stories about it; no stories were to be submitted to censorship.

Bill Shepherd, veteran United Press correspondent, had watched the Zeppelin's sortie over the city and had visited the scenes where some of the bombs had fallen. Mulling over the official injunction, Shepherd decided to try to outwit the press censor by a flank attack. Careful to avoid any mention of the Zeppelin or falling bombs, the United Press man wrote about the quiet heroism of London citizens under trying circumstances. It was not given to the average Londoner to face machine gun fire and high-explosive shells in the front line trenches, but when the war paid a visit to his home neighborhood, he knew how to deal with it. Policemen, firemen, taxi drivers, bus men went about their business with calm efficiency. Under circumstances which might have been expected to produce panic and mass hysteria, Britons kept their heads; street traffic remained almost normal, restaurants and public house patrons may have filed out on the sidewalk for a brief look around, but then they went back inside to their eating and drinking. Without once using the words Zeppelin or bomb attack, Shepherd managed to convey a great deal of atmosphere and information; indeed, he indicated that the night's events (without saying what had caused them) had greatly strengthened the purposes of the 'man in the street' to support the government and defeat the enemy. Morale in London, Shepherd wrote, was never higher than on the morning after. The censor puzzled over Shepherd's story, and then passed it for transmission to America.

The next day the United Press correspondent had an appointment to interview Guglielmo Marconi, Italian inventor of wireless telegraphy. Shepherd called at Marconi's hotel, found the inventor worn out and haggard after a sleepless night, but greatly stimulated. He explained to the newspaper man: 'I was up until an unearthly hour this morning.'

'Did you chase the Zeppelin?' Shepherd asked.

'Everywhere! I got a taxicab and I went to all the fires and saw all the horrible sights.'

Shepherd got the famous inventor to recount his night's experiences in considerable detail, and took notes on Marconi's nocturnal tour from one explosion scene to another. As the interview ended, the reporter remarked that Zeppelin and Marconi were generally recognized as two of the world's leading inventors; would the distinguished Italian scientist, on the basis of the previous night's observations, care to comment on the uses to which his fellow inventor's great work was now employed?

'Thank God,' Marconi said, 'they can't use my invention to kill women and children as they used Count Zeppelin's last night. If I were Zeppelin I would demand of my Emperor that he cease the use of my invention for such terrible purposes.'

Through Marconi's personal experiences, and his indignation, Bill Shepherd was able to give a complete and graphic account of the Zeppelin raid on London. The censor passed it on the ground that it was an interview with Marconi rather than a story of the raid, and it was published in America. Again, as in the case of Will Irwin's 'Battle of Ypres,' London newspapers picked up from the American press and reprinted the story in full, the first public acknowledgment in Britain that a Zeppelin had reached London with its bombs.

As the war entered its second year there was considerable criticism that the newspapermen were gathering their material at second and third hand, in bars and restaurants and railway stations. Their stories, it was charged, lacked freshness and authenticity. The journalists' defense was that they got as close to the war as military rules permitted, and that many honest, significant stories were gleaned in taverns and bars.

Yet more thoughtful correspondents were ready to admit, even after long experience with the armies, that their first-hand knowledge of battles was limited. Philip Gibbs said he rarely had seen any actual fighting. Once, he recalled, he watched a German counterattack when enemy soldiers linked arms and advanced slowly toward the British line until mown down by machine gunfire. He remembered the fantastic charge of British cavalry up Monchy Hill, near Arras, 'when they rode against machine gun bullets and had no chance at all.' Again, he remembered seeing British troops advancing in a snow storm to an attack on Vimy Ridge.

Most of the correspondents' work was patient slogging behind the lines—studying maps, listening to officers, reading reports, fitting the pieces together at night in their château—while the guns boomed and the horizon was lit by flashes of distant artillery fire.

Although they now had attained recognition with the Allied armies in France, the newspapermen still suffered from the tyranny of capricious censorship. Edward Price Bell of the *Chicago Daily News* summed up the case against the British War Office in a talk before the American Luncheon Club in London, November 19, 1915.

'In London, I believe, there is documentary evidence—and a great deal of it—to show that the (British) censorship justly may be described as chaotic, political, discriminatory, destructive, unchivalrous, in effect, anti-British, in effect pro-German, ludicrous, incompetent, incredible.'

He traced the history of the institution since the onset of war fifteen months before. Censorship had been organized under Mr. F. E. Smith. After his brief and 'not over-glorious' administration, the post was taken over by Sir Stanley Buckmaster. Under this hard-working official there was great improvement. 'If Buckmaster had been retained at the Press Bureau, he would have built up the best censorship any nation has known. But Sir Stanley went away . . .' Bell said he was followed by 'something scarcely distinguishable from anarchy.' Central authority at the Press Bureau seemed to dissolve. Correspondents no longer found there any responsive and dominating mind.

One of the areas in which censorship extended its confused and paralyzing grip on the press was the Dardanelles campaign. When reporters attempted to send back realistic accounts of that disastrous Allied venture, their copy was seized, or ruthlessly cut, by the censors. Some were warned against writing critical reports. Ellis Ashmead-Bartlett, frustrated in his efforts to tell the bitter truth through the columns of the *Daily Telegraph,* wrote a long letter addressed to Prime Minister Asquith detailing the mistakes and stupidities of the Dardanelles affair. Ashmead-Bartlett entrusted his letter to the Australian correspondent Keith Murdoch, who was returning to England. The Prime Minister learned about it, but when he inquired for the letter, he was told by the War Office it had been 'lost in transit.' When the ship carrying Murdoch had stopped at Marseilles, the letter had been seized by order of

Sir Ian Hamilton's chief of staff. Ashmead-Bartlett was accused of having attempted to violate censorship and dismissed from Gallipoli. His credentials were revoked and his name placed on the War Office blacklist. He went to the French front for a brief time in 1916, but his career as a war correspondent was virtually finished.

The year 1916 was a gloomy, indecisive one for the Allies. Some historians describe it as the year of exhaustion. In February, the Germans began their effort to break French resistance at Verdun, a campaign which was to continue in a series of gigantic attacks for many months. Great losses were sustained by both sides. The French made good their challenge: 'They shall not pass!' but it was a negative, expensive triumph.

A naval engagement off Jutland brought the British and German battle fleets into gigantic combat in the Skaggerak May 31. Described as the greatest naval battle since Trafalgar, it inflicted heavy losses on both and gave victory to neither.

A Sinn Fein uprising in Ireland revealed the inner stress of Britain's affairs. Lord Kitchener was lost at sea when en route to bolster Russia's flagging war effort. A British force was surrounded by the Turks and forced to surrender at Kut-el-Amarna.

After months of preparation and the war's most intensive concentration of artillery fire, the British launched their supreme effort—the attack on the Somme in July. When its initial fury had subsided, they tried to maintain the offensive and deepen the break in the German lines by the use of a new weapon—Swinton's tanks. They were momentarily effective, but the advantage of surprise was soon lost.

More and more, as the war in 1916 lapsed into a bloody stalemate, Britain and France turned to the Western Hemisphere. Only America possessed munitions and manpower sufficient to tip the scale in the Allies' favor. The people of the United States had been shocked by the sinking of the *Lusitania* the year before, and many were impatient at the exchange of notes with which President Wilson sought to protest German submarine tactics. But in May, 1916, the German Government yielded to an American ultimatum and announced abandonment of its policy of unrestricted submarine warfare. Henceforward, the Germans assured the United States

Government, submarine commanders would give warning and take measures to save the lives of crew and passengers, before sinking a merchant vessel. That assurance seemed to remove the main issue which might have brought the United States in on the side of the Allies, and as 1916 closed, such action seemed unlikely.

XII

VOT SHIP ISS DOT?

On January 19, 1917, the German Secretary of Foreign Affairs, Dr. Arthur Zimmermann, wrote confidentially to Germany's Minister to Mexico, von Eckhardt:

On the first of February we intend to begin submarine warfare unrestricted. In spite of this it is our intention to endeavor to keep neutral the United States of America.

If this attempt is not successful, we propose an alliance on the following basis with Mexico:

That we shall make war together and together make peace. We shall give general [generous?] financial support and it is understood that Mexico is to reconquer [recover?] the lost territory in New Mexico, Texas and Arizona. The details are left to you [von Eckhardt] for settlement.

You are instructed to inform the President of Mexico of the above in the greatest confidence as soon as it is certain that there will be an outbreak of war with the United States and suggest that the President of Mexico, on his own initiative, should communicate with Japan suggesting adherence at once to this plan; at the same time offer to mediate between Germany and Japan.

Please call to the attention of the President of Mexico that the employment of ruthless submarine warfare now promises to compel England to make peace in a few months.

(signed) ZIMMERMANN

With the seizure of Zimmermann's note on the Texas border by the United States Secret Service and its publication in the American press February 28, United States involvement in the war became virtually inevitable. Some formalities yet remained. The German Ambassador at Washington, Count Johann Heinrich von Bernstorff, was handed his passport and notified by the State Department that his presence was no longer desired.

The German suggestion that Mexico recover Texas, New Mexico, and Arizona from the United States was of course fantastic, but it roused the Middle West and Far West to fighting pitch. Announcement of the resumption of ruthless submarine warfare was significant. Washington waited for repudiation of the 1916 agreement before taking the final step. The question was—when would German submarines sink another passenger steamship without warning?

That winter the *Chicago Tribune* needed another correspondent in Europe. Canvassing its staff for likely material it came upon the tall, tough, able Floyd Gibbons sending back reports from the dusty campaign against the bandit Villa along the Mexican border. Summoned to Chicago for expense money and credentials, Gibbons found that the *Tribune* had engaged passage for him on the steamship carrying the discredited Count von Bernstorff back to Germany. Gibbons canceled the reservation, not because von Bernstorff would have made a stuffy travel companion but because the Germans would be unlikely to sink a steamship carrying one of their own statesmen. Seeking a vessel more likely to become involved with a submarine, the Chicago journalist switched his bags to the 18,000-ton Cunarder *Laconia*.

It would be exaggeration to suggest that as they approached the danger zone Gibbons walked the decks, shaking his fists and daring the submarines to attack the *Chicago Tribune*. Nevertheless such was his approach to war and his proud identification with his newspaper. Gibbons was a throw-back to another, earlier war correspondent, George Wilkins Kendall of the *New Orleans Picayune*. Kendall made the Mexican War of the 1840's his war, participating in cavalry charges, even capturing a battle flag, and sending back his glowing accounts to New Orleans by an elaborate relay system. For both Kendall and Gibbons, war was grand adventure, and patriotism was merged with intense devotion to their newspapers.

The torpedo struck the *Laconia* amidships about 10:30 P.M. on February 25. As the lifeboats pulled away from the sinking steamship, Gibbons was cheerful and busy. He helped the crew, volunteered to take the tiller, passed out cigarettes, kept an eye out for struggling figures in the water, and noted the behavior of men and women huddled in the small boats. When the submarine surfaced nearby, Gibbons heard the voice of a German officer inquiring the identity of the sinking steamship. That query over the dark water (Gibbons's version made it: 'Vot ship iss dot?') indicated the submarine commander had not troubled to identify the *Laconia* or give warning before firing the deadly torpedo.

It was a cold night, and the Irish Sea, as usual, was rough. Landing at Queenstown, Gibbons's first thought was to let the *Chicago Tribune* know that the ordeal in an open lifeboat had slowed his pen and warn them not to expect much until he had thawed out a bit. With that idea in mind, his opening bulletin was a personal note to the editor, but it conveyed so much Gibbonsesque flavor and drama that the *Tribune*, with commendable judgment, made it a lead-all for the front page story of the *Laconia* sinking:

> I'm here in Queenstown soaked, frozen; ice on my face, ice in my hair, dripping water on the floor. I can hardly move my fingers to write the story. I was torpedoed on the *Laconia* . . .

Disdaining sleep, Gibbons began writing his long graphic story. As he wrote, cables and telegraph wires carried the colorful details to Chicago. Within twenty-four hours Gibbons's adventure was spread across the front pages of the *Chicago Tribune,* and the submarine commander's blunt 'Vot ship iss dot?' in type almost as large as Gibbons's by-line, presented its ultimatum to Wilson, the United States Congress, and the American people. Six weeks later, the United States was in the war. It was inconceivable that any lesser result should flow from a challenge so insolently flung at the World's Greatest Newspaper and its accredited correspondent.

Gibbons thus may be distinguished as the first of a new crop of war reporters whose service began with the entry of the United States into the conflict. They would look at Europe with new perspective. Judgments of war-weary, tired journalists of 1914-16 (the Mowrers, Williams, Gibbs, Ashmead-Bartlett, Fortescue) would be put aside for fresher understanding. Everything—hospitals, Paris boulevards and bistros, the fighting qualities of our allies, the war itself—would be overhauled and appraised anew. But this new crop of correspondents would be small, at first, and the conditions under which they would work would be uncertain and difficult. The United States Government and the military authorities would profit little from the experience of their allies in dealing with the press.

When war was declared, American correspondents in Berlin packed their bags and departed, most of them through neutral countries. Paul Scott Mowrer met Raymond Gram Swing coming out of Germany into Switzerland. Swing was on his way back to the United States with his family. The Chicago newsmen passed two days together, comparing notes on the war strength of the Germans and the Allies, weighing the factors of morale, food supplies, manpower in the third year of the war. It was about the time of the Nivelle offensive. Many in France were bitter and discouraged, and the question seemed to be whether American aid could arrive before an Allied collapse.

Five weeks later, Swing was back in France. He had taken leave from the *Chicago Daily News* and was now on a confidential mission for Colonel House, President Wilson's adviser. Since the failure of the Nivelle offensive there had been reports of low morale and mutinies in the French Army. A number of regiments had refused to return to the trenches, and reports said it was impossible to count on the French for a vigorous defense, much less an offensive. Colonel House wanted someone to evaluate the situation. In addition to more formal reports received through the State Department, the colonel wanted opinions, rumors, the kind of facts and figments newspapermen exchange among themselves. The President's adviser did not want to commit a large U.S. force to France if that nation was on the verge of collapse. He wanted to find out whether there was enough Allied stability left to hold off the Germans through the summer of 1917 while the United States Army was being trained and transported overseas.

Mowrer and Swing talked the situation over in Paris. Already Swing had found France demoralized and reluctant to continue. He had talked to a number of persons—some out-and-out defeatists— and he told Mowrer the situation seemed almost hopeless. Mowrer didn't believe it was as bad as that. More experienced in dealing with the French, he made allowance for the current despondency. The French might seem depressed but they had endured much and could endure more. The arrival of the Americans, he argued, would provide the one ingredient necessary to reaffirm France's faith in her destiny and confidence in the future. Mowrer could not know how much weight Swing's report would carry with the White House adviser, but he thought he influenced his friend to carry a brighter, more confident view back to Washington.

The veteran Frederick Palmer, destined to be caught between the old and new in war reporting, was back in the United States on a lecture tour. When Congress declared war against the Central Powers on April 16, James Gordon Bennett in Paris cabled his representatives in New York to hire Palmer as chief correspondent for the *New York Herald* and its syndicate. Since August, 1914, Palmer had been foremost American correspondent in Europe, but the honor of being officially acredited representative of the three American press services—A.P., U.P., and I.N.S.—did not carry much cash. Wire service salaries were notoriously small, and Palmer had sacrificed the chance for more substantial earnings by accepting British accreditation for the U.S. news bureaus. Lecture fees had redressed the balance to some extent, but the first two years of his war service had been lean ones financially. Now the lordly Bennett offered a top salary, about $750 a week, for the duration of the war. While the contract was being drawn, Palmer made the rounds in Washington. Official doors opened readily for this distinguished figure in British officer's uniform, Sam Browne belt, and riding boots. The capital was in a fever of war preparation. The draft was getting started; huge training camps were in the planning stage; Congress was appropriating money for the military program; and the first Liberty Loan campaign was under way. Palmer traded his experience in the European trenches, his knowledge of weapons, logistics, and tactics for confidential information on plans for an American army in France.

In a small office off a corridor of the War Department, Palmer came upon an old friend from Mexican border campaigns. Major General John J. Pershing was quietly assembling a staff and working on lists of supplies he would need in France, but he had time to compare notes with the newspaperman. His appointment to command United States forces overseas came as a surprise to some senior officers, who questioned whether his limited experience in cavalry operations along the Rio Grande fitted him to direct a military force as vast and varied as America planned to send abroad. Palmer did not share these misgivings. He remembered Pershing as a level-headed, soundly trained officer, militarily correct, devoted to discipline and Army tradition.

They talked of the campaigns they had been through together and exchanged views briefly on the stalemate in Europe. Palmer wanted to know under what conditions correspondents would accompany the U.S. Army in France. General Pershing replied in effect, Why don't you come along as my press officer and write the conditions? The suggestion was discussed casually. The Government had set up a Committee on Public Information under the Colorado publicist George Creel to disseminate high-minded views and policy statements concerning the war to the press. But Pershing needed someone with practical experience to deal with correspondents at the news level, one with a sense of responsibility and enough knowledge of military affairs to know what might be printed and what must be suppressed. Already the correspondents in Washington were clamoring for interviews and information. Palmer mentioned his tentative commitment to the *Herald.* Pershing did not press for an immediate decision. Instead, he invited the veteran correspondent to accompany him and his staff on the S.S. *Baltic,* sailing from New York to Liverpool May 28 en route to France.

The voyage was, at the time, America's most carefully guarded military secret. The officers comprising the select party were to proceed to New York singly, in civilian clothing, and not even their families were to be told their plans. They were to assemble on Governors Island. A Navy tug would take them and their luggage down the harbor in the gloom and mist of a late May twilight, and somewhere in the Narrows they would climb aboard the *Baltic.*

Palmer was one of the three or four civilians invited to join this cloak-and-dagger departure. Charles H. Grasty, formerly general manager of the Baltimore Sunpapers, now a sort of executive correspondent for the *New York Times,* was another, and the socially prominent Winthrop Chanler managed to get aboard as an interpreter.

The *Baltic* dropped down Ambrose Channel and steamed away without a single mention in the press; officers and civilians maintained discreet silence. However, on the Chelsea pier for several days before the White Star liner's departure, trucks deposited crates and packing cases marked WAR DEPARTMENT, and bearing the consignment stencil in large black letters: PERSHING PARTY, A.E.F., S.S. BALTIC, CHELSEA PIER 23. Thus the secret was shared with the longshoremen and truck drivers along West Street and such enemy agents as may have frequented the waterfront saloons.

On the voyage to Liverpool General Pershing brought Palmer into the confidential circle of his newly formed General Staff. The war correspondent gave a series of informal talks on Allied methods and tactics as he had observed them, and sat late at table answering questions. Palmer had seen more of war than any of them. As they looked to him for opinions and significant facts which only a well-informed correspondent could know, so Palmer found himself attracted to the order and authority of military command. During the eight-day crossing Pershing renewed his suggestion that Palmer accept a commission and run the Press Section of G-2 under Colonel Dennis E. Nolan. By the time the *Baltic* reached the Mersey, Palmer had accepted. His decision gave him a major's salary of about $175 a month, plus certain overseas allowances, and put an end to the $40,000 a year the Bennett contract assured him. When he walked down the gangplank at Liverpool to the roars of Merseyside throngs, cheering the vanguard of American arms, Palmer had given up his war correspondent's career for the uncertain future of a commissioned officer in charge of the press.

Floyd Gibbons was the most conspicuous figure among the newspaper group around the *Baltic*'s gangplank at Liverpool. Correspondents of all the press associations in London were there to report the arrival of the American officers, but only Gibbons could recognize key figures in the party and call a personal hello to 'Black Jack' Pershing and others he had known on the Mexican border. The newspapermen trailed the Pershing party across England and reported the speeches, the cheering, the friendly welcome in the faces of the English throng for these tall, quiet, soldierly Americans. After four days in England, the party crossed the channel to find another group of correspondents waiting on the quayside at Boulogne. The French outdid the British in the warmth and intensity of their welcome. Into the journalists' notebooks and out across the telegraph wires went the happy details: the flowers, the ceremonies of welcome, the cheering at the railroad stations, the oratory. When the last bouquet had been flung and the last toast drunk, and when General Pershing had made his final bow to the crowds in the Place de la Concorde from the balcony of his hotel suite, the newspaper correspondents sent off their stories and wondered, What next?

XIII

LAFAYETTE, HERE WE COME!

Major Frederick Palmer, U.S.A., began his new career as Chief Press Officer of the American Expeditionary Forces (G-2-D) in a small office at Castellane House, 31 rue de Constantine, on the Left Bank. Temporary headquarters for General Pershing had been set up in the old mansion not far from the Hôtel des Invalides, convenient to France's principal military establishments.

In his new uniform, with its gold maple leaves, Palmer conferred with Pershing, Harbord, his chief of staff, and Colonel Dennis E. Nolan, Chief of G-2 (Intelligence) about the means of organizing his new section amid the bilingual confusion attending the American military enterprise.

Major Harbord seems to have written a memorandum expressing on behalf of the General Staff basic principles of the Army's regulations for the press. One recommendation survives in the Army files: 'Under no circumstances shall correspondents be required to write or make any statement contrary to their opinions or inclinations.'

This was a brave and sensible beginning. How simple to deal with the problem in lofty generalities. But when it came to practical details, the Army lacked both experience and imagination. One of the first decisions attempted to establish the number of accredited correspondents. Swamped by organization problems, hard up for space, short of automobiles, hampered by archaic military concepts, Pershing and his staff could not conceive of the necessity for more than twelve American newspapermen with the A.E.F. in France. How could they cope with them, keep track of them, provide communications and officers to guide them around, and censors to scrutinize their copy? One factor which influenced their decision was that the British had only five accredited correspondents with their army in France, the French only twelve with their army.

Washington agreed to having twelve American correspondents. Preference would be given to the three major press associations— the Associated Press, the United Press and the International News Service—and to those large newspaper organizations which shared their news with others on a syndicate basis. Each press association and newspaper qualifying for accreditation would be required to deposit $3,000 with the War Department to ensure payment for transport and other expenses, and as a forfeit in case of gross violation of the rules.

As Palmer worked on these details, pecking his memoranda out on the typewriter, the telephone rang, expatriate Americans and English-speaking French applied for jobs, partitions were installed, desks and filing cases moved, and electric wires strung. Visitors waited in the crowded reception room to see him. Word that the American Expeditionary Force would accredit ten or twelve newspapermen to report its affairs was an invitation to all the unattached, adventurous spirits in Paris. Among the hundred who applied was an actress.

There were some legitimate newspapermen among the scores that shuffled through the anteroom at 31 rue de Constantine. They wanted to ask Major Palmer a number of questions. When would the accreditation applications be ready? When would the first U.S. troops arrive in France and where would they train? When would they go into the front lines? Would they use French artillery and ammunition, or bring their own? It was not easy for Palmer to refuse to see old friends like Elmer Roberts and Bob Small of the A.P., Wilbur Forrest of the U.P., and Paul Mowrer of the *Chicago Daily News,* or to parry their questions. He knew much more than he could tell. Now he was the Army's man—General Staff—and Pershing's man; the newspapermen would have to wait.

A young college instructor who had worked for Herbert Hoover's Belgian Relief Organization and who spoke French fluently walked into Castellane House and was assigned to G-2-D. Lieutenant Joseph C. Green had no newspaper experience, but Palmer found him conscientious and loyal, willing to work fourteen hours a day during the formative period when help was scarce. His knowledge of French and attention to detail made him useful in many ways, but some of the newspapermen found him pedantic and stuffy. His dictatorial manner and impatience with journalistic temperament would cause trouble later on.

George N. Parks had been studying in Europe on an Amherst scholarship. He, too, walked into the hubbub at 31 rue de Constantine and asked what he could do to help. He said he could speak French and use a typewriter. Palmer gave him a desk and put him to work. He turned out to be stenographer, typist, linguist, unusually accurate and dependable. Winthrop Chanler brought his social background, friendly personality, and knowledge of French cuisine to Castellane House. Later, he became a semi-official host for G-2-D, arranging transportation, lodging and good food, and entertainment for important visitors.

With these eager and dedicated assistants, Palmer's Press Section began to function. Four automobiles were requisitioned for the use of the newspapermen, but red tape and old Army rules balked Palmer's efforts to provide enlisted men as chauffeurs. Finally he got General Pershing to sign an order hiring civilians, former Red Cross ambulance drivers, for the job.

On Morning morning, June 25, Palmer summoned the American correspondents to Castellane House. From the atmosphere of military hush and solemnity, the locked door, the methodical Lieutenant Green checking off their names on his list, it was apparent that something important was about to be revealed. Major Palmer, after a suitable pause, announced gravely that transports bearing the first contingents of American troops were approaching the coast of France. These were the First Division of veteran American regulars, the 16th, 18th, 26th and 28th regiments of the regular army and the 5th Marine regiment.

This promised to be a news event of great significance. An American fighting force was about to land on the historic soil of Europe, the vigorous New World coming to the rescue of the Old. When he had finished the brief announcement, Major Palmer handed to each of the newspapermen present a brief statement of policy and censorship rules governing the U.S. troops' arrival at St. Nazaire:

June 25th, 1917

The American Expeditionary Force depends more upon the correspondents' patriotism and discretion than upon censorship in the safeguarding of military secrets. Information given confidentially to their friends by persons, official or civilian, who have had opportunities at first hand observation is one of the most dependable sources of the enemy spy system. Therefore, correspondents are asked to make it a rule never to relate to any person, however intimate, any fact or impression which is not conveyed in their copy as censored. Correspondents will not be permitted to mention:

1. The name or location of the port of disembarkation or indicate it by any descriptive reference.

2. Names of any officers except commanders of divisions or of the Commander-in-Chief, or the names of any units.

3. Anything which will in any way indicate to the enemy the route of transports or the methods of the Navy in safeguarding their passage.

When the statement had been read aloud and its admonitions discussed in some detail, Major Palmer informed the correspondents of the special railway transportation arranged to take them to St. Nazaire, and of the time of departure. He pledged them solemnly not to discuss the matter with anyone, not even their wives, in the short time that remained before they were to start.

The departure of that first American convoy across the North Atlantic was shrouded in as much secrecy in the United States as was its impending arrival in France. War Department and Navy enjoined the newspapers to refrain from any premature announcement, and the embarkation of the regiments was carried out with discretion. However, Washington officials were aware of the historic nature of the crossing and its news significance. Several days before the convoy was to depart, the Navy notified the three principal news services to assign one man each to the job and send him to Washington for credentials, passport, and instructions. The Hearst organization (International) nominated an amiable bon vivant from Oklahoma named Daniel Dillon; conservative, quiet C. C. Lyon of the Newspaper Enterprise Association, more businessman than newshound, got the assignment for United Press. The Associated Press discovered a young man on its staff in Boston, named Stanley W. Prenosil, who understood French. Summoned to New York June 11, he was found qualified for the assignment and sent on to Washington.

The three correspondents who were to share the historic voyage met for the first time in the office of Josephus Daniels, Secretary of the Navy, at 6 P.M. the night of June 12. Secretary Daniels told them they would make the journey on the U.S.S. *Seattle,* an armored cruiser. The Secretary reminded them that everything they wrote about the crossing would be subject to censorship. They must not mention the port of departure, the port of arrival in France, the names of any officers, or the designations of regiments. All copy must be submitted to Rear Admiral Albert Gleaves for approval. During the briefing the newspapermen shook hands with a tall, distinguished-looking young man serving as Assistant Secretary, Franklin Delano Roosevelt. On their departure, Secretary Daniels handed each a letter of credentials to Rear Admiral Gleaves.

They had been directed to board the *Seattle* at the New York Navy Yard in Brooklyn, but when Prenosil went there the next morning he was told the cruiser was not at the yard, nor would yard officers at first disclose her whereabouts. Only after producing his credentials and demanding that the Yard Commandant call the Navy Department in Washington was he finally informed that he might find the *Seattle* anchored off Tompkinsville, Staten Island. On the Staten Island ferryboat Prenosil met Dillon and Lyon, who likewise had made a frustrating journey to the Navy Yard, and the three proceeded together to Tompkinsville, where a Navy launch picked them up and carried them out to the *Seattle.* They sailed early the morning of June 14.

The voyage was relatively smooth and uneventful. Theirs was the first of four convoy units each consisting of a battle cruiser, two destroyers, and five or six transports. Each newspaperman shared a stateroom with an officer and ate with the senior officers in the wardroom. They took turns standing four-hour night watches in the crow's nest with a member of the crew; otherwise, until they reached a point about nine hundred miles off the coast of France, there was little to do except watch the fast-moving destroyers and count the transports trailing behind in a long double line.

At length the monotony was broken by a submarine alert. Prenosil recalled that the night alarm sent everyone scrambling to the upper decks, where they found the cruiser increasing her speed, the transports fanning out in all directions, and all ships of the convoy exchanging messages furiously by blinker lights. The newspapermen heard several rumbling explosions which they were told were depth charges released by a destroyer, but none saw gunfire, torpedoes, or periscope wake. After an hour or two the excitement died down, the convoy pulled together and resumed its leisurely zigzag course toward France.

The three newspapermen wrote their stories the night of June 25 as the *Seattle* and its convoy lay at anchor off Belle Isle, below the port of St. Nazaire. Since the submarine alarm was the only excitement in an otherwise quiet crossing, they played it up in their dispatches. However, they reckoned without Admiral Gleaves. The admiral sent word that there must be no reference to the episode, and the correspondents had to eliminate it and rewrite their stories.

The admiral and his staff debarked early the next morning to confer with French officialdom and arrange for the docking of the transports. Lyon, Dillon, and Prenosil were not allowed ashore until noon. Meanwhile, their dispatches were held up in the admiral's suite while the admiral was being feted by the hospitable French Navy. Returning to the *Seattle* in a mellow mood late in the afternoon, Admiral Gleaves approved the three dispatches, and the correspondents left the ship about 7 P.M.

Together they scurried about St. Nazaire looking for the telegraph office. It was closed for the night. No dispatches could be cleared until the following morning. The telephone exchange, in an upper floor of the same building, also was closed. Prenosil climbed to an open window and in his uncertain French pleaded with the telephone operator to put through a call to the A.P. office in Paris. *Mais, non, M'sieur.* It was not possible.

Back on the Seattle, Prenosil told his troubles to the executive officer, Commander R. Drace White. Commander White was leaving for Paris on the night train and invited the Associated Press man to go along. Since Prenosil's orders from the A.P. were to proceed promptly to Paris, he accepted the commander's invitation. Lyons and Dillon elected to stay in St. Nazaire.

Early the following morning Major Palmer and a select group of correspondents arrived by train from Paris. Charles Grasty was there for the *New York Times,* Gibbons for the *Chicago Tribune,* Philip Powers for the Associated Press and Wilbur Forrest for the

United Press. The *New York Tribune* correspondent was a large, untidy, argumentative man named Heywood Broun. Parisian newspapers had been notified of the event, and more than a dozen elderly French journalists turned out. Three or four reporters from Fleet Street represented the London dailies and Reuter's news service.

Dillon and Lyon quickly attached themselves to this official group, and, showing their dispatches, with Admiral Gleaves' release, to Major Palmer, inquired whether they could have top priority on the cables to New York. Major Palmer had conferred with General Pershing during the train journey from Paris, and his decision was that no news of the transports' arrival at St. Nazaire could be released until the last of the four convoy units arrived off Belle Isle. Since they were traveling a day apart, at least two more days must elapse before the last transports dropped anchor.

Prenosil arrived in Paris that same morning, innocent of Palmer's ruling. Hurrying to the Associated Press office he reported to Elmer Roberts, bureau chief, and then went across the street to the cable office to file his story. The French censors found nothing objectionable; accepting Admiral Gleaves' stamp of approval, they put the story on the wires via London. There Admiralty censorship, finding the dispatch most interesting, decided to hold it up for closer examination before sending it on to the United States.

At St. Nazaire, meanwhile, the transports moved up to the docks and gangplanks were lowered. Under the scrutiny of the assembled newspapermen and a nearby gang of German war prisoners, American troops shuffled down the gangplanks and trod on the soil of France. It was indeed an historic occasion. The journalists noted the confident bearing of the U.S. infantrymen, their good spirits after the twelve-day voyage, the incredulity in the faces of the watching German prisoners. All the elements were there for a great war story, but unfortunately, in transmission to newspaper readers, a number of things went wrong. Despite Major Palmer's precautions, and his plan to release the good news simultaneously for all correspondents after the arrival of the last transport, the big story squiggled out of censorship control and dribbled piecemeal into the press.

The first offender was a Paris newspaper, *Ce Soir*. This enterprising journal, learning of the convoy's arrival at St. Nazaire and ignorant of Palmer's restrictions, submitted to French censorship a proof of its front page with the news prominently displayed under a two-column heading. The censor, aware of the precautions against premature publication, killed the story in proof. However, through some lapse of his blue pencil, or carelessness in the newspaper composing room, *Ce Soir* appeared on the newsstands with the significant front page headline:

LE PREMIER CORPS EXPEDITIONNAIRE AMÉRICAIN
EST ARRIVÉ À SAINT-NAZAIRE

Underneath, a space of blank white paper showed where the censor's pencil had killed the story. The disclosure of St. Nazaire as the port of debarkation was such a grave violation of censorship that French officials tried frantically to retrieve all the erring copies of *Ce Soir* from the newsstands. Police agents hurried around the city with trucks, confiscating the edition, but not before more than a thousand has been distributed. That night the revealing headline was the talk of Paris.

The British correspondents at St. Nazaire observed all of Major Palmer's rules, withholding the name of the French seaport and other forbidden facts, but, instead of waiting for Palmer's official release, they sent their copy to London by courier, thus escaping the press officer's scrutiny at the telegraph office. London newspapers and Reuter's service carried a brief announcement on June 28, the same day *Ce Soir*'s indiscretion was published in Paris. The London stories were brief and factual. FIRST AMERICAN FORCES LAND IN FRANCE. UNEVENTFUL VOYAGE. That night the first fragments of the big story trickled into New York, as the wire service correspondents in London forwarded brief items culled from the London press.

The next morning the cables to Paris began to crackle with pointed queries. What was going on? Had the U.S. contingents landed or hadn't they? Why should the British announce it first? Why couldn't the American people have the news? About this time the British Admiralty decided to release Prenosil's dispatch to the A.P., which had arrived from Paris thirty-six hours before. Another Associated Press dispatch from Philip Powers, which also had unaccountably escaped Major Palmer's vigilance, was also cleared through London. The two stories, complementing each other, were the first definite news to reach the United States and gave the Associated Press one of its major beats.

Unmoved by the protests and confusion, Major Palmer sat grimly on all other newspaper dispatches at St. Nazaire until the last transport of the last convoy unit dropped anchor off Belle Isle. July 1, five days after the cruiser *Seattle* had reached France with the first transports, the stories of the correspondents at St. Nazaire were finally released. In the rush of transmission one of the French telegraph operators neglected to delete the date line 'St. Nazaire, June 26 (delayed)', so it appeared on one press service dispatch to New York. Some editors caught the lapse and deleted the name, but enough printed it to nullify all the censorship precautions. Grasty of the *New York Times* declared the whole affair had been botched. Major Palmer offered to resign if Grasty would take over his job.

Meanwhile, the *Tribune*'s Broun introduced a note of whimsey in the proceedings. Just under the lead paragraph Broun had written:

Since little things are important at moments when history is being made, it may be recorded that the first remark of the first soldier to land was: 'Do they allow enlisted men in the saloons in this town?'

This raised a nice question for the censors. No other correspondent had heard the plaintive query. Broun admitted it was not literally true. But even if the first man down the gangplank hadn't asked it, the correspondent insisted the question was foremost in the minds of most of the soldiers. He refused to change it, argued that it made the soldiers human rather than dummies, and defied the censors to take it out. Since it violated none of Major Palmer's rules, the censors let it pass.

Washington now came forward with a unique contribution to the affair. On Monday, July 2, Mr. Creel's Committee on Public Information announced that the transport convoy had been attacked at sea by a number of enemy submarines and the Navy had defeated the massed U-boats in a spectacular battle.

The attack was made in force, although the night made impossible any exact count of the U-boats gathered for what they deemed a slaughter.

This was stirring stuff; issued almost on the eve of the Fourth of July, it led to a good deal of flag waving and cheering at the small-boy level. Almost immediately the bloom was taken off it by a demand for an investigation of the Navy Department. Confidential information on the convoy route must have been passed to the enemy, it was charged, to enable German submarines in such force to attack far at sea. Was it possible a nest of spies flourished in the heart of Washington? While Republican newspapers speculated on that interesting possibility, other editors demanded an investigation of Mr. Creel's sources of information. Earlier accounts had described the voyage as uneventful. The American general in charge of the convoy had stated that the trip was calm and 'nothing happened.' None of the officers or soldiers interviewed at St. Nazaire recalled a battle at sea with a massed force of submarines. Pressed for an explanation, Mr. Creel admitted that he had 'elaborated' a brief report of the crossing by Rear Admiral Albert Gleaves, presumably for patriotic purposes. He insisted that at least one U-boat had tried to intercept the convoy and was driven off.

The War Department, realizing that all was not going smoothly, directed that henceforth all news dispatches from France relating to the American Expeditionary Forces must be directed to the War Department in Washington and scrutinized there before being sent on to the newspapers for which they were intended. Secretary Baker explained:

At present General Pershing's headquarters are not organized so that he is not in a position to take care of dispatches bearing on troop movements and this can only be done here in Washington.

This rule survived only two days. Washington awoke to the fact that General Pershing's headquarters were organized and a Press Section headed by the experienced, if somewhat unlucky, Frederick Palmer, was a part of the set-up.

The most serious blunder in these misadventures was the identification of St. Nazaire as the port of debarkation. Major Palmer and Lieutenant Green decided that the slip-up occurred through lack of proper understanding with the French Bureau de la Presse and its censoring authorities. Earlier, when the matter had been first discussed, the French did not think it necessary for the United

States to set up its own bureau of censorship. France had had long experience in dealing with correspondents and the press. French military officials knew the problems and pitfalls. Why not trust everything to them and let them scrutinize all newspaper copy? The Americans thanked the French for their offer, but reminded them that a U.S. Army in France would create news problems outside their experience, problems which could be solved only by American organization and teamwork.

With the St. Nazaire incident to strengthen his purpose, Lieutenant Green called on Captain Riboulet, French Press Censor, at 110 rue de Grenelle and presented his case. The Press Section, A.E.F., desired to work closely with their French colleagues; would it not be possible to establish a desk in the French censoring office where a member of Major Palmer's staff might scrutinize not only all copy relating to the A.E.F. intended for publication in France, but also all copy originating in France, from whatever source, which referred to the activities of the American forces? This would include the copy of British correspondents and dispatches written for the Italian, Swiss, Scandinavian, and other neutral newspapers. The French agreed the idea was sound. Lieutenant Green moved in immediately and worked almost around the clock, getting the new liaison organized.

Paul Mowrer expected to cover the arrival and subsequent activities of the U.S. Army in France for the *Chicago Daily News*. He was a little put out when a new man, Junius Wood, turned up on the Avenue de l'Opéra with a letter from Victor Lawson and the blunt statement that he was the *News'* A.E.F. correspondent. Mowrer thought the *News* might at least have consulted him on the assignment in view of his long service in Europe and experience in war reporting. His resentment was softened by the realization that American troops would not go into the trenches for some months, and, while Wood must confine himself to training preliminaries, he, Mowrer, would still be sending the main war stories from the fighting front.

Wood's assignment was due chiefly to a workmanlike job for the *Daily News* on the Mexican border in 1916. Before that he had been an energetic, crusading City Hall reporter in Chicago. Like Floyd Gibbons, his chief competitor, Wood had a nodding acquaintance with General Pershing and friendly personal contact with several of the staff.

A second contingent of the First Division arrived at Brest on July 2. Mowrer in a new uniform was one of the newspaper group to report the proceedings. Like Broun, he saw the U.S. infantrymen coming down the gangplank raring for wine, women, and a chance to get at the Boche. It was his first contact with the American troops and he found them eager, tough, and confident, in contrast to the war-weary French and British. When he had finished filing his story on the arriving transports, he went directly from Brest to the Anglo-American Press Mission at Chantilly, to which he had just been accredited and where he would report activities along the whole French battle line. This left Junius Wood and Edgar Ansel Mowrer to cover the Fourth of July festivities in Paris for the *News*.

The arrival of American forces in France was dramatized in a holiday celebration in the streets of Paris. Newly landed regiments marched with their bands under the American flag. To one American journalist, they appeared gawky and amateurish in their new uniforms. The tunics were wrinkled, trousers were ill-fitting, puttees badly wound; compared to French and British veterans, the newcomers lacked military style. But French citizens were much moved to see the vigorous young men striding along the rue de Rivoli, through the Place de la Concorde and up the Champs Elysées to the Arc de Triomphe. From the sidewalks excited groups spilled onto the street to lock arms and exchange greetings with the smiling Americans. Bouquets of flowers were tossed; along the curbs, lines of school children waved small American flags. There was an elaborate Fourth of July luncheon with toasts to the United States Army, the Navy, President Wilson, General Pershing, Admiral Gleaves, and General Sibert. The Americans in turn toasted President Poincaré, the gallant French Army, General Foch. The reigning British monarch and several prominent British officers were similarly honored. The stories of the American reporters glowed with the color and warmth of France's observance of the American holiday.

Most of the American correspondents trailed the official party to Little Picpus Cemetery, where General Pershing laid a wreath on the tomb of Lafayette. There were more felicitous speeches, mostly in French. Chief spokesman for the United States Army was Major Charles E. Stanton, A.E.F. paymaster, who was fluent in French and had the natural eloquence of an old-fashioned orator. A good part of Major Stanton's address was drowned in the roar of low-flying military planes, mistakenly ordered to embellish the occasion. Yet most of those present heard the stirring apostrophe as he concluded by facing the marble slab and addressing the French General who had fought in the United States' Revolution:

Lafayette, nous voilà!

There were calls at this time for some remarks by General Pershing. An orderly came forward and laid a large flower wreath on the low railing that surmounted the oblong slab. As Pershing bent down and pushed the wreath over the railing to its proper place, the cries for a speech were repeated. The general straightened up and those near him heard him utter a few phrases in English to the effect that Major Stanton had spoken for all Americans and that it was an honor to stand at the tomb of Lafayette.

The phrase 'Lafayette, we are here!' found its way into one or two of the newspaper stories. Few of the correspondents thought the Picpus ceremonies worth more than a couple of paragraphs. A speech by the obscure Major Stanton of the Quartermaster Corps was not worth quoting in a day so overflowing with color and famous personages. Nevertheless, the phrase struck a right note. Floyd Gibbons, who may have had it second-hand from one of his officer friends, attributed it to General Pershing. Afterward, when the phrase was attributed to Pershing in scores of newspapers, it was pointed out that the newspapermen would not have been permitted to credit the statement to Major Stanton under a censorship ruling issued by Major Palmer that same day, prohibiting the mention of any officer by name except General Pershing, General Sibert, and Admiral Gleaves. Pershing said later he could not recall having used the phrase *Lafayette, nous voilà!* at Picpus. Major Palmer said Major Stanton had written and uttered it 'for General Pershing.'

Major Robert R. McCormick, publisher and part owner of the *Chicago Tribune,* called at Castellane House early in July and was taken by Palmer to see General Pershing. McCormick had come overseas to command a battery of First Division artillery, and he made a fine erect figure in his military gear. In the course of the brief talk in Pershing's office, Palmer said one of his chief problems was that none of his assistants had experience in dealing with newspapermen. He had been so long away from the U.S. that he, too, was ignorant of the younger generation reporters being sent over to cover the war. He needed someone in the Press Section who could distinguish legitimate journalists representing responsible newspapers and the adventurers, amateurs, and irresponsibles who wanted excitement.

Major McCormick recalled that a very able *Tribune* man named Mark Watson had just finished a course in an officers' training camp in Illinois. He said Watson would make an excellent assistant. Pershing, impressed by McCormick's recommendation, called a stenographer and sent off a cable, requesting that Watson be detached from present duty and ordered to report to A.E.F. headquarters in France.

New faces appeared among the correspondents assigned to cover the A.E.F. in Paris. In addition to Broun and Junius Wood and the rambunctious Gibbons, those on hand for the Fourth of July ceremonies included Lincoln Eyre of the *New York Morning World,* a tall young man of aristocratic family who spoke fluent French and knew the European scene; J. Westbrook Pegler, a thin, freckled youngster in his early twenties, representing the United Press at $37.50 a week; Robert Small, who had been covering the British front for the A.P. through that last disastrous year and was sick of the whole business; Raymond Carroll of the *Philadelphia Public Ledger,* who kept so much to himself that he became known as the Hermit Crab; the veteran feature writer Herbert Corey; another Philadelphia journalist, Reginald Wright Kauffman. Wythe Williams of the *Times* and Wilbur Forrest of the United Press dropped in frequently at Castellane House to ask for an interview with Pershing and to question Palmer about the A.E.F. training program. Newcomers wanted to consult him about their new uniforms and passes. With the experience of the British and French to guide them, Palmer and Nolan decided that since the accredited correspondents were to be confined to a select few, they should wear a conventional Army officer's uniform with Sam Browne belt and green brassard or arm band with a letter 'C.'

They would not be required to salute officers, but might, if the occasion required, return the salutes of others. By the time Bastille Day came on July 14, the corps of American newspapermen had not only grown to nearly twenty but were dressed in smart new outfits befitting their calling.

This new class of semi-military figures promenading around Paris, patronizing restaurants and bars, climbing in and out of taxicabs, did not set well with some old-school Army officers. They found the idea irregular and unmilitary. Major Palmer was stopped on the street by Brigadier General William H. Allaire, the U.S. Provost Marshal charged with policing the Paris scene for the A.E.F. The brigadier had recently been annoyed at seeing a party of war correspondents strolling in the seeming irregularity of their attire. He was especially enraged by their Sam Browne belts.

The general's testy complaint expressed the resentment a good many West Pointers must have felt toward these newspaper hybrids at this stage of the war. They wore military plumage and enjoyed privileges, yet had no responsibility, no duties. Some were paid as much as general officers. None appeared to be subject to any kind of discipline. The Army had never had this special class of privileged drones before.

As he recalled the encounter in his memoirs, *With My Own Eyes,* Major Palmer outmaneuvered the general by quoting military protocol.

'They are in uniform,' Palmer said, 'because that is in the regulations, a copy of which I sent you as Provost Marshal; and they have Sam Browne belts because all the accredited correspondents of all the Allied Armies wear them. The belt shows they are not privates who are expected to give salutes. They have not the insignia of rank of officers because they do not take salutes and are not officers—all to establish their position under Army control, just as your stars on your shoulders establish yours, or crossed rifles show a man is an infantryman. After reading the press regulations, General, I suggest you hurry up your own regulations for which we have been waiting to our embarrassment. In order to avoid arrest by the Provost Marshal, we should like to know what we are likely to be arrested for.'

Palmer's exchange with the Provost Marshal emphasized the need to get the correspondents out of Paris to some convenient place where they could settle down and work. While the formalities of accreditation were going forward at 31 rue de Constantine—the first two, Ray Carroll and Junius Wood, were officially approved July 9—Palmer and Nolan canvassed the French countryside in the general area selected for A.E.F. training for a suitable headquarters.

On the morning of July 19, 1917, the newspapermen found on the Press Section bulletin board at Castellane House a bulletin which marked the beginning of a new chapter in their war careers:

July 19, 1917

All accredited correspondents will please come to this office at 11 o'clock on Saturday morning, July 21st, and they will go to their headquarters near the American training camp at 7:30 Monday morning from the Gare de l'Est.

All correspondents
1. Are advised to have telegraph credit cards.
2. Can carry small cameras.
3. Are advised to buy a No. 6 Tarride map, which is that of the region where he will live.
4. Should have typewriter, large or portable, plenty of copy paper, carbons, writing paper, etc.
5. Should take plenty of tobacco, cigars, cigarettes.
6. Should have a small rubber bath tub.

XIV

NOTHING NEW AT NEUFCHÂTEAU

On Monday morning, July 23, a group of newly accredited American war correspondents climbed on the train at Gare de l'Est and said au revoir to Paris. Under the chaperonage of Major Palmer they were off to their new press headquarters at Neufchâteau, where, it was presumed, they would soon begin actively covering the historic spectacle of American troops entering the fighting war. The newspapermen looked smart, if a little self-conscious, in their new uniforms. They could be distinguished from regular army officers by their green sleeve brassards and varied luggage. Portable typewriters, supplies of paper and tobacco and collapsible rubber bathtubs detracted somewhat from their martial appearance.

Some had misgivings about leaving the amenities of Paris for the simple life in an obscure provincial town. However, war has its hazards, and the move into the valley of the Meuse 250 kilometers east and a little south of Paris seemed a logistical step toward the battle lines. At Neufchâteau, safe from the distractions of the boulevards and Paris night life, they would watch the first two infantry divisions of the A.E.F. in training under French instructors and war conditions. Indeed they likewise would be undergoing training for combat duty as they scrambled about the barracks and drill fields and journeyed along back roads and through muddy trenches.

When they arrived at Neufchâteau, after a four-hour journey, they were conducted to the Hôtel de la Providence. The proprietress, Mme. Duvernet, watched the members of the press straggle in with their bags and typewriters. A self-possessed woman of middle age, with white hair and sangfroid, she was pleased to receive a distinguished group of American journalists, press officers, and chauffeurs under her roof, but she would keep an eye on them. By way of welcome, a little vase of fresh flowers waited in every room.

Neufchâteau was to be the principal field headquarters for A.E.F. correspondents for the next eight months, and a branch headquarters for nearly six months longer, but when the first contingent arrived the town was completely devoid of war's excitement. One other American in uniform had arrived at Neufchâteau before them. He was a medical officer, setting up a laboratory to test drinking water and milk in communities where the troops would train. Except for his bottles and test tubes, the town held no sign of military activity.

Gondrecourt, where the First Division would train, was almost an hour's drive by automobile on a winding road to the northwest. Chaumont, where General Pershing was about to establish his G.H.Q., was another hour's drive or train ride off to the southwest. The First's artillery camp at Le Valdahon, near Besançon and not far from the Swiss border, was half a day's journey due south. The vacuum in which the newspapermen found themselves was temporary, but not accidental. General Pershing and his staff had talked the matter over with General Sibert; they did not want the newspapermen too close to G.H.Q. or division headquarters; they might become a nuisance with their questions and interviews. At this stage of the A.E.F. program, the West Pointers preferred the correspondents kept at arm's length.

Some of the newsmen transplanted from Paris contrasted their accommodations at Neufchâteau with the headquarters of the Anglo-American press mission at Chantilly. There the correspondents lived in a requisitioned château two miles out of town on the Paris road. The walls were hung with Flemish tapestries, and the oversize bathrooms had modern plumbing. Collapsible rubber tubs were not needed. A service bar was convenient both to the library and billiard room. A squash court had been laid out behind the stables. On the wide lawns peacocks spread their feathers as in the old days. The cook had been assistant chef at the Ritz. Americans sharing the good life there included Paul Mowrer of the *Chicago Daily News,* Wythe Williams of the *New York Times,* Berry of the Associated Press and Henry Wood of the United Press. Their liaison were three French cavalry officers of noble lineage,

Captain de Courcel, Lieutenant de Liederkerque and Lieutenant de Chabannes.

One day the owner of the château, a handsome but somewhat flighty young French nobleman, paid a visit to the correspondents' mess. During the conversation the young man, who wore the uniform of a corporal in the French supply service, expressed concern at the great loss of life suffered by his country and stated that as a patriotic duty he was doing what he could to make up the deficit. After the war, he told the correspondents, he intended to undertake the work of repopulation more systematically, developing a section of his extensive estates in the Gironde with small cottages scattered among the dunes. In each of these rustic retreats he would install a healthy young peasant woman for breeding purposes. It was his plan to visit each regularly in turn, and show no favoritism. About twenty, he thought, would be a proper number.

At Neufchâteau the accommodations were neither luxurious nor picturesque; no crystal chandeliers, grand piano or squash court; no wacky young French aristocrat to enliven their table talk. Yet the Hôtel de la Providence possessed a certain provincial charm. An Alsatian porcelain stove warmed the downstairs parlor on chilly days, the brasswork was polished, and a pleasant odor of soup simmering on the back of the stove wafted up the stairwell. The rooms were clean and the beds comfortable.

The correspondents established their mess on the second floor. Food came up from the hotel kitchen, ordinary French fare, always soup, veal and potatoes, salads and vegetables, embellished by whatever delicacies the current mess officer picked up at the local *charcuterie*. Each correspondent served in turn as dictator of mess affairs. When his turn came, he could load the table with his own brands of cheese, sausage, smoked fish, and other specialties. Later on, the tendency of some to introduce rare and bizarre items in the menu led to ill feeling on the part of those who maintained that the mess officer should concern himself with good plain cookery and plenty of liquor.

A day or two after their arrival the newspapermen discovered a beautiful young French girl, Henriette Moratille, on the kitchen staff and persuaded Mme. Duvernet to assign her exclusively to their mess. Sixteen-year-old Henriette was a refugee from Conflans, then held by the Germans. Her innocence and gentle manner gave a refreshing tone to the newspapermen's table talk. All took an interest in her welfare. Henriette's special knight errant and protector was Westbrook Pegler. His attention to her was platonic, but so marked that the girl's mother suspected a war romance was budding and warned the young man against the terrible uncertainties of *la guerre*. Henriette's sister, Suzanne, also passed dishes and ladled soup at the mess, and a third servant named Angel—estimated to be an aging 35—cleared off the dishes and brushed up the crumbs.

As for the rest of the town, it possessed few attractions and little history. There was a brewery and a local newspaper and four or five blocks of small retail shops. Several branch-line railroads converged there, but none ran direct to Paris. If you followed one of the main streets up a hillside for a third of a mile, you came to an open place, or square, with a statue of Joan of Arc. Neufchâteau paid honor to the Maid because she was born only a few miles north. The meadows of Domrémy, where she saw her visions in the sky, were only half an hour's ride away. But the newspapermen could not put any of this in their stories. It would pinpoint the U.S. training area.

The Sunday after their arrival, the correspondents heard a stir outside their hotel and saw two staff cars drive up to the door. American flags and 2-star pennants fluttered from the windshields, and the newsmen recognized the rigid figure of the Commander-in-Chief. General Pershing was looking for a place to establish his own headquarters and acquainting himself with the whole training area. In his party were Major (Major-General) James G. Harbord, his chief of staff; Colonel de Chambrun, French aide and interpreter, and Captain George S. Patton, aide. They did not stay long or talk about their errand. Pershing had nothing to say to the newspapermen, and his manner was a little aloof. Harbord, who kept a diary, made a brief note of the occasion:

At Neufchâteau we found a rather depressed little group of Americans. They were the correspondents of our great American newspapers, starving for news.

Within a day or two some crumbs of news materialized. Conducted by automobile to Gondrecourt the correspondents were permitted to watch men of the First Division at their training exercises. Most of it was familiar training camp routine, digging trenches, crawling under barbed wire or across a ploughed field, thrusting bayonets into dummies.

It was at this phase of the war that the correspondents, searching for a suitable nickname for the U.S. infantryman to match the British 'Tommy Atkins' and the French '*poilu*,' tried out the term 'Sammy.' No one knows who first started it, but the nom de guerre derived from America's classic cartoon figure 'Uncle Sam.' By common consent the newsmen put it to work. 'Sammies' excel at throwing the grenade because of their baseball boyhood. 'Sammies' win the hearts of French small fry with gifts of gum and candy. 'Sammies' entertain French instructors with a picnic, American style. 'Sammies' blow up their own trench by mistake. 'Attaboy!' and other U.S. slang was explained to bewildered French by 'Sammies.'

Presently it occurred to the correspondents that the American soldier did not look like a 'Sammy' or behave like one. In print, 'Sammy' was completely phony. Officers and men grumbled about it, and no one mourned when 'Sammy' was quietly dropped overboard, the first American casualty of the war.

Life at the Hôtel de la Providence settled to a quiet routine. Breakfast, with a big bowl of chocolate, then off by motor to Gondrecourt, to watch the swarms of men in khaki at their war games; lunch at some officers' mess; then the long ride back to Neufchâteau, where they would try to work out some fresh angle to put on the cable for the next day's papers. Late in the afternoon the correspondents' typewriters made a mild clatter in the two upper floors of the Hôtel de la Providence as the men set down the day's impressions. What they wrote concerned the trivial preliminaries of war, not its essence, but the American public was hungry for tidings—any tidings—about its army in France.

Floyd Gibbons and one or two others became bored after a week of this and went back to Paris. A newcomer, Thomas L. Johnson of the *New York Sun,* arrived to report that Press Headquarters in Paris had been moved from the rue de Constantine to 10 rue Ste. Anne, just off the Avenue de l'Opéra and much more convenient to Harry's New York Bar.

Johnson reached Neufchâteau just in time for an important story. General Pétain came down to review the First Division, and the correspondents were permitted to tag along as he watched the Americans go through their paces. Afterward, addressing the officers, he was enthusiastic in his praise. What spirit! How confidently they went about their work! What excellent condition! Why, they looked ready to go into the trenches immediately. This sounded fine to the American newspapermen, who made copious notes. In the process of writing their stories and clearing them through censorship, their education progressed. General Pétain wanted the French to believe that the Americans were about ready to take over, and they would soon be relieved. The national morale was low; it was his job to bolster it, however he could. This statement about the fitness of the American troops and their readiness for combat was so important that two of Pétain's staff went to Neufchâteau from Gondrecourt to see that the newspapermen got the general's glowing statement in detail and to make sure it cleared.

U.S. press officers and censors were less enthusiastic. They had the word by telephone from G.H.Q., where Pétain's motives were better understood. After some discussion, the censors reluctantly passed the story; Pershing was unhappy about it. The American soldiers were not ready to go into the front lines, but Pétain's prestige and his desperate need to reassure the French carried the day.

A week later 'Papa' Joffre arrived to review the troops. No longer in active command of a French army, Joffre still was a popular figure, respected in France and well known in the United States. After watching the First Division march and go through its new routines, the marshal was brought to Neufchâteau by officers from G.H.Q., who dined and wined him at the Hôtel de la Providence. Afterward, Colonel Nolan prepared a statement for Joffre's signature. The American troops looked fit, the statement said, and their training was progressing. The Americans were keeping their promises and doing everything within reason to assist the Allied cause. But it would be unwise to rush them; the troops would go into the fighting line when the Americans were ready.

This statement was handed around to the newspapermen, and the balance was redressed.

There were more desertions to Paris. Floyd Gibbons shuttled between Paris and Le Valdahon, where Major McCormick and his battery were in training. Heywood Broun's wife had arrived in France, and the *Tribune* man spent much of his time in Paris too. Carroll got the wanderlust and disappeared from Neufchâteau to hunt for material on his own.

Green complained to Major Palmer in a memo:

1. I have found it almost impossible in your absence to obtain any news from the chief sub-departments (at G.H.Q.) for the Press Correspondents.

2. It is extremely important that we should supply these correspondents with news, not only to ensure our keeping in touch with them, but in order that through them we may keep public opinion in America properly informed.

3. I suggest that you request the C in C to instruct the Chief of Staff and the heads of departments to provide your assistants with any items which they may think suitable for publication.

> J. C. GREEN, 1st Assistant
> Press Section

At that early stage Green discovered the difficulties of gathering news from military men concerned with their own affairs. But he lacked experience; he didn't know what questions to ask and he confused the function of press officer with that of reporter.

The removal of G.H.Q. from Paris to Chaumont in August, the growing impatience of the French at the deliberate pace of American training, and the growing restlessness of the correspondents at Neufchâteau all combined to produce that rare event—a Pershing press conference.

Palmer sent out notice a day in advance. The 'regulars' motored over from Neufchâteau. The 'Parisites' hurried down by train. A full complement of sixteen accredited correspondents gathered in General Pershing's office in Chaumont, with Colonel Nolan and Major Palmer on hand to listen and keep order.

The Commander-in-Chief gave a little talk on the qualities he wanted to develop in the American soldier. These young men were being asked to give up much of their freedom and personal liberty, placed under strict discipline, required to obey instantly and without question. But this did not mean they were to be turned into automatons. He wanted discipline and obedience, but he wanted the men to think, too, and to know why they were fighting. He was pleased with their progress in training. They were rapidly learning, under experienced French instructors, the rudiments of trench warfare, with emphasis on spade and grenade and barbed wire. But with all due respect to the French, he wanted the American soldier to rely more on his rifle, and know what he must do in the open, fast-moving infantry attacks. The A.E.F. training program, Pershing said, must prepare for the time when the Western Front would be broken and the war return to the phase of movement and vast maneuver.

Robert Small of the A.P. broke in at this point to suggest that the general might want to reconsider his terms. Many Allied leaders had come to believe that the front could not be broken. That conviction was based on greater experience than Pershing's. If the general talked offhand about breaking the Western Front and was so quoted in all the newspapers, would it not sound like Yankee boasting, or at least, overoptimism?

General Pershing turned in his chair and fixed the A.P. reporter with a slow, cold stare. When he spoke, his words had an icy edge.

'Of course the Western Front can be broken. What are we here for? We and our Allies together are going to break it. You may quote me as stated.'

The general had no small talk or laughter for these infrequent meetings with the press. He was impatient with any interruption, anything that took him from his desk. Only those few, like Floyd Gibbons and Junius Wood, who had served with him on the Mexican Border felt at ease in his presence. To the others he was unnecessarily grim. Watching the tight line of his mouth and the set of his jaw, they saw the fixed purpose of military command and the harsh spirit of censorship. In one sense, he was their enemy. Later, when the newspapermen became aware of the incessant scheming and pressure by the French and British to feed American troops piecemeal into the line, of his determination to hold them together and fight as the United States Army, and of the supply failures, the jealousies and back-biting in Washington, many of them understood him better and made allowance for his grimness. But for others to the end, he was tough Black Jack, arrogant, a cold fish.

The Pershing interview cleared the air a bit and gave the newsmen fresh insight into the training problems at Gondrecourt. For several days they covered the camp's activities with special attention to rifle and open warfare. Then the late summer doldrums set in again. This was training, not war. More went back to Paris.

The rest climbed in the press cars and rode down to the artillery camp at Le Valdahon. General Peyton C. March showed them around, talked about the relative merits of French and American field guns and explained what artillery was about. His manner was friendly and his talk so frank that one correspondent inquired whether they could use the material he was giving them.

Of course, General March replied. He said they could even give the location of the camp. The Germans knew it anyway. The fire of the big guns could be heard across the Swiss border, and spies with powerful field glasses could undoubtedly keep track of the camp's activities. General March didn't worry about this. When the Germans had sent some planes over to bomb the camp, his antiaircraft batteries had gained useful target practice. The peppery March hoped the Boche planes would keep coming, so his men could gain experience shooting them down. As for the rest, the reporters could write anything they liked about his camp with a single exception. Recently some of his batteries had begun using a new improved model of the French 155's. This gun had not yet been captured by the enemy, and since it represented a new principle in design, he wanted it kept quiet.

This was a refreshing experience for the reporters. But as they filed out of General March's office with his carte blanche in their ears, Major Palmer remained behind. He told General March, when they were alone, that the Commander-in-Chief, Colonel Nolan and he, Palmer, had laid down certain principles and prohibitions for the press, and that one of them was that no mention be made of the location of any training camp. Likewise, the general had talked a little too freely about his artillery. Palmer reminded him that the censorship rules adopted early in July prohibited the mention of details of batteries and observation posts, 'aerial photograph methods, new types of guns, new types of shells, any reference to ranging, especially to ranging mechanism.'

So, despite General March's easy manner and liberality, the trip to the artillery camp produced only anemic generalities.

Young Pegler did not accompany his associates to Gondrecourt one day. On their return to Neufchâteau that afternoon the others found the U.P. man pounding the typewriter and learned that he had ridden over to Chaumont. By 5 P.M. the rumor was all over the Hôtel de la Providence that brash young Pegler had obtained an exclusive interview with General Pershing at G.H.Q. As the hour for filing approached, the worried correspondents appealed to Major Palmer and Lieutenant Green. The United Press man, they said, should be made to disgorge. Pegler was summoned. Was it true, that he had gone to Chaumont and gotten in to see Pershing? Reluctantly, Pegler said yes. An interview? What happened, what did he say? The U.P. man looked thoughtfully at the ceiling, as if wondering how much of the confidential tête-a-tête with the Commander-in-Chief he should disclose to his colleagues. They waited with pencils ready; there was a long, anxious interval of silence while Pegler pondered. Then:

'I got in to see the general. I said: "General Pershing, I'm Pegler of the United Press. Can you give me a statement on the general situation?"

'He looked up from his desk. "Pegler," he said, "Get the hell out of my office." '

Not long after this, the correspondents at Neufchâteau made a curious discovery. In the small Paris or Continental edition of the *Chicago Tribune,* a story appeared which related the experiences of a young newspaperwoman at an army camp in France. From the text it was clear that the camp was Le Valdahon, near Besançon. The name signed to the dispatch was 'Peggy.' A few days later another 'Peggy' story appeared. The young woman seemed to be having a very interesting time knocking around the training camp, hobnobbing with officers, watching the boys march, and listening to the boom of the big guns. No woman had been accredited to the A.E.F. What was going on here? In one of her dispatches, Peggy confided to the *Tribune*'s readers that she was staying at the big army camp as a guest of the commanding general and with the special permission of the Commander-in-Chief. The stories were chatty and informal, mostly about the adventures and problems of a young woman in the midst of several thousand men busy with martial affairs, the problems of keeping her hair curled and lingerie in order, and similar feminine touches. However, the harmless rambling nature of the Peggy stories did not prevent the correspondents at Neufchâteau from making an issue out of the case.

Junius Wood was particularly concerned when he learned that the 'Peggy' stories were being published in the *Tribune*'s main edition in Chicago. His own paper, the *Chicago Daily News,* questioned him about the breezy girl correspondent.

L'affaire Peggy turned out to be a blessing in disguise to the press corps at Neufchâteau. It came at a time when ennui, frustration, and monotony weighed heavily on the occupants of the Hôtel de la Providence, and not even the cheerful, gracious Henriette could dispel the discord and tension. The correspondents were dissatisfied with the transportation arrangements. They accused the press officers of using the cars for their own convenience. In *Editor & Publisher* someone discovered an advertisement of the *Philadelphia Evening Ledger,* asserting that their man, Henri Bazin, was the only correspondent to receive the Croix de Guerre. Bazin tried to pass it off as a joke, having only a minor decoration in no way connected with the war, but the others were sarcastic and bitter. Bazin wrote to Major Palmer protesting against the drunkenness and rowdy behaviour of several correspondents at Vittel and Neufchâteau, disassociating himself from such conduct. Wood had had several rows with Lieutenant Green over censorship, on one occasion snatching back several letters rather than permit Green to read what he had written to his wife and mother. The correspondents who remained faithfully at Neufchâteau criticized the restless 'Parisites,' and those who moved around accused the Neufchâteau regulars of being lazy. Palmer was accused of being stuffy and officious, and of failing to keep them informed. Censorship was getting worse. Now, by a ruling of Colonel Nolan, the reporters were forbidden to write that the French people made occasional gifts of wine to U.S. soldiers, for fear such mention would rile the Anti-Saloon League and the W.C.T.U. back home.

Into this atmosphere of acrimony and unrest the Peggy affair came as a refreshing breeze. Where men find a common threat to their livelihood and dignity, they stop fighting among themselves and unite against the foe. In this case, Major Palmer and his assistants were as indignant as the correspondents over the privileged lady correspondent at the artillery camp. The wires began to vibrate with official inquiries. Le Valdahon, 10 rue Ste. Anne, the *Chicago Tribune* office at 420 rue St. Honore, and G.H.Q. at

Chaumont—all were put on requisition to enlighten the Chief Press Office about Peggy.

Peggy turned out to be Mrs. Henrietta Hull of El Paso, Texas. In civilian life she had worked for the *El Paso Morning Times,* and in 1916 had followed U.S. forces for a time during the trouble along the Mexican Border. She may have been the only newspaperwoman to serve as a correspondent during the Rio Grande campaign. The military life seemed to appeal to her and with a letter from the publishers of the *El Paso Morning Times* and one or two smaller Southwestern journals, she turned up in Paris in July, 1917.

Mrs. Hull's newspaper connections impressed the staff at 10 rue Ste. Anne. The Press Office arranged for her to visit some Army installations and see some of the French sectors. But she was ill when the tour started and could not go. Several days later she called at the office of the *Chicago Tribune* in the rue St. Honore and was introduced to Major McCormick, who happened to be in town. The major was favorably impressed by the young Texas newspaperwoman and suggested to the *Tribune's* Paris edition manager, Joseph B. Pierson, that Mrs. Hull might contribute some 'women's angle' stories for their paper. Mr. Pierson, who was about to start out on a tour of U.S. Army camps in the interest of *Tribune* circulation, invited Mrs. Hull to go along. When she pointed out that she had no pass, Mr. Pierson said that the *Chicago Tribune* credentials which he carried, including a rare pink pass for the operation and fuel for a motor vehicle, would no doubt suffice.

Away they went and in time arrived at Le Valdahon, where, it will be recalled, Major McCormick commanded a battery. The sentries were not very happy about admitting a female without proper credentials to the artillery camp, but the magic of the *Chicago Tribune* got Mrs. Hull through the gate and past a number of sentry posts. However, the post adjutant insisted that the young woman could not have the freedom of the camp without some credentials stating who she was and why she was there. He was particularly concerned because General Pershing had arrived to inspect the camp and confer with General March. What happened next may best be explained in Mrs. Hull's own account of the affair:

I had no pass and the Post Adjutant laid the matter before General March. The result was that I was invited up to the mess hall to have tea with the two generals and tell them all about it.

I explained to General Pershing that I wasn't accredited—that my poor little paper couldn't afford to have me accredited and that as my opportunity to visit the American camps had been lost when I was ill, I had decided to go home. He (General Pershing) said it wasn't necessary, and that I mustn't leave now when the story was getting bigger all the time.

Someone in the crowd of staff officers suggested that I work in the Y.M.C.A. cantine or get a position in the Quarter-Master's office—both of which General Pershing approved. He said I couldn't write about the troops unless I saw them and as long as I wasn't accredited that was a good way to be with them. He also instructed Major Collins to see if some arrangements couldn't be made so that I could work as a secretary with General Headquarters (!) At that point General March suggested that I come to the artillery camp and in the course of the conversation that followed it was decided that I should help with the work at the Y.M.C.A. . . .

Mrs. Hull admitted that her situation was somewhat ambiguous since she had no standing either as a legitimate canteen worker or as a correspondent. But she was quite ready to work out some satisfactory compromise:

I am writing to General Pershing to ask him to O.K. my application for war department credentials. Major McCormick has offered me the great opportunity of my life but I know that he cannot have two accredited correspondents for the big *Tribune,* so I am going to explain to the General that if he will permit it, I can be accredited for the Army (Paris) edition.

As for the unchivalrous correspondents who had objected to her activities at Le Valdahon, Mrs. Hull pointed out that she had always been a small-town newspaperwoman and never considered herself a competitor of the big-city journalists; if they wanted to write Peggy stories for their papers, why, said Mrs. Hull, they had her permission to go ahead and do it.

When all the facts were in hand, Major Palmer considered the matter, discussed it with Colonel Nolan, and then wrote a memorandum reviewing the affair for General Pershing:

If the privileges which she says have been given to her have been authorized by the Commander-in-Chief and by the Commanding Officer at Le Valdahon, then she is receiving privileges which have never been given to any individual representing any daily paper with any European army during the present war; privileges, indeed which are granted only to distinguished writers who use their material for lectures or for books or magazines, and do not enter into competition with the accredited news correspondents.

The *Chicago Tribune,* Paris Edition, has not wanted for representation, if it would make use of its privileges. It has a regularly accredited correspondent, Mr. Floyd Gibbons, who has been absent from the accredited correspondents' headquarters since the first week in August —throughout the months of August and September.... At the same time the *Chicago Tribune* has, by a special arrangement, made use of the articles of Mr. Heywood Broun.

The complaints against Mrs. Hull on the part of the accredited correspondents are unanimous. They add ... that the work she is doing is undignified.

If the Commander-in-Chief of the Expedition is to accredit correspondents by invitation, it will be equally gratifying to the Chief of the Press Division if, when such invitation is given, he be informed through the regular channels.

Mrs. Hull says that she was present at a luncheon given by Generals Pershing and March, when both Generals invited her personally to be their guests with the Army. The fact of her having received such an invitation has been widely advertised in her own paper.

It is therefore requested that some official authorization of Mrs. Hull's exact standing be given to the Chief of the Press Division, as soon as may be convenient, in order to regulate the situation which has resulted from her assignment to the Artillery Camp.

FREDERICK PALMER

On that note the affair ended. It had taken several weeks to round up the facts in the case, but finally Mrs. Hull packed up her gear at Le Valdahon and returned to Paris. Whether General Pershing replied to the lady's request for accreditation to the *Tribune's* Paris Edition, or referred it back to G-2-D without recommendation, the records do not disclose. No accreditation was forthcoming, and Mrs. Hull sat out the balance of the war by the Seine.

Another item in the *Chicago Tribune,* Paris Edition, caught the eye of the correspondents at Neufchâteau. This, too, involved the work of an unaccredited lady journalist. A story about an enemy air raid on an unnamed American aviation base appeared on the front page under the by-line of Mlle. Many de l'Estang. The German planes came over at night and dropped quite a number of bombs. The loud explosions, the glare of flames, the rattle and bang of antiaircraft fire, the excitement and tension all were described vividly by Mlle. de l'Estang.

Investigation disclosed that Mlle. de l'Estang was the sixteen-year-old secretary of Mr. Joseph Pierson. On his circulation trips through the American camps and bases, the *Chicago Tribune*'s Paris manager found it convenient to take his youthful and attractive secretary along as interpreter. When the military authorities issued a rare pink pass to Mr. Pierson, authorizing him to operate and refuel his motor vehicle in American camp and base areas, it was with the understanding that he would confine his activities to *Chicago Tribune* circulation and business affairs and would under no circumstances act as a newsgetter. Having passed with his secretary through the dangers and excitement of an air raid, Pierson saw no reason why Mlle. de l'Estang, who was bound by no such agreement, should not set down her impressions for the paper. Major Palmer and the correspondents at Neufchâteau objected to such a loose interpretation of the rules, and Mr. Pierson was warned that if he wanted to keep his pink pass, Mlle. de l'Estang must confine herself to secretarial duties and interpreting and give up the joys of authorship.

One rainy September morning the newspapermen overheard the New England voices of some new American troops bewailing the 'No Tabac' signs in shop windows. The Twenty-sixth Division—with men from Boston, Springeld, Fall River, New Bedford, Hartford, and Down East—were finding their places in the Lorraine training area. A part of the division, which had landed in Liverpool, had lost most of its baggage in the hurried journey across England. The men had not been paid in more than a month, and nearly all of them were out of tobacco.

When the correspondents tried to write about the new arrivals, censorship put up the bars. Under a recent censorship ruling: 'The presence of new bodies of troops in the training area may not be mentioned except by special permission.' No such special permission was forthcoming from Chaumont, and the presence of the New Englanders in France went unheralded.

Something was needed to keep the accredited correspondents cheerful and busy. Lieutenant Green organized a motor tour of Army installations in outlying training areas. Recently the Army had installed great bake ovens near Dijon where millions of loaves of bread—American style—would soon be turned out each week for the growing A.E.F. The proposed tour would not only take in the bake ovens and mammoth supply bases, but some historic old châteaux. Itinerary and details were worked out carefully by the methodical Lieutenant Green.

The three-car caravan left Neufchâteau on schedule and proceeded to Chaumont for lunch, maintaining a fixed order: Car No. 18, first; No. 4, second; No. 20, third. The drivers were directed to stay as close together as possible, avoiding each other's dust. Car No. 20 was half an hour late leaving Chaumont on the afternoon leg, and did not arrive at Dijon until the others were already in the hotel having dinner. In his report to Major Palmer, Green gave painful details of the scene. The dining room of the Hôtel de la Cloche was filled with respectable French bourgeois at their evening meal. The uniformed occupants of the first two cars were quietly finishing their soup when in strolled the occupants of Car No. 20. The correspondents in the laggard car—Lincoln Eyre of the *New York World,* Junius Wood of the *Chicago Daily News,* and Dan Dillon of International News Service—greeted their comrades boisterously. As they took their seats at a nearby table, it was apparent that they had paused somewhere along the road for refreshment. Presently one of the later arrivals—Lieutenant Green thought it was Eyre—began to toss pellets of bread at the correspondents of an adjoining table. This was embarrassing to Lieutenant Green and other sober members of the party, who thought the boisterous antics would create an unfavorable impression on the local French diners. Afterward, so Lieutenant Green was told, the correspondents attended a theater, where the behavior of the occupants of Car No. 20 again was so noisy that others in the party, Mr. C. C. Lyon and Major McCain, left rather than be identified with them. The next morning, Green charged, he waited half an hour past the starting time for laggard members of Car No. 20 and then drove off to inspect the bake ovens without them. There was an unpleasant scene on the sidewalk in front of the Hôtel de la Cloche upon their return, when Eyre accused Green of running the tour for his own convenience, without consulting the correspondents.

That afternoon the tour of the historic old châteaux proceeded without the occupants of Car No. 20. Wood, Eyre, and Dillon preferred to dispense with Green's guided tour and explore the French countryside on their own. When the two groups returned to Neufchâteau two days later, there was a decided coolness between them.

In a long report to Major Palmer, Lieutenant Green preferred charges against Lincoln Eyre and Junius Wood. He recommended that they be suspended and their credentials withdrawn. Eyre was charged with being intoxicated and conducting himself in a manner calculated to lower the tone and dignity of the American Expeditionary Force. Wood's moody temperament and his continuous rows over censorship were cited by Lieutenant Green as evidence of his unfitness to serve as an accredited correspondent. Green's statement was supplemented by other press officers and one or two correspondents who were annoyed by the defendants' behavior.

However, Mr. Green's case was greatly weakened by one particular. He accused the wrong man of throwing the pellets of bread across the dining room of the Hôtel de la Cloche. It was Dillon of the I.N.S., not Eyre of the *World*, who had committed this lapse of etiquette. Dillon not only accepted the blame for this episode but admitted having partaken of strong liquor on the ride from Chaumont to Dijon. His detailed statement gave pause to military officialdom at a time when it appeared that two of the most capable correspondents were about to be unfrocked and sent home.

As Dillon recalled the adventurous afternoon, their car, No. 20, had first paused at a wayside liquor store to enable Junius Wood, current mess officer, to lay in supplies of whiskey and rum at prices more reasonable than those prevailing at Neufchâteau. Later, along the road, they came upon Car No. 4 halted by tire trouble. Its occupants were reclining at the roadside while the driver wrestled with an inner tube. Naturally, Dillon explained, he and his companions paused to lend advice and encouragement to the stranded ones.

While standing about [Dillon's statement explained] I had the brilliant idea that a drink of rum would do me good after an all-day ride. Unselfishly I communicated my inspiration and it was hailed by cries of 'Hear! Hear!' Showing the deference due to a press officer, I handed the bottle first to Mr. Griffith, who after taking a copious draught, passed it along to the others.

Dillon said he had quaffed a goodly portion of the rum at the roadside and arrived at the Hôtel de la Cloche feeling no pain. He exonerated Eyre of misconduct in the dining room.

I can only say from the depth of my sack cloth and ashes that it was I, Daniel Dillon, who committed this personal and professional conduct which might have injured the morale or discipline of our soldiers. As I happened to toss a few crumbs at my roommate, Mr. Lyon, seated at an adjoining table, you, Mr. Eyre, of course, had no interest in my playful antics and at no time used your powerful right arm to hurl these dread grenades.

Dillon also claimed the distinction of being the only one in the party who had told Lieutenant Green his chaperonage was puerile and stupid. On his testimony, the case against Wood and Eyre collapsed.

The colorful Dillon did not remain long as the I.N.S. correspondent nor did he write much, but there were few dull moments while he was a member of the correspondents' mess. On one occasion he had difficulty making out an expense account to explain his outlays for two months in rural France. By great persistence and imagination he managed to account for all except $250. After some thought, he made one final entry:

Entertaining General Pershing—$250

Major Palmer, who found it necessary to scrutinize the correspondents' expense accounts as well as their copy, protested vigorously at this item, saying it reflected on the Commander-in-Chief, as if newspapermen found it necessary to entertain him lavishly to win his favor. Some compromise may have been reached, but the affair gave Dillon lasting fame among his comrades of the press.

There was indeed something unique and undisciplined about these correspondents, something that gave freshness and vigor to their work. They would not conform. No two were alike. Junius Wood, City Hall reporter, temperamental and tempestuous; the whimsical Broun, scornful of military abracadabra; youthful Pegler, always wanting to know why? and how come? Lincoln Eyre, aristocratic and intelligent, scornful of bureaucratic stupidities; Dillon, the Irish bon vivant from Oklahoma; war-wise Wythe Williams, veteran of Paris and the Marne; flamboyant and incredible Floyd Gibbons; thoughtful and humorous Tom Johnson; Ray Carroll and Reg Kauffmann, the Philadelphia individualists; elderly, Francophile Henri Bazin. How was it possible to control these unpredictable journalists with a little book of rules? Pershing did not understand the urge that drove them, but he learned to use them later on. Palmer should have understood, but he had put on a uniform and had a major's leaves on his shoulders. Correct and dignified, he did not approve their careless behavior, forgetting that they had little else to occupy them, and he was intolerant of the youth and brashness of some of them.

After the collapse of the charges against Wood and Eyre, Lieutenant Green went back to Paris, where at 10 rue Ste. Anne his conscientious attention to detail was better appreciated. A new man came to Neufchâteau as field censor. Gerald Morgan, veteran correspondent and companion of Richard Harding Davis in the early months of the war, had taken a course at officers' training camp and now wore the bars of a first lieutenant. Able, experienced, friendly, and at ease with the newspapermen, he filled a long-felt want at Neufchâteau.

The minor squabbles and temperamental storms among the newspapermen at Neufchâteau were obscured at length by the gloomy turn in Allied affairs. Censorship could soften but could not conceal the accumulation of military and political failures. In Russia, the Kerensky Government, pledged to continue the war against Germany, had been overthrown and the collapse of the whole Russian front was imminent. The great British attack at

Passachendaele had bogged down in bad weather after the expenditure of thousands of lives and mountains of ammunition.

The French were disheartened by the failure of the Nivelle offensive. On the Italian front, German propaganda had weakened Cadorna's army and paved the way for the disaster at Caporetto.

The American newspapermen discussing the implications of these gloomy reports wondered whether United States forces would arrive at the battle line in time to save the Allied cause. For a few weeks in the autumn of 1917, it seemed touch and go.

XV

THE FIRST GOES INTO THE LINE

Fall and frost; autumn chill and rain. Making rounds of the camps, the newspapermen found that some of the crusading glory had gone out of the war for the men in the ranks. The adventure of the ocean voyage, the excitement and strangeness of the French towns had passed. Monotony and homesickness set in. Somebody discovered something called nostalgia. A few patients turned up in hospitals whose illness was an intense longing for home. A little of this could be written but censorship forbade the newsmen to dwell on it or make it appear significant.

Like the correspondents, the men in the camps were growing tired of training monotony and looking forward to the time when they would start fighting. For the newspapermen this was the great day. Everything else was merely prelude to the time when American troops would enter the front lines and come to grips with the enemy.

Colonel Nolan and Major Palmer both had assured the accredited correspondents that when the date was set for an American division to take its place on the battle line, they would be notified. But October came and was half gone, and still no word.

Heywood Broun had gone to Paris and was A.W.O.L. On October 19, Frederick Palmer wrote to him:

Your leave was up on the 18th and though you have not returned we have heard nothing from you. I may say that it is important that if you do not return within the limits of your leave a request be made for its extension. Otherwise we shall hardly be running our office systematically. Again, if we did not know where you were, you might miss something quite worth while.

Floyd Gibbons and Ray Carroll were missing, too. Palmer sent Gerald Morgan to try and round them up. Both had been last heard from at the artillery camp at Le Valdahon.

The note to Broun and the effort to bring Gibbons and Carroll back to Neufchâteau suggest that the Chief Press Officer knew something important was about to happen, but no word of advance warning was vouchsafed to those who remained at press headquarters. On October 22 they went out on their customary rounds. One group took the familiar road to Gondrecourt, another made a longer journey down to the artillery camps and the bake ovens at Dijon. Returning from this trip, near Langres, the correspondents overtook a wagon train headed north. The wagon drivers asked the correspondents if they had heard the news. What news? Why, the First Division was going into the line. It occurred to the youngest newspaperman in the group, the scrawny U.P. cub Westbrook Pegler, that Colonel Nolan and Palmer had conspired to send them off on a wild goose chase to Besançon and Dijon, so that they would not be around when the great event occurred.

The correspondents who passed most of the day at Gondrecourt likewise were ignorant of the big news until late in the afternoon. Although they had talked to the officers, and lunched at a staff officers' mess, no one had mentioned the impending move into the line. After leaving Gondrecourt, on the road back to Neufchâteau, their chauffeur remarked casually that the First was getting ready to move. He had learned it from the buck privates with whom he had talked while the correspondents were hob-nobbing with close-mouthed officers.

The two groups of correspondents arrived back at the Hôtel de la Providence about the same time and confronted Major Palmer with their tidings. He appeared genuinely surprised. Although he knew something of the kind was imminent, he had not been advised of the date and knew little more than the reporters.

A telephone call came through from Paris. Lieutenant Green told Major Palmer he had just heard a rumor from a friend at the French censor's office. A French politician was going to announce in the Chamber of Deputies the next afternoon that an American division was going into the trenches to take its place beside the French Army. The Paris newspapers naturally would be happy to have such an important item and the politician would achieve a coup.

The correspondents reminded Major Palmer that when the first U.S. troops landed in France four months before, the news had reached the United States through the British press. Now it appeared that the entry of U.S. troops in the trenches would be announced by Paris news agencies. Again, they pointed out bitterly, accredited American correspondents would be left holding the bag.

Major Palmer climbed in his staff car and rode over to Chaumont. Colonel Nolan was not in his office; General Pershing had gone to Paris. The press officer got in to see Major Harbord, Chief of Staff, who listened thoughtfully to his problem. Two telephone calls were put through the Chaumont switchboard, one to locate General Pershing, another to the French High Command. A French interpreter got on the wire. High military authority and the presiding officer of the Chamber of Deputies combined their powers to muzzle the ambitious politician.

After Major Harbord hung up the telephone receiver, he and Palmer talked over the implications of the approaching event. The Commander-in-Chief, Harbord said, was aware of the newspaper interest in this first move into the line, but he hoped they would not make it sensational. Actually, the First Division would be undergoing the final phase of its training in this quiet sector of the line. The American people should not be led to expect great battles and great victories out of this simple operation, nor should the French be encouraged to hope for a quick end to the war. Harbord reflected the views of General Pershing and Colonel Nolan. The talk was friendly; Palmer had heard much of it before and was in complete agreement.

Back at Neufchâteau that night, Major Palmer reassured the assembled newspapermen that no premature disclosure would be made in the French Chamber of Deputies. Motor cars would be ready at noon the next day to take them to Einville, not far from the quiet sector at Arracourt, where the First Division would go into the line. Palmer repeated Harbord's injunction against overdramatizing the occasion and expressed the hope that they would keep it in perspective. The correspondents did not take kindly to this advice. If the entry of the First Division in the line was of no importance, why had Chaumont kept it so secret? If Colonel Nolan and Palmer would not take the newspapermen in their confidence, they must not expect them to take seriously admonitions against sensationalism.

On their arrival at Einville behind the Arracourt sector the next day, after a drive of 75 kilometers, the correspondents learned that their view of the American troops entering the line was to be extremely limited. The French still exercised command over the area, and French rules for dealing with the press prevailed. The American correspondents would not be permitted to march in with the First Division or even to circulate freely among the men. They were under the constant supervision of 'conducting officers' who restricted their movements and answered their questions in monosyllables.

It was night when the troop movement into the forward area began. A light rain had begun to fall. The correspondents were herded in a group at a crossroads, where they could watch the long infantry columns moving forward. A few hundred yards ahead, at the edge of a field, was the communicating trench which would lead them in the rain and darkness to the front line, where they would face the enemy. Near where the newsmen were standing a tavern door stood open and an oblong of yellow light fell across the road. As the infantry columns moved forward, the men crossed the lighted space and each turned for a last look at the warmth and comfort of the roadside tavern. The correspondents saw in these glances a wistful good-by as they crossed the threshold to war. There was some desultory artillery fire, and a few rockets and flares up ahead, over no man's land.

Back at division headquarters the reporters were briefed on the operation by Colonel Campbell King, Chief of Staff of the First Division. He explained that one battalion of each regiment was going in, the remainder being billeted in the rear to await their turn. The whole thing was under French supervision; no U.S. officers above the rank of major were accompanying the troops into the trenches or directing the relief. The division also was being supported by its own artillery—the 5th, 6th, and 7th Field Artillery—which had been training at Le Valdahon.

'By the way,' Colonel King remarked, 'you boys are a little late, aren't you? Two other correspondents came up with the artillery two days ago.'

The colonel's casual announcement had the effect of a Jack Johnson (that is, a powerful explosive shell named after the current heavyweight champion). Carroll, the Hermit Crab, had been staying at Le Valdahon, and Gibbons had been summoned there from Paris several days before by Major McCormick. Both of these had advance information about the move into the line, and they had accompanied the batteries on the journey north from the training camp, by-passing Major Palmer and the press headquarters at Neufchâteau. If they had been able to get any of their copy out, Gibbons and Carroll would have a clear beat on the biggest story since America's entry into the war. But the two still had to deal with censorship.

The lone wolves turned up at Einville late that night, demanding that their stories be cleared for immediate release. The other correspondents demanded that Gibbons and Carroll be 'impounded' and escorted back to Neufchâteau, where they should be required to write their stories and take their turn with censorship. Furthermore, since they had absented themselves from Press Headquarters, they should not be permitted to send out any material relating to the First Division, but only about the artillery camp where they had chosen to hide out. The indignant reporters drew up a petition presenting their case, and Palmer, annoyed that Gibbons and Carroll had tried to evade his authority, sustained them.

The matter was still in abeyance, but during the ride back to Neufchâteau it developed that Gibbons and Carroll, for all their enterprise and early foot, had missed the real story. All they had was some idle chatter and local material picked up among the 'horse-lines,' artillery material which had none of the drama and interest of the infantry moving into the trenches at night. Finally, the two culprits were asking hopefully for a 'fill-in' on the trench scenes as the correspondents' caravan arrived at the Hôtel de la Providence.

Now, as the men began to get their stories in shape, Palmer ruled that the three press associations would draw lots first to determine the order in which their 100-word bulletins or flashes would be filed. After that, all qualified correspondents would draw to determine the order of sending their stories, limited to 500 words. Gibbons and Carroll, being disqualified, could not file until all the others had cleared.

Gibbons's fury was directed alternately to Major Palmer and to the other correspondents who had obeyed the rules. He called them lazy and contemptible fat cats who waited for the news to fall into their laps, while real reporters got out and dug. They were a disgrace to the profession. As for Palmer, the Chief Press Officer would find out whether he could discriminate against the *Chicago Tribune* and get away with it. He would summon Major McCormick; he and Major McCormick would lay the case before General Pershing; they would appeal to the War Department in Washington; Congress and the U.S. Senate would have the whole story. 'He summoned thunder clouds of influence,' Palmer later recalled, and of course, he threatened to have the Chief Press Officer fired.

Carroll assumed an attitude of injured innocence. Henri Bazin was not satisfied with the drawing arrangement. He thought it unfair that the press associations, after getting clear priority for their flashes, should then be permitted to draw lots with the other correspondents for their longer stories. He argued vehemently but in vain. At length a compromise was arranged whereby Gibbons and Carroll were restored to some degree of parity with the others, and the drawing of lots began.

Tom Johnson, the quiet correspondent of the *New York Sun,* was first among the newspaper group; Gibbons and Carroll were well down the list. Bazin was last.

Major Palmer meanwhile had been at work on a historic document—the official announcement of the troops' entry into the line. With one eye on the military sensibilities at Chaumont, he wrote the first American communiqué:

In continuation of their training as a nucleus for instruction later, a contingent of some battalions of our first contingents, in association with veteran French battalions, are in the first line trenches of a quiet sector on the French front. They are supported by some batteries of our artillery, in association with veteran French batteries.

The sector remains normal. Our men have adapted themselves to actual trench conditions in the most satisfactory manner.

So with becoming modesty and official vagueness, the world was informed that the A.E.F. had taken a small place in the front line, and the war moved into a new phase.

Now that the First Division was in the trenches, there was work to be done. The motor cars left the Hôtel de la Providence early in the morning for the long ride to Einville. At division headquarters they would get hot coffee and pick up their French conducting officers. A mile or two behind the front lines at Arracourt they would hear the occasional exchange of desultory artillery fire and watch the helmets bobbing along the communication trenches. There was not much to see. From some of those on outpost duty the correspondents learned what it was like at the front. They looked out across fields of wet dead grass without seeing any trenches or Germans. On Sunday morning it was so quiet the Americans looking across hypothetical no-man's land could see Lorrainers going to church.

Among the items of news was that the first shell in the American sector had been fired by Battery C, Sixth Field Artillery, from a French 75. The gunner who sent the missile on its way was reported to be red-headed, and one correspondent made him out to be a red-headed, left-handed Irishman. Pegler thought this a little too pat, so he tramped around to Battery C and learned that the gunner was a black-haired Czech who had pulled the lanyard or pressed the button with his right hand. By this time the historic shell case, properly engraved, was on its way to Washington, gift of General Sibert to President Wilson.

Four days after they entered the line the American troops captured their first prisoner. This seemed to be a real news story, and the correspondents shook off their conducting officers and went to work on it.

The prisoner's name was Leonard Hoffman, and he was in the hospital. The details of his capture did not reflect credit on American arms. The twenty-year-old Hoffman was a mail orderly of the 3rd Machine Gun Company, 7th Regiment, First Landwehr Division, Third Bavarian Army Corps. He had wandered off with his mailbag and, getting lost behind the American lines, had surrendered to the first patrol that challenged him. In that first encounter with the American troops he had suffered a minor bullet wound, not serious enough to prevent him from raising his arms in surrender. While he stood, helpless and wounded, with his arms above his head, some of his excited captors rushed up and thrust their bayonets in his chest.

The correspondents found him in the hospital, seriously wounded. The best surgeons in the Medical Corps had examined him and all the resources of American medical science were marshaled to try and save his life. He lingered a day or two and died.

When the correspondents tried to tell the story of the capture and death of Leonard Hoffman they encountered a new phase of censorship. Major Palmer ruled that the facts could not be disclosed. Enemy propaganda would make too much of the incident of a helpless, unarmed German mail carrier being bayoneted by bloodthirsty Americans, Palmer said. The moral they would draw from it would be to fight to the end rather than surrender to such savage adversaries. The Associated Press carried only this brief mention of the incident:

The first German prisoner of war taken by the A.E.F. died today in an American field hospital, having been shot when he encountered an American patrol in No Man's Land in front of the American trenches.

The newspapermen could give the name of the first American wounded by German fire. He was Lieutenant D. H. Harden, 26th Infantry Reserve Corps, struck in the knee by a piece of flying shrapnel.

The first night raid by the Germans on the American lines, two days later, left three U.S. soldiers dead, with their throats cut. The correspondents got details of the raid, but they were not permitted to write that the enemy had cut the throats of American soldiers. Major Palmer ruled that this would give an unfair picture of German war methods. Throat-cutting was standard trench-raid procedure for all armies, to prevent struggle or outcries. So the censors would not pass the throat-cutting details unless the correspondents explained that the French and British used the same methods.

In one sense, the two incidents—bayoneting a helpless prisoner and savagery in a trench raid—counterbalanced each other. But they left the American correspondents feeling more helpless in the clutch of censorship. They also prevented the American people from learning the grim facts of war.

The entry of the American troops in the front line near Arracourt —the French called it the Sommerville sector—had not produced the big story the correspondents hoped for. Caught between the strict chaperonage of the French and Palmer's high-minded censorship, their accounts were strained and trivial. As the novelty of the long motor journey between Neufchâteau and Einville wore off, their work again sank to dull routine. The 'Parisites' were soon back in Paris.

Major Palmer had other problems than those difficult censorship decisions at Arracourt. The Associated Press wanted an investigation of the Press Office to find out who was gossiping about the contents of A.P. dispatches. The complaint, brought by Elmer Roberts, suggested that other press association men were learning about the A.P. file through the careless talk of the censors. Palmer had to look into that and issue a warning to the staff.

A New England reporter, Frank Sibley of the *Boston Globe,* turned up in Paris and wanted a pass to go with the Twenty-sixth Division. Looking up the records, Palmer found that Charles H. Taylor, publisher of the *Globe,* had first inquired about credentials for Sibley back in August, when the New England troops were about ready to leave for France. At that time there had been an exchange of views between the War Department in Washington and Pershing in Paris.

In its ruling on the *Boston Globe* application, General Pershing and the War Department had established an important policy dealing with the press.

It is regretted very greatly [H. P. McCain, Adjutant-General, informed Publisher Taylor] that no such permission can be given. The conditions in France are such that only a very limited number of newspaper correspondents can be permitted to be with the American forces.

An arrangement has been worked out whereby it is hoped that the 15 correspondents accredited to General Pershing's headquarters will be able to cover the entire country with their news from the front. A larger number than this could not be permitted with deference to the military situation.

General Pershing thinks it inadvisable to accredit correspondents to local units. Such assignment would, it is thought, cause undesirable rivalry among correspondents and make it difficult to maintain a uniform policy throughout the Army. Also newspaper praise of individual officers and local units would be detrimental to discipline and the work of the censors would be immeasurably increased by permitting correspondents from the several states to accompany their troops. It will therefore be impossible for the War Department to make any larger provision for newspaper representation than has already been made.

Palmer remembered the case very well. The *Boston Globe* application had been the first from a newspaper seeking credentials to cover a single division; the ruling had established policy and the matter was presumably settled. Yet here was Sibley in Paris, with a letter from George Creel. He had come over on the French steamship *Touraine* late in September and had camped in the outer office at 10 rue Ste. Anne for three weeks, waiting to see Major Palmer. Palmer kept him waiting two more weeks and then blamed the adverse decision on Colonel Nolan. Still Sibley refused to give up and go home. Finally, he got permission from G-2-D late in October to visit the Twenty-sixth Division for two days at Neufchâteau.

Lieutenant Colonel McCormick of the 5th Field Artillery (and the *Chicago Tribune*) dropped in at Chaumont one day and in the course of a talk with Major Palmer and General Pershing, inquired what had happened to his recommendation about getting Mark Watson into the Press Division. The general said he had sent a couple of cables to the War Department, asking for the young man, but nothing had come of it.

'Why, he's right here in Chaumont,' Lieutenant Colonel McCormick said. 'I talked to him by telephone this morning and I saw him a few minutes ago in an office just around the corner.'

Lieutenant Watson was soon located in the Quartermaster's Office, where he had been on duty for several weeks, only 200 feet from Colonel Nolan's office. Watson said he had been greatly pleased in August when at Camp Grant, Illinois, he received orders to report to the Commander-in-Chief in France. However, when he reached Chaumont, no one had any idea who wanted him or why he had been detached and sent to France. Watson had assumed that it had something to do with artillery because that was his specialty, and had occupied most of his time in training camp.

Because he was now a quartermaster, he was assigned to the Chief Quartermaster and had passed most of September and October trying to trace lost quartermaster personnel. At last his status was straightened out, and Lieutenant Watson was assigned to G-2-D as assistant to the Chief.

At Neufchâteau, Major Palmer called on Major General Omar Bundy, who had been designated by G.H.Q. some weeks before to command the training area. The general's greeting was unfriendly:

'I hear you have established yourself here with a lot of newspaper reporters,' Bundy said sharply. 'Why haven't you reported to me? Don't you know that I am in command of this region—that I am your superior?'

Palmer dealt with the testy Bundy as he had with the indignant Allaire in Paris early in July. He reminded him of regulations.

'I was established here weeks before you came, sir, by order of my Chief at G.H.Q. As I read the regulations, G.H.Q. is supreme, and it can place any of its representatives anywhere it chooses. I am directly under the Chief of Staff Section, sir, and if I reported to you for instructions and you gave me instructions, we would both be violating regulations, sir.'

General Bundy thought about it for a moment and turned to the young West Pointer standing behind his chair. The aide agreed with Palmer. 'Maybe so,' the general said. 'Maybe I have been unnecessarily curt.'

In November Palmer was summoned to Chaumont. The problem of the newspaper corps again was reviewed in Pershing's office. Events of the last few weeks had increased the correspondents' discontent. Some echoes of their grievances were heard in the War Department, in Congress, and in newspaper editorial columns. Palmer was the storm center of the controversy. Beginning with the contretemps at St. Nazaire in June, G-2-D had shown itself to be singularly inept or unlucky, or both. The catalogue was long. Minor irritations included the special privileges accorded Peggy Hull at Le Valdahon, and attempts to discipline Wood and Eyre after the trip to Dijon. The Press Division had failed to keep the correspondents informed on the First Division's move into the front line. What military necessity (its *raison d'être*) prompted

G-2-D censorship to suppress all mention of gifts of wine by the hospitable French to American soldiers? Censorship rulings in the Hoffman bayoneting and the trench raids raised new questions about military control of the news. Other departments of the military establishment might blunder and improvise, make mistakes and suffer lapses with impunity, protected by Army protocol. But G-2-D's shortcomings stirred those whose business it was to protest and expose and bring shortcomings out in the open. Something had to be done, and General Pershing did it.

Major Palmer was detached from duty at G-2-D to undertake a confidential mission for General Pershing in the United States. When he sailed from Brest on the S.S. *Mount Vernon* (formerly the German *Kronprinzessin Cecilie*) in December, Colonel Edward M. House, President Wilson's personal representative, was a fellow passenger. In his new role, Palmer answered Colonel House's questions and brought him up to date on problems and policies at Chaumont. Arriving in the United States, he reported to Secretary Baker in Washington, paid a call at the White House, and talked confidentially to Senator William E. Borah, Senator Hiram Johnson, and other members of Congress who were critical of Army affairs and wanted censorship abolished. At Oyster Bay, N.Y., he passed an afternoon with Colonel Theodore Roosevelt, another forthright critic of the nation's war policies. When he returned to France in February, Major Palmer carried back some War Department directives authorizing General Pershing and Colonel Nolan to relax the rigid censorship rules. This was his last function for the press and G-2-D. Henceforward, he would be attached to the General Staff as Pershing's confidential agent, observer, and adviser.

With Palmer's departure the stormy first phase of G-2-D's existence came to an end. Palmer had organized the department, written its rules, engaged its personnel, formulated its basic censorship policies. To that complex task he brought considerable experience and energy and complete integrity. But the newspapermen who came under his rules found him stuffy and aloof. They were not impressed by his distinguished career dating back to Queen Victoria's jubilee. He might once have been the world's foremost war correspondent, but now the younger newspapermen found him in league with the brass, as arbitrary as any West Pointer in his military judgments. They envied him his inside knowledge and resented his failure to communicate what he knew.

As for Palmer, he failed to understand the brash, restless generation of journalists 1917 had brought to the war scene. They were young—Pegler was only twenty-three—impatient, impulsive, inexperienced. Most of them had never seen a war or heard a shot fired in anger. They had no respect for military men or military procedures. They drank and gambled. The task of controlling them, censoring their copy, enforcing rules and discipline among them was formidable. Palmer made a good try, but he failed. And now the military would take over.

YOU CAN'T WRITE THAT!

From Neufchâteau November 14, Herbert Corey wrote to his friend Henry W. Suydam in care of the American legation at The Hague. The three-page letter told the newspaper gossip of Paris and Chaumont and Neufchâteau. Junius Wood was rowing with the censors again. The boys were having a lot of fun with Henri Bazin over the Croix de Guerre which his Philadelphia paper and *Editor & Publisher* had conferred on him. Henri said it was all a joke. Corey didn't think much of the military leadership of the A.E.F.:

> The West Pointer promises to be the biggest joke of the war. He is ignorant, arrogant and in an advanced state of mental decay. The younger officers may grow out of it. The older are, I think, hopeless. Our staff is viciously incompetent and is covering up the incompetence which it may suspect by a huge pretense of desk-slamming and cursing.

Corey was one of the older group of correspondents, more experienced and war-wise than the 1917 arrivals. In spite of the fact that he had once been a stagecoach driver for a livery stable— perhaps because of it—his judgments generally were sensible and shrewd. His confidential letter to Suydam may be considered symptomatic of a growing feeling among newspapermen about military inefficiency and arrogance in France. With more freedom to observe and to write honestly about what they learned, the growing tension and resentment might have eased. But no such forthright comment was possible under the rules laid down by Palmer and G-2-D.

Westbrook Pegler, the youngest of all the correspondents and the most impressionable, had a long talk with Lowell Mellett, U.P.'s Paris man, about some things that disturbed him. Pegler had watched a growing procession of funeral corteges wind over the hills around Neufchâteau. Men in the training camps were dying of pneumonia because of inadequate shelter, clothing, and hospital care. From his own observation and talks with officers he learned that when the men returned to their billets at night they were often soaked through with rain. Many of the billets were sheep barns. The only heat came from charcoal braziers and small stoves so smoky that windows and doors had to be thrown open to dispel the fumes. There was no way to keep warm, no way to dry their clothing, no extra clothing or dry underwear to change into. As the weather turned cold and rainy, pneumonia deaths were rising.

Pegler recalled the censorship lapse at St. Nazaire on the arrival of the first American troops; Colonel Nolan's promise to keep them informed about the movement of the First Division into the front line, and the failure of that promise; the lapses and injustices, the petty tyranny of censorship. He criticized the military judgment which decreed that American infantrymen must spend fifteen minutes to half an hour each day winding spiral puttees around their legs from ankle to knee, a device which the British had adopted to protect against snake bites in India.

On Mellett's advice, Pegler wrote down his long indictment of the American military command in France in the form of a letter to Roy Howard. Mellett would take it to London on his next trip and show it to Ed L. Keen, European manager for the United Press. The two would talk it over and, if the facts seemed to warrant, Keen would try to forward it to Howard in New York.

Censorship and the supply failure were the main topics of conversation wherever newspapermen gathered. The conviction was growing that censorship was being administered in the narrow interest of the military clique rather than in the interest of the American people. Colonel Nolan's ruling that gifts of wine from the French people to American soldiers could not be mentioned was an odd example of how censorship served political considerations. Palmer's rulings on the bayoneting of the German prisoner Hoffman and the throat-cutting in German trench raids showed censorship as a tool of propaganda. Restrictions, prohibitions, and delays, the unfitness of some censors for their work, erratic judgments of others, made it almost impossible for American news-papermen to do their job; at least, such was the burden of the correspondents' talk.

In Paris in the fall of 1917 some of the more indignant and aggressive among them decided to form an organization to make their protests effective. Whitney Warren, the architect, was a lead-ing spirit in bringing the group together. They called it The Ameri-can War Publicity League in France. Hutchins Hapgood was its first, and only, president. Its membership included many of the leading correspondents then in France.

The American War Publicity League in France wrote to G.H.Q. at Chaumont asking for an appointment with General Pershing. A delegation was named to wait on the Commander-in-Chief, A.E.F., and discuss its program. The general was busy and declined to meet the delegation. Actually the league had only one idea to suggest. That was Wythe Williams's proposal that censorship be removed from the military organization and set up under a capable civilian head who would consider the rights and interests of the American people as well as the requirements of military discre-tion. The civilian censorship thus constituted would be responsible directly to Congress.

It is doubtful whether General Pershing would have been favorably impressed by that proposal, however forcefully presented. He already had to deal with a Committee on Public Information which was trying to set up an office in France and widen its scope. He was not entirely satisfied with the way censorship was working but it was not his nature to give it up because it creaked, or be-cause some civilians were disgruntled about it. He refused to deal with the league, and its activity reverted to café talk. The war moved on.

Some newspapermen continued the fight as angry individuals. Pegler was one. Another was Reginald Wright Kauffman. Ac-credited as a representative of the *Philadelphia North American,* this journalist also had other connections including the Red Cross, the Y.M.C.A. and George Harvey's *North American Review.* Harvey, one of Woodrow Wilson's original supporters in 1912, had broken with the President and was critical of the way the Ad-ministration was running the war. Kauffman also was in cor-respondence with Theodore Roosevelt, another critic of the

Administration who was writing a newspaper column and contributing to *The Outlook*.

All newspaper copy sent by cable required censorship approval. Likewise, mail stories for newspaper publication were supposed to be officially scrutinized and stamped. But it was possible to send confidential material back by friends returning to the United States. In addition, not all the letters dropped in the mail boxes in Paris came under the censor's eye. Kauffman learned that only one letter in five, on an average, was examined by the French postal censors. When he decided that conditions in France justified defiance of the A.E.F. censorship, Kauffman worked out a system of getting his reports back through the mails. Five copies would be made of each article or confidential report and one would be posted in each of five separate Paris *arrondissements*. French officials had great admiration for Theodore Roosevelt, Kauffman was told, and a letter addressed to the former President at Oyster Bay, New York, was likely to be immune to scrutiny or seizure. The system worked. All through the fall and winter of 1917 Kauffman scattered his reports, most of them addressed to T. R. at Oyster Bay, in the outlying Paris mailboxes. Most of them reached their destination. Roosevelt would make notes of the material and then forward the typescript to Mr. Van Valkenberg of the *Philadelphia North American,* who would then revise the article for publication. Eventually Army Intelligence became interested in Kauffman's activities and assigned agents to trail him in Paris, but they were not able to interrupt the transmission of his reports.

Heywood Broun was another who evaded censorship and refused to be bound by G-2-D regulations. On one occasion he told Lieutenant Green and Lieutenant Guy T. Viskniskki at 10 rue Ste. Anne in Paris that he had mailed articles to the *Tribune* in New York without submitting them to censorship. He said he did not consider the accredited correspondents' agreement signed by him as binding upon his conscience, as he had been obliged to sign it in order to accompany the Army and therefore considered it an engagement signed under compulsion. He also told the two press officers that in any case he would not permit a breach of personal honor to stand in the way of the national interest.

Broun had ways of expressing his contempt for military authority which did not require evasion of censorship. He considered

Pershing arrogant and cold fish, and he expressed his views in barbed comment which the censors could not expunge, although its import was clear. It was well known that a warm personal relationship existed between French *poilus* in trenches and General Joffre, a relationship expressed by the affectionate term 'Papa Joffre.' After watching the U.S. Commander-in-Chief review an infantry division, Broun wrote: 'The soldiers of the A.E.F. will never call Pershing "Papa." ' Again, relating that General Pershing had returned to Chaumont after a trip among the camps, he wrote: 'General Pershing completed his tour of inspection yesterday morning. The American Army is doing as well as could be expected.'

Palmer recalled that Broun seemed to be amused that he, Broun, was in uniform. When he wasn't in open revolt he was smiling at the whole ridiculous routine of salutes and drills and all the stage business of war. The *Tribune* reporter had a special little salute for Palmer as he laid his copy on his desk, a salute which Palmer thought 'conveyed a sort of teasing irony.'

Broun returned to the United States in December, disgusted with the way the war was being run, disgusted with war itself. He had not yet exhausted his capacity for indignation when he reached the *Tribune* on Nassau Street. Now he could write without a censor looking over his shoulder.

Since their arrival at Neufchâteau, Colonel Nolan and Major Palmer had encouraged correspondents to visit the growing network of supply bases centering at Tours. General Pershing wanted the American people to know not so much what had been accomplished, but what a tremendous job remained to be done to supply the A.E.F. in France. On these trips, shuttling between Neufchâteau, Chaumont, Troyes, Orléans, Tours, Blois, Lyons, Dijon, the newspapermen learned somewhat more than the military intended. The facts came from a variety of sources.

A distinguished surgeon from Johns Hopkins who had been brought to France to organize and administer base hospitals told one correspondent that the hospital supply situation was desperate. He had given an ultimatum to the top brass at Chaumont: if the surgical equipment and supplies were not loaded on the next ships leaving the United States for France, he would quit and go home and tell the American people why. Many men in the Rainbow

Division were ill. Two hospitals with their equipment had been taken over from the French for use while U.S. ones were building. Now these had to be returned and four hundred sick men had to be evacuated to other hospitals. The United States Medical Corps had not yet received its allowances of ambulances. Available at the time were only the Fords borrowed from the American Ambulance Corps on duty with the French, for which there were no extra tires or spare parts. When the first ambulances did arrive from America in the late fall of 1917, their papier-mâché sides had a tendency to disintegrate in the rain. The camp hospital for the Forty-second Division, nearing completion, had to be abandoned.

Talking with officers at Chaumont the newspapermen learned that the First Division had gone into the 'quiet sector' near Arracourt lacking adequate clothing, rolling kitchens, and trucks. An essential article of diet, dried fruit, was missing from infantry rations; the men were short of soap and candles. Something was wrong with the first American-made gas masks. Tom Johnson learned that the masks were cumbersome and hard to put on. More important, the First Division staff had almost been asphyxiated during their final drills because the masks had failed to function, because some vital gadget was missing or did not work.

Another Chaumont report was that Pershing had cabled Washington to stop sending to France bath bricks, book cases, bath tubs, cabinets for blank forms, office desks, floor wax, step ladders, lawn mowers, settees, stools, and window shades. Instead he wanted more winter clothing, heavy socks and underwear, oversize boots and shoes. Washington evidently considered his requisitions excessive. Monthly allotments were far below requirements; sometimes urgent cables were disregarded. One explanation was that the clothing and other supplies were needed at training camps in the United States.

From St. Nazaire and Brest came tales of shipping blunders. One ship which arrived at St. Nazaire with 300 tons of badly needed steel carried it back to the United States as ballast. One that arrived in the United States with sand ballast in its hold, brought the sand back to France instead of urgently needed supplies. Fifteen thousand tons of sawdust crossed the ocean for a cold storage plant in France when there was plenty of sawdust available only a few miles away.

By mid-November all the newspapermen at the front knew that the military effort in France was being undermined by a grave shortage of supplies, and they surmised that the stupidity and incompetence responsible for the shortages flourished on both sides of the Atlantic. Tom Johnson, Junius Wood, and Herbert Corey uncovered significant facts about the supply situation and submitted stories to censorship at Neufchâteau. Gerald Morgan sent his stories to Chaumont. Within a day or two the three correspondents were ushered into Pershing's office. The general knew them to be conscientious newspapermen and talked frankly about the problem. He agreed that their facts were in the main correct. It might be a good thing if the American people were jolted into a realization of the immensity and complexity of the task before them. However, matters of policy were involved.

Several days later, after discussing the matter with Harbord and Nolan, Pershing sent a carefully worded cable to the War Department in Washington:

REGRET THAT SHORTAGE OF QUARTERMASTER SUPPLIES AND FAILURE OF THAT DEPARTMENT TO BUILD UP BALANCED RESERVE HERE, COUPLED WITH UNUSUALLY SEVERE WEATHER HAS GIVEN GROUND FOR CRITICISMS WHICH HAVE REACHED PRESS CORRESPONDENTS RESULTING IN SUBMISSION OF ARTICLES WHICH CENSOR HAS HELD NOT BECAUSE OF MISREPRESENTATION BUT IN ORDER TO AVOID APPEARANCE OF OUR PRESENTING THROUGH PRESS MATTERS ALREADY SENT YOU OFFICIALLY. SUPPRESSING THESE DISPATCHES SUBJECTS US HERE TO CHARGES OF KEEPING BACK INFORMATION WHICH PRESS REASONABLY CLAIM AMERICAN PEOPLE IS ENTITLED TO KNOW. SUCH NEWS MUST UNDOUBTEDLY REACH PUBLIC IN SOME MANNER AND I BELIEVE THAT CONTROLLED NEWSPAPER CRITICISM OF QUARTERMASTER CORPS OR EMBARKATION AUTHORITIES IS PREFERABLE TO LACK OF CONFIDENCE BY COUNTRY AND PRESS THAT MIGHT RESULT FROM PERSISTENT SUPPRESSION OF CRITICISM. AS CRITICISM SEEMS INEVITABLE, PROBABLY BEST NOT WAIT UNTIL IT IS PUBLISHED FROM HOSTILE SOURCES BUT ACCEPT IT FROM FRIENDLY SOURCES INSTEAD. RECOMMEND THEREFORE RELEASE TO CORRESPONDENTS HERE ARTICLES INVOLVING TEMPERATE CRITICISMS ON SUPPLY DEPARTMENTS WHERE THEY ARE KNOWN TO BE WELL FOUNDED. EARLY ACTION REQUESTED.

PERSHING

The reply from Washington reached the Commander-in-Chief at Chaumont six days later. The answer was 'No':

> THE SECRETARY OF WAR DIRECTS YOUR CONSIDERATION OF THE
> FACT THAT CRITICISMS OF THE DIFFERENT DEPARTMENTS IN THE
> NEWSPAPERS AS RELEASED FROM YOU MIGHT BE CONSTRUED AS
> CRITICISMS BY YOU THROUGH PRESS WHICH WOULD BE UNFORTU-
> NATE AND GIVE FALSE IDEAS. OF COURSE MISTAKES HAVE BEEN
> MADE AND DELAYS OCCURRED DUE TO THE LACK OF FACILITIES FOR
> CARRYING OUT PROMPTLY THE BIG PROBLEM THAT IS PRESENTED
> BUT IT IS THOUGHT THAT THESE MISTAKES ARE BEING RECTIFIED
> AS FAST AS CAN BE DONE.
>
> BIDDLE

In this exchange General Pershing and Secretary Baker disclosed how muddled official thinking had become about censorship. Official interference had corrupted the flow of news. The original purposes of censorship had become involved in bureaucratic punctilio. Here was tacit agreement between Chaumont and Washington that every censored news dispatch from France was suspect; that the news, instead of reflecting the honest discoveries of the reporter, was becoming a semi-official, semi-military agency serving the purposes of the bureaucracy which controlled it.

The Commander-in-Chief's warning that news of the supply failure was likely to reach the public in some manner was well founded. While the matter was still under debate at Chaumont and Washington, two United States congressmen returned home from a tour of the Army camps in France. At Washington, Representative Clarence B. Miller of Minnesota dictated to reporters in his office a statement concerning the War Department's failure to supply the A.E.F. American soldiers abroad, he said, lacked guns, clothing, 'nearly everything required by troops in the field.' Representative Porter H. Dale of Vermont said he found American troops without guns, blankets, boots, and other equipment. The congressmen blamed Major General Henry A. Sharpe, Quartermaster, for most of the supply deficiencies, and Major General William Crozier, Chief-of-Ordnance, for the lack of modern field guns and rifles. Spokesmen for the Administration could only point out that the congressmen critics were Republicans.

Heywood Broun's article in the *Tribune,* 'Supply Blunders Hampered First U.S. Units in France,' written after his return to the United States, told the story of the supply situation in more detail.

There was a mild flurry in Washington. Senator Borah and Senator Norris talked about a Senate investigation of censorship. Newspaper editorials denounced the Administration for using military necessity to conceal its mistakes.

It was a long cold winter for the four American divisions in France—the First, Second, Twenty-sixth (Yankee), and Forty-second (Rainbow). In after years the men of those four outfits formed a veteran group apart from all that came after. They were tough; they had survived. The others could talk about Cantigny, Château-Thierry, St. Mihiel, and Meuse-Argonne, but those were merely battles.

The newspapermen did what they could, but the story of that winter could not be written. The British Admiralty censors caught Pegler's letter and sent it back to Chaumont. A little later Roy Howard was asked to send a replacement; Pegler was no longer *persona grata* at G.H.Q. He was too young, Pershing thought; he lacked experience. Kauffman got away with his protests a few weeks longer, then he, too, lost his credentials with the Army. Broun was suspended and fined.

They couldn't do anything to Herb Corey. His letter was not for publication. But the Section Économique of the Ministère de la Guerre picked it up and turned it over to Army Intelligence, where his barbed comment on the ways of elderly West Pointers was buried in the files.

On winter afternoons the correspondents made the rounds of the muddy A.E.F. camps near Neufchâteau to watch the familiar training exercises. A few would arrange to be dropped off at Troyes, where they could take a train to Paris. The rest would go back to the Hôtel de la Providence to peck at their typewriters or sit around the porcelain stove and read their mail. War was mostly waiting.

XVII

REBELLION AND REPRISALS

Frank Sibley of the *Boston Globe* moped in Paris waiting for Army permission to go to the Twenty-sixth Division camp. Since his arrival in France nearly three months before with a letter from George Creel, he had had only two days with the Yankee troops at Neufchâteau. Major Palmer, mindful of an earlier decision by the War Department denying limited accreditation to the Boston newspaper, saw no reason to change the ruling on a letter from George Creel. Sibley thought Palmer's handling of the case arbitrary and curt.

Now Palmer was gone. His departure, and the consequent reorganization of the Press Section, gave Sibley an opportunity to reopen his case. He by-passed G-2-D and wrote a letter to General Harbord, Pershing's Chief of Staff.

Sibley reminded General Harbord that he had lived with the Twenty-sixth Division at its New England training camp the previous June and July, reporting its activities in homely detail for the *Boston Globe*. The people of New England, he thought, hadn't lost interest in their sons and brothers now that they were in France. On the contrary, more than ever they wanted to know what was happening to them. It was impossible for the press associations to carry detailed accounts of the Twenty-sixth's activities in France; they were concerned with the whole A.E.F. and the whole war. Nor could New York, Philadelphia, and Chicago correspondents be expected to devote time and effort to New England troops.

Surely the A.E.F. was now sufficiently organized in France, Sibley wrote, to take care of a single newspaper correspondent or two with each division. Living with the Twenty-sixth, he would not interfere with the work of the accredited correspondents at Neufchâteau, or compete with them. But he would provide a useful and effective link between the Yankee troops in France and their folks at home.

This sounded reasonable to General Harbord. He picked up the telephone and called Twenty-sixth Division headquarters. Sibley? *Boston Globe*? Yes, General Edwards remembered him from training camp. Good man. No, the general had no objection to his coming to the division. He thought it a good idea to have a newspaper correspondent around the camp so that New Englanders back home could keep track of their boys.

Harbord's decision was prompt and favorable. Sibley got his pass, signed by the chief of staff. This did not mean that he was 'accredited'; he could not wear the green armband with the red 'C,' or cover the whole A.E.F. But he was free to live at the Twenty-sixth Division camp, observe its training, and report the little incidents and adventures that occupied the American soldier in France. Sibley's persistence and Harbord's common sense had made a start toward the kind of newspaper coverage America needed in the winter of 1917-18.

Colonel W. C. Sweeney of the General Staff took over as head of the Censorship and Press Division, and another regular Army officer, Major E. R. W. McCabe, went to Neufchâteau as chief field officer for G-2-D. Major McCabe did not know much about newspapermen or their work but he knew how to get along with people, and he relied heavily on the experienced, capable Gerald Morgan. One of McCabe's early problems dealt with the influential and sensitive Associated Press.

Late in the fall of 1917 a new Associated Press correspondent joined the group at Neufchâteau, replacing the war-weary veteran Robert Small. The new man, Norman Draper, took his work and the prestige of his employer so seriously that he made himself unpopular with the other correspondents. He claimed special privileges and prerogatives. His contention was that because the A.P. served the largest group of newspapers in America and reached a circulation greater than all the others combined, he should have access to all the news gathered by the other correspondents and should be given first place in filing priority.

Soon after McCabe took charge at Neufchâteau, an important news development brought a minor crisis in the press censor's office. Half a dozen other correspondents were already in line with their copy when Draper arrived and demanded first place for the Associated Press. He asserted his claim, with the customary arguments to Lieutenant Morgan, who was not impressed, and then turned to appeal the case to the new officer in charge, Major McCabe.

'What seems to be the difficulty?' McCabe inquired. Morgan explained that Draper had arrived late but insisted on filing first because of the importance and great circulation of the Associated Press.

'The Associated Press has ninety million readers,' Draper said, 'more than all the rest of these put together. It is the biggest news organization in the world. Ninety million.'

McCabe considered the situation briefly, while the other correspondents watched and waited.

'Well, Ninety Million,' he said to Draper, 'I'm afraid you'll have to get back in line and take your rightful turn behind the others.'

This got McCabe off to a good start with the other correspondents and gave Draper his definitive nickname. From that time on, he was 'Ninety Million.' Draper told a number of the special correspondents he expected them to share all their news with him. He pointed out that the Associated Press was entitled to the local news of all its newspaper members and argued that the same rule should apply in the field. Nobody at Neufchâteau agreed with him. Later the other correspondents learned that in his zeal to serve the Associated Press he tipped the French telegraph operators at the Bureau-Poste to let him scan the carbon copies of stories filed by others, and occasionally lifted items of special interest. His activities caused a group of the independent correspondents—Tom Johnson, Junius Wood, Lincoln Eyre, Henri Bazin, and later Herbert Corey —to form a combination against him. Working together they could cover more territory than was possible for a single man, and, by sharing their news at night, they produced more complete and better rounded reports.

An aggressive young officer with the distinctive name of Guy T. Viskniskki arrived in France and because of his newspaper background was assigned to G-2-D as press officer and censor. As soon as he had gotten his bearings at Chaumont and Neufchâteau, he proposed to Lieutenant Colonel Sweeney that the Army begin publication of a weekly newspaper for the troops. Others had advanced the same idea, and Colonel Nolan had mentioned it tentatively at one or two General Staff meetings. But no one had pressed it with as much purpose and confidence as Lieutenant Viskniskki. To back up his proposal, the young officer submitted copies of *The Bayonet,* the Eightieth Division Training Camp weekly which Viskniskki had organized and managed back in the United States. Impressed, Lieutenant Colonel Sweeney ordered the young man to Paris to find out about paper and printing facilities. In four days Viskniskki was back at Chaumont with a detailed plan. He had found enough newsprint to make a start, arranged for printers, Linotype machines, stereotyping, and press work. Also, he told Lieutenant Colonel Sweeney, he had discovered four enlisted men with newspaper experience who would form the nucleus of a business office and editorial staff.

About this time, Tom Johnson ran into another *Sun* man on the street in Neufchâteau. Boz Hawley was in the 101st Machine Gun Battalion of the Twenty-sixth Division, but Johnson remembered him as the young Yale man who had come down from the *Hartford Courant* to take a job on the *Sun* two or three years before. Hawley showed Johnson a little magazine, *The Tripod,* which he was getting out for his machine gun outfit. Johnson found it readable and lively and wrote a little piece about it for the *New York Sun.* The censoring official who passed on the story was Lieutenant Viskniskki, and he asked Johnson to bring *The Tripod* editor in for an interview. As a result, Hawley was drafted from the Machine Gun Battalion to help Viskniskki organize *The Stars and Stripes.* Practically unaided the two produced the first issue on February 8.

The problem of restless correspondents still plagued the press officers at Neufchâteau. Floyd Gibbons and Ray Carroll were off again; Kauffman passed most of his time in Paris. Wythe Williams of the *Times* rarely appeared at the Hôtel de la Providence. To bring the strays into line and compensate the faithful, Gerald Morgan issued a new ruling. After February 1, he decreed, no correspondent who had not been at press headquarters for two preceding weeks could file any material based on official releases until all those who had remained at Neufchâteau had filed their stories. Again Carroll protested, arguing that such a restriction penalized those who went out and worked, rewarding the lazy ones who hung around the Hôtel de la Providence waiting for the telephone from Chaumont to ring.

Lieutenant Morgan's memorandum, posted on the bulletin board January 12, was a warning that the correspondents had better stay close to headquarters; something was about to happen. A day or two later, Floyd Gibbons turned up at Neufchâteau from Paris, hinting at big news, demanding the latest word from Chaumont. By this time there was no room at the Hôtel de la Providence. Gibbons shopped around town and found a tolerable lodging in the local brewery. Other correspondents could cover the war from châteaux, hotels, taverns, and lean-tos; only Gibbons availed himself of a furnished room in a brewery. The accommodation pleased him; he kept it until he returned to the United States the following August, and then turned it over to his successor, Frazier Hunt.

Something was stirring. On January 19 the First Division moved into the front line again, not for advanced training this time but for keeps. The scene of this new American take-over was a 'sector northwest of Toul.' The correspondents had sufficient warning this time and made the long motor journey north from Neufchâteau on January 18. They expected to watch the veteran Americans relieve a tired French division. But at the last moment, press officers reported the French command decided that the U.S. correspondents were not to watch the march. They could only observe the movement of the First Division from a point about ten miles in the rear.

It had been nearly three months since the entry of the first American troops into the line in a quiet sector near Arracourt. That story with all its problems, limited observation, and harsh censorship had turned out badly for the newspapermen. Now the old frustrations were at work again. Most of the correspondents made the best of it, picking up what color and detail they could ten miles behind the front line trenches, piecing the story together from what they knew and what the briefing officer told them.

A group of four—Wythe Williams, Herbert Corey, Reginald Kauffman, and Naboth Hedin, correspondent for the *Brooklyn Eagle*—motored back to Chaumont and got in to see Colonel

Nolan. Again American troops were going into the line, they told him, and again the French command was preventing the correspondents from seeing and reporting the event. Nolan agreed their protest was justified and called the French general in command of the Toul sector. There was some delay—the French did not do things hastily—and at 6 P.M. the word came back. Accredited American correspondents could watch the First Division take over the 'sector northwest of Toul' and move in the forward area without French officers at their heels.

While awaiting this decision at Chaumont, the reporters learned that General Pershing, instead of motoring up to Toul for the take-over, was about to board the evening train for Paris. Assuming this portended some important news development, Williams and Kauffman decided to trail the general to Paris, while Corey and Hedin would return to the 'sector northwest of Toul' and observe events there for all four. Nothing much came of the train ride to Paris; Pershing's errand was routine, or too confidential to be disclosed to the press.

When Kauffman and Williams rejoined the newspaper group at Toul two days later, they were informed that the censors would not pass their 'eye-witness' stories of the take-over, because they had not actually witnessed the scenes. This led to another angry wrangle. Kauffman protested that two days before, the press officers, accepting the French rule keeping them out of the forward area, had suggested that they fabricate their stories from scraps and pieces. He had done so, writing his dispatch in advance from limited observation and filling in with what he learned from Corey and Hedin. The protest went unheeded. Kauffman's copy and Williams' dispatch for the *Times* were both rejected.

The other correspondents who had witnessed the take-over fared little better. For some reason not at first apparent, G.H.Q. made no formal announcement of the entry of the First Division into the 'sector northwest of Toul.' Without such announcement from Chaumont, no newspaper accounts could be released for transmission to the U.S. Finally it occurred to some of the correspondents that the War Department was determined to soft-pedal this latest involvement of U.S. troops. One theory was that Washington officials wanted to avoid criticism for sending troops into the line to bolster French morale. Another was that, as the Administration had announced some months before that it had a 'fighting Army' in France, it did not want to dispel the impression that U.S. troops had been in the front line trenches since the previous October. Whatever the obscure motives of officialdom, censorship decreed a news stalemate on the entry of the First Division into the line northwest of Toul. Meanwhile, Kauffman had made five copies of his rejected dispatch and mailed them, with other confidential material, in five different Paris *arrondissements*. Herb Corey sent back an indignant cable to the manager of Associated Newspapers, and Williams protested to the *New York Times*.

On February 5, seventeen days after the Toul sector had been occupied, an official announcement from G.H.Q. was posted on the bulletin board:

American officers have been authorized to state that the sector of the Western Front taken over by the U.S. Army is in the Lorraine, to the Northwest of Toul.

With that brief notice, the news stories written on January 19 were finally transmitted to America, and the American people learned what the Germans, the French, and the British had known for more than two weeks.

George Pattullo drove over from Chaumont one afternoon with some confidential news for Westbrook Pegler. The United Press man was about to be relieved, and another man, Fred Ferguson, was on the way from New York to replace him. Pattullo, whose connection with the *Saturday Evening Post* and amiable character made him a trusted figure at G.H.Q., had heard from officer friends that Pegler's youth and inexperience counted against him; also, there was some talk of an indiscreet letter. Pegler knew then that his letter to Roy Howard had been picked up by the British Admiralty Censorship and forwarded to Chaumont. No formal charges were brought against him: the matter seems to have been arranged by a cable from General Pershing to Roy Howard, suggesting that an older and steadier newspaperman would better represent the U.P. with the American Expeditionary Forces. At all events, Pegler was through. He packed his gear at the Hôtel de la Providence, said good-by to his fellows and to Henriette, and climbed into a car for Troyes and Paris. Some weeks later, in London, he enlisted in the U.S. Navy.

Pershing had looked into Heywood Broun's case, too. Since December, Colonel Nolan's G-2-D files had been accumulating Broun's extended reports, written for the *Tribune* after his return to New York. The series ran all through January, mostly in the Sunday edition; none had been submitted to censorship. Broun's correspondence revealed a whimsical, sympathetic interest in the common soldier and something approaching contempt for the generals. He related the case of one 'Sammy,' whose post of duty was a remount station far in the rear. His principal duty was to administer pills to sick mules. He was homesick; he didn't like his work or the mules; he didn't know which side was winning the war. For nearly a column in the *Tribune,* Broun's pen described the boredom and frustration of this Yankee in France. Where generals were involved, Broun dipped his pen in acid and made them out more ridiculous than heroic. Somebody in the press section at Chaumont collected the Broun pieces in a folder and added marginal notes and comment. A statement was prepared for General Pershing's signature. An example was to be made of the *Tribune* man; he had defied censorship, his correspondence was frivolous and indiscreet. The idea was that the Commander-in-Chief would publicly rebuke Broun and revoke his credentials, thus serving notice on the other correspondents and the press generally that the A.E.F. would tolerate no monkey business.

The statement denouncing Broun and his works was on Pershing's desk when Frederick Palmer returned to Chaumont from his mission to Washington. The general tossed it over to Palmer to read. The former press officer, now confidential adviser, read it and shook his head. Pershing could not afford to make Broun's case a personal issue. If he publicly castigated the *Tribune* man, the public would remember Broun's observation that the American soldier would never call Pershing 'Papa.' Some would see in the general's rebuke delayed revenge for the reporter's barb.

Pershing thought about that and tossed the statement aside unsigned. Without benefit of the Commander-in-Chief's comment or signature, Broun's credentials were revoked, and the Government took possession of $1,000 which the *Tribune* had posted for him, because he had violated censorship. The whole thing was done quietly and the capable Wilbur Forrest switched from the United Press to become the *Tribune's* correspondent with the A.E.F.

Reginald Wright Kauffman's long fight against the military censorship came to a head about the same time. A cable dispatch from the Secretary of State in Washington complained:

> REGINALD WRIGHT KAUFFMAN SENDING TO PHILADELPHIA NORTH AMERICAN VICIOUS ATTACKS ON EXPEDITIONARY FORCES. FIND OUT IF HIS ARTICLES ARE SUBMITTED TO CENSORSHIP WITH VIEW OF EXPELLING KAUFFMAN.
>
> LANSING

The Secretary's request stirred G-2-D to action against the Philadelphian, but the timing was off. When Colonel Sweeney demanded the surrender of Kauffman's credentials, the journalist said he had already surrendered them to Secretary of War Baker three weeks before with a letter explaining why he would no longer serve with the A.E.F.

I take this action [Kauffman wrote Secretary Baker] because the present military censorship in France violates the only rules and obligations on which it is based: those detailed in Article VIII Field Service Regulations, U.S.A. (corrected to April 15, 1917) and those implied in the credentials issued to war correspondents by your department under the provisions, restrictions, privileges and promises of which my appointment was made. These violations in my opinion render it impossible for a conscientious correspondent to perform those duties to the public which his profession imposes.

The Philadelphian was not permitted to leave the Army's jurisdiction on such a note of high purpose and outraged professional dignity. The Army ruled that he was not resigning but being expelled. The Adjutant General's department was called to prepare a brief documenting Kauffman's violations of censorship, high crimes and misdemeanors; the Government possessed the American's $1,000 bond. The Philadelphia journalist remained in France, however. He found a helpful ally in Vice Admiral Henry B. Wilson, and with Navy approval continued to send back mail reports to George Harvey, Theodore Roosevelt, and his Philadelphia paper.

A third correspondent to be dismissed for willful violation of censorship was the veteran Wythe Williams of the *New York Times*. His offense did not touch the A.E.F., but G-2-D ruled he had violated the spirit of his accreditation agreement by sending an article to *Collier's Weekly* without submitting it to censorship. The article on 'The Battle of the Ridges' blamed French politicians for the disastrous failure of the Nivelle offensive on the Chemin des Dames. Williams, who had received his confidential information from Clemenceau, maintained that since the article did not affect the A.E.F. he was under no obligation to submit it to American censorship. However, at Chaumont Pershing and his staff ruled that the article had embarrassed Franco-American relations and disclosed military policies affecting the whole Allied cause. Exit Williams. The new *Times* man who turned up at Neufchâteau to replace him early in March was a stocky, scrappy young reporter named Edwin L. James, usually called Jimmy.

Colonel Nolan's intelligence department sometimes looked into the affairs of correspondents other than those of the accredited group at Neufchâteau. When Ellis Ashmead-Bartlett, veteran correspondent of the *London Daily Telegraph,* applied for credentials to cover the A.E.F. in March, G-2-D put operatives to work on his journalistic record. From the British War Office, Nolan's men learned that Ashmead-Bartlett was recalled from the Dardanelles 'for attempting to violate censorship and for *improper conversation.*'

Sir Ian Hamilton's report on the British journalist described him as a 'well known war correspondent who possesses considerable gifts and is able to write dispatches on military events with great clearness and descriptive powers. Unfortunately he is not to be trusted. He has the habit of criticism and sees everything from a most pessimistic standpoint.'

Supplementing these adverse British sources was a report from one of Colonel Nolan's men in Paris. Ashmead-Bartlett had moved from the Ritz Hotel to an apartment at 59 rue Spontini. 'This address is that of a person named Dell, a British subject and a notorious défaitiste who was before and during the early part of the war correspondent for the *Manchester Guardian*. When this paper was obliged to modify its own défaitiste attitude it could no longer afford to employ Dell and we understand that ever since he has been out of employment. Lieut. Green called at Dell's apart-

ment and found a salon composed apparently exclusively of
défaitistes. He thinks he remembers having met a Mr. Bartlett
there . . .'

The evidence was overwhelming. General Pershing said 'No.'
Such a man should not be accredited to the A.E.F. This whole
affair must have been rather painful to Lieutenant Morgan, who
remembered Ashmead-Bartlett as a boon companion of Rheims and
Senlis adventures with Richard Harding Davis and Granville
Fortescue in 1914. Subsequently, General Pershing's categorical
'No' was modified. Ashmead-Bartlett could not be accredited as a
correspondent at the front, but he might have a special pass to
visit the warehouses, bake ovens, and docks of the Services of
Supply in the rear areas. So the war career of the brilliant and
temperamental Ashmead-Bartlett, which had started out so gal-
lantly on the Vienna Express with 11 pieces of luggage on an
August night three and a half years before, ended ignominiously in
the drab backwash of the A.E.F. and in the damning files of
G-2-D.

Not all G-2-D investigations into the affairs of correspondents
turned out so grimly. A happier fate awaited the case of Paul
Scott Mowrer, Percy Noel, and the 2,000 francs.

Percy Noel occupied an unique place among the American newspapermen in France. He was the only one of several hundred correspondents to carry a pink pass. One of the first to go to France
in 1914, he enlisted in the British Red Cross when he learned that
a newspaperman was *persona non grata* at the front. Invalided out
in 1915, he worked for the *Chicago Daily News* in France and
Italy, and when the U.S. entered the war he was one of Mowrer's
most experienced men. He specialized in aviation, being at home
in all the military airfields. The extraordinary thing about Noel's
career was his pink pass. This authorized him to drive his own
motor car anywhere in British, French, or U.S. areas and entitled
him to fill the tank with military petrol.

Noel's first car—a Chenard-Walcker—which he had acquired
soon after his arrival in France, caught fire while he was running
errands for the British Red Cross during the Battle of the Marne.
But by this time, Noel's right to operate a motor vehicle in the war
zones was firmly established. In 1915 he acquired a used Model T
Ford and by patient negotiation acquired a brand new Ford at

Neuilly in 1916. By 1917, when he journeyed to Blackpool, England, to meet arriving troops of the A.E.F., he had acquired an almost new 9-h.p. Delage. With the connivance of friends at 10 rue Ste. Anne, the Delage was registered as a military vehicle, and Noel's pink pass was renewed with the understanding that he would not drive in the forward areas and would use his vehicle only for legitimate purposes. One reason why the Press Office extended these accommodations to Noel was that he had proved helpful in showing visiting British correspondents around the U.S. airfields at a time when G-2-D could not spare vehicles or conducting officers. By the end of 1917, Noel had become a semi-official host for the A.E.F. Press Section and an experienced air guide, as well as the *Chicago Daily News* authority on aerial combat and reconnaissance. He lived with his family at Blois, convenient to the dispersed U.S. airfields.

On Feb. 16, 1918, Paul Scott Mowrer wrote from his Paris office to his associate at Blois:

MY DEAR PERCY:

Yes, we are receiving regularly your reports (of) cables, etc. for which thanks. I enclose a check for 2,000 francs as per your request of February 12. Please mail a receipt for this amount to Miss Murphy, and oblige,

Yours truly,

PAUL SCOTT MOWRER

The note with its accompanying check was picked up in the Paris post office, where the censors, finding the message obscure, directed it to Press Division, Intelligence Section, Hôtel Ste. Anne. Someone there should have recognized the names Mowrer and Noel, and understood the transmission of funds, but by this time G-2-D had filled up with new, uncertain officers. One of them readdressed the note to the Commanding Officer, Military Police. The spy investigation was on. Military Police read the note, looked at the check, and referred the matter to the Assistant Provost Marshal, A.P.O. 717. It turned out that this was none of his affair. He sent the matter on to Major R. L. Weeks, Assistant Provost Marshal, A.P.O. 702. Eventually someone at Chaumont recognized the correspondents' names and decided there was nothing sinister in the transfer of 2,000 francs from Paris to Blois. The spy hunt ended. Mowrer's note was dropped in the *Daily News* file at G-2-D and the check forwarded to Noel, who was annoyed at the delay but never knew he was under suspicion as an enemy agent.

Slowly, as winter ended, the restrictions of censorship were being relaxed. Early in February, a new day began for the correspondents. On February 2 Lientenant Morgan wrote to Colonel Sweeney:

I believe in gradual liberalization of all censorship restrictions. In the American zone, the correspondents are under no restrictions except those imposed by Division and Brigade headquarters.

The *Philadelphia Evening Ledger's* Henri Bazin was one of the first to take advantage of the new freedom. Since October the newspapermen had been waiting eagerly to share life in the front line trenches with American troops and write first-hand about it. Now that French restraints were removed, the correspondents edged up to the sector northwest of Toul and sniffed the smells of trench life and dug-out cookery. Bazin turned in for censorship at Neufchâteau a long mail story, 'Eight Days in the American Trenches.' Lieutenant Morgan read it thoughtfully and reminded the elderly Philadelphian that he had passed only about two hours in the forward area. Bazin admitted that his stay in the trenches had been limited, but in those two hours he had interviewed eight soldiers. Their composite experiences, expanded and enhanced with detail, made up the full eight days. On that technical defense, Morgan passed it.

Other correspondents soon learned to take what the soldiers told them with a grain of salt. Many of the infantrymen—especially First Division regulars—were tough, disciplined soldiers, but irresponsible romancers when out of the trenches. Officers were more reliable.

Supplementing the more liberal policies put into effect under the new regime at G-2-D, Colonel Palmer brought back from Washington a memorandum worked out with Secretary of War Baker, allowing the correspondents more freedom and relaxing some of the more arbitrary censorship rules imposed by the War Department.

About the same time General Harbord approved a recommendation from Lieutenant Colonel A. L. Conger, Acting Chief of the Press Section, that correspondents be permitted to write about casualties and activities of troops in the line, since the casualty lists were being given out in Washington and the Germans knew U.S. troops were in the line.

The correspondents appreciated their new freedom, but they complained at the long distance they had to travel daily from Neufchâteau to reach the American sector northwest of Toul. On February 21 they drafted a petition and presented it to Lieutenant Gerald Morgan, Acting Chief Press Officer.

Dear Sir: The following accredited correspondents respectfully request that Press Headquarters be transferred from Neufchâteau to some point nearer the American sector, such as Nancy or Toul.

In making this request we feel that at the present time it is essential for us to be in the closest possible touch with the sector Northwest of Toul, known as the American sector.

We further feel that we can demonstrate that under the present arrangement from ½ to ⅔ of the time of all correspondents is absolutely wasted, due to the wholly needless miles we are forced to travel.

We respectfully urge that permission be granted a committee representing the correspondents to put our case before the proper military authorities.

HERB COREY	FRED FERGUSON	FLOYD GIBBONS
LINCOLN EYRE	THOMAS M. JOHNSON	RAYMOND G. CARROLL
C. C. LYON	HENRY G. WALES	
J. W. WILLIAMS	NORMAN DRAPER	

Transmitting the request to Colonel Sweeney at Chaumont, Lieutenant Morgan recalled that a similar petition by the correspondents the previous October had been turned down by General Debenay, the French commander of the area.

'One point I should like to mention again,' Lieutenant Morgan wrote. 'The temptations to drinking and to women at Nancy might well cause us difficulties with certain of the correspondents . . ."

The move to Nancy was not approved.

XVIII

BIG BERTHA AND LITTLE CANTIGNY

It was March, 1918. The days were growing longer. Winter was almost over. Transports were coming across the North Atlantic steadily now in great sprawling convoys. At St. Nazaire and Brest and Bordeaux, at Liverpool and Cardiff and Plymouth, the Americans streamed down the gangplanks by thousands. The supply service got better. Hospital equipment arrived; so did the missing prunes, apricots, soap, and candles.

Secretary of War Newton D. Baker came down the gangplank of one of the transports March 10 in France to see how things were going. The correspondents interviewed him in General Pershing's office at Chaumont and learned things were going well. He spoke of the triumph of American convoys over German submarines, praised the Navy, told the correspondents about the morale and determination at home. The French and British had borne the brunt of the early years; now the Americans were to make their growing strength felt in the battle lines. Secretary Baker reaffirmed the U.S. policy of having the A.E.F. fight as an American army and praised General Pershing's firmness in refusing to allow our troops to be fed piecemeal into the line under French and British command. Most of this had been said before, but the fact of its reaffirmation by the Secretary of War at American Army headquarters in France gave it fresh impact. The correspondents dutifully wrote down Mr. Baker's observations as if these profound truths had just been uttered for the first time.

Some of the correspondents wanted to trail around with the Secretary of War on his tour of the training camps and bases, but Major Palmer said that would be impractical. Instead, Palmer made the trip at Mr. Baker's side and later reported to the newspapermen as much as he thought prudent to disclose about where he had been, what he had seen, and whom he had shaken hands with. A carefully guarded secret was the Secretary's excursion to the American front line trenches, northwest of Toul. Accompanied only by General Harbord and Major Palmer, Mr. Baker disappeared from circulation for three days, and the newspaper correspondents were chagrined to learn later that he had donned a helmet, gas mask, and overalls and walked through a mile or two of trenches in that quiet sector.

Since February there had been rumors of a great German offensive in the spring. Tom Johnson was one correspondent who got authentic advance information about the situation. At Neufchâteau one night Johnson ran into a young officer from New York who was badly in need of transportation. Major William J. Donovan, later known as 'Wild Bill' Donovan, had been training with British intelligence and now had been ordered to report for duty as staff officer at the headquarters of the First Corps under General Hunter Liggett. Donovan did not relish this assignment; he wanted to get back with his battalion of the 165th Infantry (the old 69th, N.Y.) of the Forty-second Rainbow Division. If he could reach the Forty-second Division camp that night, Donovan thought he might wangle a change in the orders and get back with his old outfit. If Tom could provide the transportation, Donovan offered to tell the newspaperman something likely to develop into important news.

Johnson got a car from the correspondents' pool and in the ride to Forty-second Division headquarters learned that Donovan had picked up some significant information during interrogation of a German prisoner captured by the British a day or two before. The prisoner told of the preparations being made by the Germans for the spring offensive. They were confident they could break the Allied line before American help could be effective. New weapons, new tactics were to be used; great surprises were in store; fresh divisions, released from the Eastern front by Russia's collapse and the treaty of Brest-Litovsk, would batter Allied resistance to pieces. So said the talkative prisoner. Donovan had made a detailed report to British intelligence, and Chaumont knew about it. The German drive, he told Johnson, would begin any day.

The blow fell March 21. What the prisoner had forecast almost came true. While German tanks and infantry masses broke the Allied line in Picardy, German shells fell out of the sky on Paris. A hastily summoned council of war appointed General Foch supreme commander. Secretary Baker and General Pershing conferred at Chaumont and America's role was promptly and clearly defined. Pershing offered to the Allied High Command all of America's troops and resources, without reservation, for the duration of the crisis.

For several days the news was grim, and the worried censors fussed and sweated over what could be told and what must be suppressed. Meanwhile, the First Division was ordered up to Picardy, where the German assault was most threatening. The newspapermen could not say what units of the A.E.F. were ordered to support the broken line, or where they were going. As one correspondent expressed it, about all they could do was to write about 'American troops moving in all directions.'

French censorship decided nothing would be gained by trying to suppress the news that German shells were falling in Paris streets. Too many people knew about it, too many had seen the explosions and heard the screams of the wounded civilians. The correspondents took some of the sinister menace out of the situation by naming the mysterious monster 'Big Bertha.' They were able to count the time intervals between shells, report the damage they did, and speculate on the location and type of gun capable of reaching the city from such a great distance. It was known that the German position nearest Paris was about seventy miles away. Maximum range of the largest guns known to military science was about twenty-two miles. Thus in their ignorance and confusion the military theorists and newspaper correspondents argued whether the Germans had smuggled their big gun inside the Allied line and had it hidden in a cave, whether the great distance was achieved by firing the projectile beyond the earth's atmospheric envelope, or whether some new propulsive force had been discovered.

Wilbur Forrest sent a story to the *Tribune* suggesting that the long-range bombardment might be due to a new projectile, which, fired in the conventional manner, gained new thrust in mid-flight by a second rocket-like explosion. He called it a 'relay shell.' Ordnance experts scoffed at the theory, and other newspapermen compared Forrest to Jules Verne. Time proved, however, that

Forrest was on the right track, and his relay shell would come forty years later to dominate military thinking as the intercontinental ballistic missile.

The long-range shell struck a Paris church on Easter Sunday, killing scores of bewildered French worshippers. In the ensuing panic, enhanced by night attacks by Gotha bombers, nearly a million persons left Paris. Forrest got his wife and small son out to the suburbs. Floyd Gibbons suggested Dijon as a likely place to relocate wives during the crisis, and the idea appealed to Lincoln Eyre and Tom Johnson. The three correspondents collected their wives and hand baggage and in one of the press Cadillacs journeyed down to Dijon. The ladies were installed in the Hôtel de la Cloche, renowned for its snails and scene of the correspondents' pranks which had so pained Lieutenant Green the previous autumn.

Returning to Neufchâteau, the three newspapermen found press headquarters in turmoil. Correspondents were packing to accompany the First Division to Picardy, where, it was assumed, one of the war's great battles soon would be fought. Gerald Morgan was going along to censor their reports, and another censor was being sent from Paris to British headquarters. Meanwhile a skeleton staff and three wire service men were remaining at the Hôtel de la Providence to cover developments at Chaumont and Gondrecourt. There was a dispute over automobiles. More cars were needed to transport the party to Picardy, but those remaining behind wanted the Cadillacs left at Neufchâteau. Lieutenant Colonel McCabe ruled that only the three press association men would be attached to First Division headquarters; the other correspondents were distributed among the units, two to a regiment. The uncertainty of the First's assignment complicated press arrangements; nobody knew what telegraph lines would be available for their copy. Yet the newspapermen had greater freedom of movement, and a better understanding prevailed with the press officers than on any previous operation. Whatever happened, they would be able to see it and write about it.

The trouble was that nothing much happened. The First Division was not thrown in to plug the German breakout; it was moved up behind the Montdidier sector and held in reserve. Press headquarters were established at Chaumont-en-Vexin, then moved to Maisoncelles. Later they were shifted to Chepoix. The newspapermen waited and grew restless. They could not write anything, or even inform their editors where they were or why they must remain silent.

Early in April the British and French, under Marshal Foch's direction, closed the gap and blunted the German drive. By April 15 the Germans realized they had not the reserve strength to achieve a final decision and settle down again to static warfare.

In May the correspondents were permitted to disclose for the first time that American troops were in the Montdidier sector in Picardy, where they finally had made contact with the enemy.

Meanwhile, as fresh selective service divisions finished basic training and crossed the North Atlantic, more American newspaper editors decided to send reporters to France. The War Department received letters from newspapers in Rhode Island, Nebraska, Missouri, Pennsylvania, Ohio, Maryland, New Jersey, and California. Its customary reply was to refer to the decision in the *Boston Globe* case. General Pershing does not want any more correspondents with the Army; he does not want 'local' correspondents with each division. But the newspapers were not discouraged. They persisted. George Creel gave them the blessing of the Committee on Public Information. A few got limited permission from Secretary of War Baker. They might go to England and France, and they might see some of the A.E.F. training camps, bases and hospitals. But they must not expect accreditation or hope to get to the front line or live with the Army.

Late in March the first of the new crop began to embark. Clare Kenamore came over for the *St. Louis Post Dispatch,* Walter S. Ball for the *Providence Journal. The Red Cross Magazine* sent Frazier Hunt. Sibley had broken the ice. There was no stopping them. William Slavens McNutt and Arthur Ruhl came to France for *Collier's Weekly.*

One transport brought Webb Miller of the United Press, Otto P. Higgins of the *Kansas City Star* and Adam Breede of the *Hastings* (Nebraska) *Daily Tribune.* Miller had already seen wartime service in London and Paris; now he was returning to Europe after a conference with Roy Howard. Adam Breede, owner and editor of the Nebraska daily, wore a flowing Windsor tie and a wide-brimmed hat. He resembled a Texas cattleman. He had traveled all over Europe and hunted big game in Africa. Otto Higgins, too, bore the stamp of the West. He was a big, bear-like man who had learned newspaper work as a police reporter in Kansas City's Northside, had a strong desire to bet against the dice in all crap games and was full of conviviality. Higgins smoked home-made cigarettes, which he rolled himself from a ten-cent package of Bull Durham. In distinguished company, Higgins invariably attracted attention when he poured out the Bull Durham, shaped the flimsy cylinder in his huge paws, and licked the paper to seal it. As he finished the ritual, Higgins would invariably ask whoever was watching, 'Would you like a cigarette?' Before the confused onlookers could think of a safe reply, Higgins would thrust the homemade tissue twist in his mouth and, reaching in his back pocket, pull out a gold cigarette case from which he would offer the others his own private brand with gold monogram 'OPH,' a special blend of Turkish and Greek tobacco. He carried a swagger stick with a silver handle, which was hollow and always held a small drink or two of brandy.

As these three arrived in England, Webb Miller explained that under War Department regulations they would not be permitted to send long messages home or tell where they were. The customary thing, he said, was just to send a three-word message: ARRIVED SAFELY, LOVE. But American newspapermen rarely do the customary thing. Breede and Higgins held a parley at the Liverpool dock. Breede, uncertain whether he would wear the Army uniform in France, had brought over only one pair of pants, which were getting a little baggy. He wanted to send back to Hastings for another pair, but was uncertain, in view of Miller's warning, whether the message would be too long. Higgins suggested that he dispense with the 'Arrived Safely, Love' and send merely a brief request for the pants. That message, Higgins contended, would assure the folks at Hastings of his safe arrival and would also conform to the Allied demand for brevity.

That night British intelligence, puzzled over a cryptic cable message: SEND OTHER PANTS PRONTO. ADAM BREEDE, assigned one of its operatives to check on the Nebraska editor. Obviously this was code. He located Breede and Higgins at the Strand Palace Hotel in London and kept them under fairly continuous surveillance for several days. They were trailed across the channel. G-2 in Paris picked up the scent. For nearly a month the combined resources of British, French, and American secret services endeavored to learn what Adam Breede meant by his mysterious cable. Eventually, when he had become well known at 10 rue Ste. Anne, a casual question disclosed that there was nothing secret or sinister about his message from Liverpool to Hastings, Nebraska: he simply wanted another pair of pants.

Higgins and Breede made themselves at home in Paris and soon learned the shortest distance between their hotel, 10 rue Ste. Anne, and Harry's New York Bar in the rue Danou. In May, with other recent arrivals they were given special passes and sent on a tour of airfields and bases—Blois, Tours, Saumur, St. Nazaire, Coëtquidan, Gievre, Issoudun, Nevers, Dijon, Is-sur-Tille. They were part of a growing procession of miscellaneous visitors. Beginning about the time the German March offensive was halted, a steady stream of men and women on various pretexts and errands got the necessary approvals in Washington and crossed the Atlantic to view the great military pageant in France. The more important were shepherded about the training camps and bases by Major Palmer. Nearly all of them checked in at 10 rue Ste. Anne for their passes and did their sight-seeing under the auspices of G-2-D. The General Staff, which less than a year before refused to accredit more than fifteen correspondents, now opened the floodgates, or permitted George Creel's Committee on Public Information to open them, and organized conducted tours, all for the ostensible purpose of keeping the American public informed.

The visitors covered a wide range of interests and in some cases their connection with the war effort was not clear. There were, among others, Robert M. McBride, editor, lecturer and magazine writer; Keith A. Murdoch, London manager and editor of the United Cable service of Australasia; the Reverend Joseph H. O'Dell, preacher, who wanted to do articles on the A.E.F. for *Outlook* and *Atlantic Monthly*; Judge Ben Lindsay of the Children's Court, Denver, Colorado, friend of George Creel; Edwin G. Pipp, editor-in-chief, *Detroit News*; Burton Holmes, lecturer; Louis Raemakers, cartoonist; Lester G. Hornby, artist; E. C. Rauck, special correspondent writing a book; M. Gaston Riou, connected with the French Foreign Office, who wanted to write a number of studies of American troops; Harold Godwin, representing a commission of the Daughters of the American Revolution; Rabbi Abba Hillel

Silver; Griffin Smith, representing the *Paragould* (Arkansas) *Daily Press*; Elinor Glynn, novelist; Professor Kemp Smith of Princeton University; W. B. Trites, who planned to write articles on aviation for *McClure's Magazine*; R. L. Barrett of the U.S. Shipping Board; Henry Seidel Canby, Yale professor; G. W. Coleman, chairman of the War Commission of the Baptist Church; and Frank Gardner, automobile engineer, personal friend of James Gordon Bennett.

In May, field press headquarters in Picardy were shifted from Chepoix to the small city of Beauvais. It was now possible to write guardedly about the First Division in action in the Montdidier sector, and occasionally some news trickled in from other sources. The word was passed that Captain Archie Roosevelt, youngest son of the former President, had been wounded in action. This created quite a stir at press headquarters. 'Ninety Million' Draper was one of the first to seek a ruling from Lieutenant Morgan.

'Captain Roosevelt has been wounded,' he said. 'It happened several days ago. Can't we send something on it?'

Morgan said 'No.' The rule was very definite. Nothing on casualties; only after they had been announced in Washington.

A new arrival, Fred Ferguson of the United Press, was interested in the case, but he bided his time. When Draper and the others had gone, he asked Morgan whether Captain Roosevelt had received the Croix de Guerre. Morgan thought he had. Ferguson remembered a ruling on decorations, and he quoted the section to the censoring official:

3. In the case of Allied army decorations [the] citation . . . is considered as news. Such a citation can be published by the American correspondents. . . . This news will not originate officially with the American G.H.Q. but if it comes to the attention of the Press Officer at G.H.Q. will be promptly communicated to the Field Hdq. of the Press Section.

'I would like to send the United Press a little story on Captain Roosevelt receiving the Croix de Guerre, giving just that fact, and of course, the citation,' Ferguson said.

Morgan called Mark Watson at Chaumont. Watson looked up the rules and said, 'As long as Ferguson's story is based on the decoration, not on Roosevelt being wounded, it's OK.'

The Associated Press did not enjoy being beaten on the Archie Roosevelt story, and Melville Stone, its veteran general manager, raised a rumpus with General Pershing, Lieutenant Colonel Sweeney, and McCabe, as well as with his own man, Norman Draper. Even after the facts were explained to him, he didn't like it. This was the first of a long series of A.P. headaches and frustrations, most of them due to the energy and resourcefulness of their chief adversary, Fred Ferguson. The new U.P. man was small, friendly, a good listener, and, in his quiet way, a most efficient newspaperman.

One of the first moves made by the Associated Press to meet its opposition was to increase its staff. John T. Parkerson was accredited as an A.P. correspondent on March 30, at the high point of the German spring offensive, and a third man, Charles S. Kloeber, was added some weeks later.

In April, while his colleague Draper and most of the other American correspondents were immobilized in Picardy, Parkerson picked up an interesting item about a couple of chaplains serving with the Twenty-sixth (Yankee) Division, which had taken over the sector northwest of Toul.

When the complete story of this engagement is told [Parkerson wrote] the bravery of the regimental chaplains will be an outstanding feature. One of them, Father William J. Farrell of West Newton, Mass., aged 35, went to the assistance of a battery when four men were killed, carried up ammunition, helped keep the gun going all Saturday night. He was wounded with three others Sunday morning but refused to have his wound dressed until he carried Myron Dickinson, aged 19, of Bridgeport, Conn., one of his wounded comrades, to a dugout dressing station. Father Osias Boucher of New Bedford took charge of cooking, washing and carried on the work of serving hot soup, etc. to the soldiers.

This was the kind of human interest story all the correspondents wanted to get. It had names, real people, action, heroism, the stuff of something that might be called Americanism. Parkerson must have been proud of it, and when the Associated Press put it on the national wire, it was published not only in New England, but in half the newspapers of the United States.

But the Associated Press jinx went to work on this story too. A day or two after publication, General Pershing received a cable from General Peyton C. March in Washington. This was the same March who had commanded the artillery camp at Le Valdahon in 1917. The two generals did not see eye to eye about A.E.F. training methods, and March made no bones of the fact that he did not regard Pershing as properly qualified for his high command. In the early winter months Secretary Baker had written to Pershing asking for recommendations for the post of Chief of Staff in Washington, and the general, mentioning one or two he believed qualified, suggested March for *assistant* chief of staff. The peppery March, however, had returned to the United States and so impressed the Secretary and others in the War Department that he was appointed to the top post in Washington. He still did not think much of Pershing's leadership and devoted some time in his new job to measuring his own authority, as defined in the regulations, against that of a mere general having command in the field.

General March's cable called Pershing to task for the A.P. story about the two chaplains.

'This seems to constitute a violation of the laws of war,' General March said. 'The incident might be used to our detriment as pro-German propaganda.'

Technically, General March was correct. Chaplains and Red Cross people were noncombatants. The rules of war said thus and so. Chaplains could not serve hot soup or carry the wounded to dugout dressing stations. They certainly could not pass ammunition to keep the guns firing.

General Pershing should have pointed out to March that sometimes in war, as in ordinary life, men rise above the rule books and produce extraordinary results. But he was a rules-book man himself, and there it was in black and white. On the spur of March's complaint, Pershing put aside his other work to inquire how G-2-D censors had approved such an outrageously irregular story, and to send to all divisional commanders an order reminding them that chaplains were not to pass ammunition or perform other war-like tasks. The investigation set in motion at Chaumont disclosed that the story about the two chaplains had been written by the new A.P. man, Parkerson, on the basis of a commendation issued at the Twenty-sixth Division headquarters by General Edwards himself. By the time the investigation was completed and a formal report prepared for Washington, the war had entered a new phase and March's querulous complaint was blotted out by the smoke and din of battle.

In a cable from Chaumont to the War Department on May 10, General Pershing announced the beginning of a daily communiqué covering the activities of the American Expeditionary Forces for the preceding 24 hours:

> CONSIDERING THE SIZE OF OUR FORCES NOW IN FRANCE AND THE INCREASINGLY IMPORTANT PART BEING BEGUN BY THESE FORCES IN THE OPERATIONS NOW IN PROGRESS ON THE WESTERN FRONT AND THE NECESSITY ON THAT ACCOUNT OF ISSUING AN AUTHORITATIVE OFFICIAL STATEMENT FROM THESE HEADQUARTERS REGARDING THESE ACTIVITIES, IT IS DEEMED ADVISABLE TO BEGIN ISSUING AN OFFICAL COMMUNIQUÉ FROM THESE HEADQUARTERS FOLLOWING IN GENERAL THE LINES OF THE OFFICIAL COMMUNIQUÉS ISSUED FROM THE HEADQUARTERS OF THE ALLIED ARMIES IN FRANCE.

The announcement, posted on the bulletin boards at Neufchâteau and the field press headquarters at Beauvais, was welcome news to the American correspondents. Now, for the first time, they would have an official, timely report from G.H.Q. on all engagements of American arms. They did not expect the daily communiqué to do their reporting for them. They knew it would be vague and general; nevertheless, it would reflect the General Staff's daily view of the war's progress and greatly aid the newspapermen in maintaining perspective.

The first communiqué, issued May 15, must have disappointed those who looked for important news developments. The launching was a routine affair.

> May 15. A. North of Toul and in Lorraine there was marked increase of artillery activity on both sides. Today two of our aviators brought down three German machines. There is nothing else of importance to report.

Supplementing that brief, perfunctory statement was a second section of more general information which could be made public at the same time.

B. In Lorraine May 12 three snipers, scouts of intelligence service, went out in camouflage sniping suits to find German sniper and encountered 18 enemy at strong point near dug-out. They shot four of whom one appeared to be an officer, secured valuable papers and retired under heavy fire. One failed to reach our lines and Major commanding sector sent three officers and four men to find him. This patrol also penetrated enemy's line and reached strong point attacked by first patrol. Here enemy was now in force and our patrol was driven back by hot rifle and grenade fire. On reaching lines one man of this patrol also found missing. Two officers who went out to find him killed enemy scout and brought back body for identification purposes. The man missing from second patrol has not been found but third intelligence scout of first party has returned.

The first day's historic communiqué also contained confidential information transmitted in code to the War Department in Washington, but withheld from the press in France. This included such intelligence comment as: 'Since April 15, the enemy has realized that the offensive begun March 21 could not be carried out to a decision with his worn troops and the number of remaining fresh reserves. Since that date only local attacks have occurred . . . The enemy's policy has been one of resting and reconstituting his exhausted divisions . . .'

Thus was launched the daily communiqué of the American Expeditionary Forces in France. It had taken them almost a year to get around to it. It would be issued every night, generally around 9 P.M., and the newspapermen would wait for the telephone call from Chaumont. Some would look over the press officer's shoulder as he typed the pages, searching for something that could be lifted and put into the night cable for America. Much of the time the communiqué held nothing new, nothing worth sending, but occasionally, as on the night of May 28, it was worth waiting for.

May 28. A. This morning in Picardy our troops attacking on a front of one and one fourth miles, advanced our line and captured the village of Cantigny. We took two hundred prisoners and inflicted on the enemy severe losses in killed and wounded. Our casualties were relatively small. Hostile counter-attacks broke down under our fire.

Cantigny! A town so small you hunt in vain for it on the map of France. Yet here, among the cluster of houses and small patchwork of streets on May 28, 1918, American troops made their first planned, full-scale attack of the war and accomplished what they set out to do.

The correspondents who had remained at Beauvais, waiting for something to happen, at last were rewarded. Of the eight who learned about it in advance, three or four followed close behind the attacking troops. Tom Johnson of the *Sun,* Wilbur Forrest of the *Tribune* and Jimmy Hopper of *Collier's Weekly* got an outline of the battle plan the night before from the First Division operations officer, Major George C. Marshall. The French had sent over additional batteries to increase the First artillery fire power, and the combined guns were to start neutralization fire on hostile artillery at 4:45 A.M. There would be increasing volume of preparation and diversion fire for an hour and a half, and at 6:40, behind a rolling barrage, the veteran Twenty-eighth Infantry and a battalion of the Twenty-sixth were to advance into the little town.

Johnson and Forrest stayed up all night to watch the preparations and follow the jump-off. Hopper went in with the infantry. The companies kept formation and moved in even lines behind the tanks. By 8:00 A.M. the first German prisoners were streaming back.

Hopper went far enough into Cantigny during the first attack to round up a group of bewildered Germans and herd them toward the rear. He was very businesslike about it, giving orders like an officer.

The Cantigny attack resulted in the capture of more than 200 prisoners, and advanced the line held by the Americans from 300 to 1,600 yards. This was considered a very substantial gain. Jimmy Hopper's adventure caused comment at press headquarters.

This was the first time an American correspondent had performed such a feat. Johnson and Forrest knew about it and thought it would make a wonderful story. For the next couple of days they kept after him to set it down on paper, his story about capturing the German prisoners. Hopper said that he had not written it yet because he had some other 'stuff' to get off first.

Johnson and Forrest asked what other 'stuff' could be as important as Cantigny and the prisoners. Hopper replied that he first had to write a story about a nun.

The methodical Hopper, not being under the daily deadline

pressure which spurred the other reporters, liked to reflect on his stories and keep his material in chronological order in his notebook. Thus, his adventures in Cantigny had to wait their turn on his type-writer while he dealt with the quiet heroism of a nun.

For three days the correspondents concentrated their energies on the Cantigny affair, interviewing officers who had led the attack, talking to the wounded, keeping close watch on the Germans' un-successful efforts to retake the village. Cantigny! Cantigny! Cables and telegraph wires hummed with the name and all America was learning where it was on the war map and trying to pronounce it. But by the time the people back home had embraced the little town and learned to pronounce it, another name began to crowd Cantigny out of the headlines. This new name had a ring, too: Château-Thierry.

XIX

NIGHT RIDE TO CHÂTEAU-THIERRY

The crisis at Château-Thierry developed quickly and unexpectedly. On May 31 Junius Wood of the *Chicago Daily News* and Ray Carroll of the *Philadelphia Ledger* were at First Division headquarters, following up the Cantigny story, now nearly three days old. They heard a piece of news that drifted in by telephone. The Second Division had been alerted and set in motion by the French high command. Nobody knew for sure why, but the report was that there had been a German breakthrough on the Chemin-des-Dames between Rheims and Soissons.

A press car with driver waited outside and the two newspapermen climbed in. They could either turn back to Beauvais and find out what Captain Morgan knew about it, or, to save time, go direct to Gisors and try to pick up the division there. They drove to Gisors. Most of the Second had already left. The newspapermen trailed along.

Meanwhile, Wilbur Forrest had driven down to Chantilly a day or two after the capture of Cantigny. He was at home here at French press headquarters, having passed several months at the comfortable château on the Paris road as one of the correspondents accredited to the French front.

The *Tribune* man found the newspapermen at French press headquarters indifferent to the Cantigny affair. What was Cantigny? A set piece: a little exercise arranged for publicity purposes. While the American force (less than a division) was seizing that small and unimportant French town, Ludendorff had launched his Blücher attack between Soissons and Rheims. The Germans had broken through on the Chemin-des-Dames—a supposedly secure Allied position—and were already across the Aisne. Soissons had fallen.

A glance at the map showed an alarming bulge. The press correspondents at Chantilly knew that the Second Division, A.E.F., had
been alerted. From the atmosphere at Foch's headquarters they
knew the situation was grave.

Forrest climbed in a French press car with Paul Scott Mowrer.
In a little more than an hour, bucking military traffic, they reached
the Marne and half an hour later ran into the Germans' plunging
advance at Dormans, a river town northeast of Château-Thierry.
The encounter—they narrowly escaped capture—confirmed the
gloomy reports: this was a breakthrough of major proportions.
Forrest and Mowrer, familiar with the map from months of intensive study, suddenly realized that the German thrust was aimed at
Paris and that very little Allied defensive force was poised to stop
them. For the first time since September, 1914, the Germans were
swarming along the Marne.

At Château-Thierry, to which the two correspondents in their
press car hastily retreated from Dormans, following the road south
of the river, Forrest and Mowrer saw something that stirred their
pulses—American troops: trucks with American insignia, a motorized American machine gun company deploying in the outskirts
of Château-Thierry. There was something in the path of the on-
rushing enemy after all.

That same morning, about the time Forrest and Mowrer were
setting out from Chantilly, two hundred miles away on the edge of
the Vosges mountains at Neufchâteau, two other American correspondents climbed into their car in front of the Hôtel de la
Providence. They planned to ride up to Gondrecourt, see what was
stirring there, and then go on to Châlons-sur-Marne later in the
day. With them was a conducting officer, Lieutenant Wilson.

Both men were newcomers. Don Martin had received his credentials only two weeks before, the first correspondent to be accredited for the *New York Herald*. A middle-aged newspaperman,
he had covered politics in New York, Albany and Washington for
the *Herald* before coming to France. Edwin L. James, his companion, was the newest correspondent for the *New York Times,*
accredited in March when Wythe Williams was suspended.

There was little news at Gondrecourt. A new division had moved
in and its training was routine. But the newsmen did pick up a

disquieting report of the German breakthrough. They decided to push on to the Marne.

Somewhere at a cross road above Gondrecourt their car was forced to one side of the highway by the swift passage of a train of military vehicles. This was the 7th Machine Gun Battalion (motorized) of the Third Division. The men in the newspaper car yelled after the hurrying vehicles to find out what was up. The word came back: there's a big fight, and we're going to be in it. The press car trailed along in the dust of the machine gunners' trucks. They were headed northwest. In mid-afternoon, they came to the Marne at Château-Thierry at just about the same time that the German advance reached the northern outskirts of the town. After consultation with the French commanding officer, the machine gun battalion moved up and established themselves at the bridge, commanding the river crossing.

Thus, quite by accident, four American newspapermen were present that eventful afternoon when the machine guns of the A.E.F., co-operating with a battalion of French colonial infantry, stopped the German advance.

Below Senlis, still hunting for the Second Division rendezvous, Junius Wood and Ray Carroll encountered a succession of French M.P.'s along the road. They were not helpful at first. The newspapermen demanded directions to the Second Division headquarters, and the French, convinced that this small group had legitimate business with the American troops, finally directed them to a place called Montreuil-aux-Lions.

Montreuil-aux-Lions was a rendezvous for the Second Division command, and its temporary headquarters. The French had been very secretive about the division's destination. A new brigadier general, James G. Harbord, arrived there to take command of the Marine Brigade. He had been Pershing's chief of staff at Chaumont and had a sound knowledge of the over-all war picture, but here he was, pitched into an emergency situation, taking over command of troops that knew nothing about him, and facing a situation about which he knew very little.

Wood and Carroll made their way to Montreuil-aux-Lions that night, and so did Wilbur Forrest, following some ammunition trucks. The first impressions they had were of hundreds of tired men sleeping by the roadside and of an officer with a hoarse voice, standing on the tailgate of a truck, shouting: 'Everybody within sound of my voice, help unload this ammunition!'

Everything happened in a few hours. Chaumont must have known what was going on. It may have occurred to Colonel Sweeney at G-2-D sometime during the day to notify the accredited correspondents through Captain Morgan at Beauvais. But there wasn't much to tell them, except that there had been a German breakthrough somewhere along the Noyon-Reims sector south of Soissons, and the Second Division was being rushed toward the hole. The French wouldn't tell anybody at first where they were sending the Americans. The Second's trucks were spread over a dozen roads, the division was scattered over sixty miles of French countryside without knowing where or when it would come together. At key junction points, French M.P.'s would hand road directions to the drivers: 'Proceed to X, where instructions will be given you.'

Late in the afternoon, word finally reached the correspondents at Beauvais, where they were still preoccupied with Cantigny. At least six were there in the field press headquarters when Captain Morgan got a telephone call from Paris, saying that the French had sent for the Second Division and planned to use it somewhere in the line. So what? The news was vague at first. Even when it developed a little later that the Second was converging in the neighborhood of Château-Thierry and the Third's 7th Machine Gun Battalion was there, too, the press men remained calm. They were still at work on the Cantigny follow-up stories. But the situation changed with the next telephone call. A voice said: The German drive seems to have changed direction. Some of the advanced elements are over the Marne. They are pushing southwest toward Paris. If Paris was to be saved, it was up to the Americans. This might turn out to be quite a story after all. Another telephone call from rue Ste. Anne: Wood and Carroll were at Second Division headquarters at Montreuil-aux-Lions; so was Forrest. Two other correspondents were reported with the 7th Machine Gun Battalion. Colonel McCabe was in Paris.

The daily communiqué came over the wire from Chaumont.

The enemy has been again completely repulsed by artillery fire and infantry action in attacks against our new positions near Cantigny. . . . Artillery fighting continues actively there and in Lorraine where it includes the use of gas shells. There is nothing else of importance to report.

Nothing about the Second Division; nothing about Château-Thierry. And, of course, nothing about Paris being doomed unless the Americans made a stand.

Another bulletin from 10 rue Ste. Anne: Wood had just telephoned to find out if there would be a censor at the press office in Paris to handle their copy. The answer was 'Yes.' Wood and Carroll were expected from Montreuil-aux-Lions around midnight.

That afternoon when the first reports reached Beauvais, the correspondents reminded each other that they were all in the same boat. Except for a few strays, the flower of the American press corps was at Beauvais. They were obeying orders, co-operating with the press officers, following the prescribed routine. It seemed unlikely that G-2-D would let important events take place without declaring them in.

Yet, here they were, 80 kilometers northwest of Paris, more than a hundred from Château-Thierry, scooped on the biggest story of the war.

Lincoln Eyre asked Captain Morgan's permission to talk to Colonel McCabe by telephone. The connection went through to rue Ste. Anne and McCabe's voice came on the wire.

The *New York World* man outlined the problem of the newsmen at Beauvais. For nearly two months, he told McCabe, they had stuck with the First Division behind the Mondidier sector, and not until the Cantigny attack, three days before, had they been able to produce a real story. All that time they had stayed in line, always in touch with their press officers, conforming to the regulations. Now it appeared, they were to be penalized for obeying the rules.

Eyre called the roll, for Colonel McCabe's benefit, of the correspondents at Beauvais. All the wire service men were there— John T. Parkerson, A.P.; Fred Ferguson, U.P.; Newton C. 'Archie' Parke, I.N.S. Also Tom Johnson, *New York Sun;* Herb Corey of the Associated Newspapers; and finally, the *New York World,* Eyre himself. He did not know under what circumstances Wood and Carroll and Forrest (Eyre knew nothing then about Mowrer and James and Martin) had learned about the Second Division move and followed it to Château-Thierry, but he did know that they were off the reservation. They had acted without the co-operation or knowledge of G-2-D, and it did not seem fair to reward their irregular conduct by giving them a big lead over the faithful at Beauvais.

The cool, resourceful Eyre made out a convincing case, but McCabe saw the other side of it too. So far as he could determine, Wood, Carroll, and Forrest broke no rules in getting to Château-Thierry; they had acted impulsively and energetically, rather than irresponsibly. Whatever they wrote would be subject to the most rigid censorship, but it would be unfair, he thought, to penalize them for getting the news first.

Eyre suggested that G-2-D had failed to keep the correspondents at Beauvais properly informed. They depended on the Chief Press Officer to advise them of important events, but apparently their trust had been misplaced. Now they were being penalized on one of the biggest stories of the war, not for being lazy or careless, but for putting their faith in McCabe, Morgan and Company.

McCabe listened thoughtfully and proposed a compromise, calling Captain Morgan on the line again for consultation. How long would it take the correspondents at Beauvais to get to Château-Thierry? Three or four hours, depending on the traffic and whether they got lost. How long to round up their story and get back to Paris? Another four hours, maybe five. Very well, McCabe said. He didn't know when the French were going to issue their communiqué—probably around 11:00 A.M. But he would hold everything up until noon. That gave Eyre and his fellow correspondents twelve hours. After noon tomorrow, he would release whatever Wood and Carroll and Forrest had ready just as soon as the communiqué came out; the others could file next as soon as they arrived.

Eyre's persuasive talk had won a temporary reprieve. About midnight, in three press cars, the six correspondents started for the Marne. They rode all night along roads choked with Army traffic, getting directions from military police, reading signposts with pocket flashlights. Around daybreak they found division headquarters at Montreuil-aux-Lions. An officer named Brown, who had not slept for 36 hours, told them how the Second had came into position and stopped the Germans cold. No doubt about it, the Americans had saved Paris. Tom Johnson and Lincoln Eyre drove on up the Paris-Château-Thierry road to find the front. It was slow going, for the road was choked with supply trucks and rolling kitchens. They got out and walked and came to a turn in the road where Marines were dug in on both sides, lying beside their machine guns. They asked a sergeant where the Germans were, and he said: 'Just keep on around that bend in the road and you'll run smack into them.' There wasn't much firing, the troops on both sides had outrun their ammunition supply. The two correspondents saw some Marines signaling across a field with wig-wag flags. The war had climbed out of the trenches at last.

Back in Paris at 10 rue Ste. Anne, the correspondents crowded around McCabe's desk and watched the stamping of the sheets that determined priority on the wires. The French communiqué had been issued, signaling the release of the big news all along the line. For the Americans, this was more important than anything that had happened so far. The censors permitted the U.S. correspondents to say that the Americans had stopped the German drive on the Marne and saved Paris.

Jimmy James and Don Martin got back to Neufchâteau late that afternoon, not knowing that press headquarters had been shifted to Paris. Neither had had any sleep for two days. They had traveled nearly 400 miles and had followed the 7th Machine Gun Battalion into the streets of Château-Thierry, watched them set up their guns and go into action.

'Where have you been?' 'Ninety Million' Draper asked.

'Go to hell,' said Jimmy James, without malice.

Draper wandered out to the sidewalk where Lieutenant Wilson was taking his gear out of the car. 'I hear you had quite a ride,' he said.

'Yes,' the lieutenant said, adding that they had followed the 7th M.G. Battalion right up to the Marne and that the Yanks had stopped the Germans cold. The A.P. man got out his pencil. 'Tell me more,' he said. Wilson told him all about it.

The indignant James wrote a long angry protest to Colonel McCabe. He and Martin had returned to Neufchâteau from their arduous journey, and their unsuspecting conducting officer had spilled all the details to the Associated Press man who demanded the news as his right.

Draper immediately grabbed the stolen goods and wrote a piece which he tried to send urgent—thus of course getting to New York first the story which Mr. Martin and myself spent two days and rode more than 400 miles to get.

Martin, newest of all the accredited correspondents, sent a cable to his managing editor in New York:

Have Ohl [*Herald* correspondent in Washington] take censorship matter up Washington. Impossible to send real news. Correspondents hobbled everyway imaginable. Situation inexcusable. Must be remedied. Press treated absolutely no consideration. Details letter.

Presumably his letter told about the affair of Lieutenant Wilson and Norman Draper. Draper himself complained bitterly about the state of affairs at Neufchâteau. It was supposed to be the Chief Press Center of the A.E.F., yet no word had been forthcoming there about the movement of the Second Division, nor anything about the Third; and when the French finally released the news in Paris that the enemy had been stopped on the Marne by American forces in co-operation with the French, nobody remembered to pass the information along to the correspondents at Neufchâteau. What they were able to write about it did not pass censorship and get on the cables until several hours after all the other correspondents' copy had cleared. The war had in fact left Neufchâteau behind. A few correspondents would linger on at the Hôtel de la Providence after June 1, and occasionally the town would be a stopover between the front and Chaumont, but its significance for the press had ended.

The situation around Château-Thierry May 30-31-June 1 made necessary a hurried shift in arrangements for the press. Beauvais and Neufchâteau were too far away to serve as headquarters in the crisis along the Marne. Sensibly, Colonel McCabe established press headquarters in Paris at 10 rue Ste. Anne. There, for a few days, censors and correspondents worked around the clock. It was possible to reach Montreuil-aux-Lions in an hour and a half, Château-Thierry in two hours from Paris. Communications were excellent. The American forces were giving a good account of themselves, Paris was saved, and the correspondents could break the harsh grind with a good dinner and a taste of gay city night life. It was too good to last.

The French worried at the possibilities opened up by daily commuting between Paris and the battle scene. It would be difficult, French intelligence believed, for all the correspondents to remain discreet, considering the vital information they possessed and the temptations of city life. If the boulevards were not in fact swarming with spies, the case of Mata Hari could not be ignored. The war correspondents knew too much. They would have to quit Paris.

Most of the American war correspondents looked back on that week—May 31-June 7—and remembered it after other memories had faded. It had a special, positive character. At Cantigny the week before, they had come out of a long, smoky tunnel to a clearing. The war had taken on new meaning and vigorous pace. The stuff they were writing now really counted. A few of the correspondents, looking back, realized that in their enthusiasm they overplayed the situation along the Marne, giving the Americans too much credit for saving Paris and overemphasizing the role of the Marines. But at the time, they were caught up and swept along by events, and the events called for flag-waving and superlatives. At the time it seemed that the 7th Machine Gun Battalion and the Marine Brigade *had* saved Paris. The censors at 10 rue Ste. Anne agreed and permitted the newspapermen to say as much. (Neither correspondents nor G-2-D realized that Marshal Foch had ample French reserves posted on both flanks, waiting for the Germans to overextend themselves south of the Marne. What the Second and Third Divisions had stopped at Château-Thierry was not an enemy attack in force, but a probing action designed to learn how fast and how far the French were withdrawing across the Marne. The Germans had put out feelers and they had fought very well, but it was no great feat to stop them. Paris never had been in danger.)

The correspondents were not greatly at fault for overplaying the Marines. That lapse, if it was a lapse, was due largely to an old frustration. Censorship had forbidden them to identify any of the divisions; they could not write that American troops in any given action were from New England or Texas; they could not distinguish between branches of the service such as infantry, artillery, signal corps, cavalry; they could not refer to regiments or battalions, only 'units' or 'elements' of United States forces. Nor could they distinguish between the Regular Army (First and Second Divisions and part of the Third), the National Guard (Twenty-sixth 'Yankee' and Forty-second 'Rainbow' Divisions), and the Selective Service (draft) divisions.

When the Marine Brigade went into action at Château-Thierry for the first time on May 31, it occurred to the correspondents that this was a special branch, like the Air Force or the Navy. This being so, why couldn't it be identified, since its identification would convey no useful information to the enemy?

The question was first raised at 10 rue Ste. Anne. Colonel McCabe telephoned to Colonel Sweeney at Chaumont, who may have referred the matter to Colonel Nolan. Back came the ruling—and Colonel Sweeney took full responsibility for it—that the correspondents could mention the Marines by the generic term, without indicating their strength or naming individual units, after the enemy learned they were in the front line. The correspondents made the most of that when the Marines were given the task of clearing the Germans out of Belleau Wood. This was a difficult assignment because of the rocky, wooded terrain which enabled the enemy to plant machine gun nests. The job took about three weeks, and all that time the Marines dominated the headlines. The regular infantry regiments of the Second Division were fighting valiantly and advancing northwest of Château-Thierry, but little attention was paid to them. The Marines got most of the credit and practically all the glory. The resulting discord, which was reflected in lowered Army morale, did not become generally known, but the effects were serious enough to be analyzed in official reports.

The initial organized attack on Belleau Wood began early in the afternoon of June 5. Most of the correspondents knew about it and drove out from Paris that morning to follow the assault. Johnson, the *Sun* man, found a place on a slight rise near Marine Brigade headquarters. Nearby, a French artillery observer was scanning the terrain through a pair of 'scissors' (a slang word for binoculars on a tripod). He spotted some Germans moving at the edge of a field half a mile away and jumped around like a dancing puppet in his excitement, called out *'Boches là!'* About this time a press car drove up and the tall figure of the *Chicago Tribune*'s Floyd Gibbons got out. He was followed by an officer Johnson recognized as Lieutenant Arthur Hartzell. Hartzell had been on the cable desk of the *New York Sun,* and after a course in officers' training camp had come overseas as a first lieutenant. Previously attached to the 9th Infantry, Second Division, because of his newspaper training he had been transferred to G-2-D. By arrangement with the French, a conducting officer accompanied each press car from Paris to the front, and Hartzell was assigned to the *Tribune* vehicle. The two men planned to watch the attack together with Major Berry. Before leaving 10 rue Ste. Anne, Gibbons wrote an advance for the *Tribune,* based on what he had learned about the attack, picturing the Marines charging ding-dong, hell-for-leather into the wood and putting the Germans to flight. It was a dramatic, colorful Gibbons story, and he expected to fill in authentic detail when he returned to Paris that night.

Hartzell and Gibbons stopped for a word with Tom Johnson. They said they were headed for Lucy-le-Bogage and asked the *Sun* correspondent whether he wanted to go along. Johnson said, 'No thanks.' He would watch the jump-off through the Frenchman's 'scissors.' Besides, he had been warned against Lucy. Dave Bellamy, still another old *Sun* man, now a lieutenant in the 6th Marines, had passed by a few minutes before on his way to Brigade headquarters. Lucy-le-Bogage was a hot corner, he said, alive with Germans waiting for something to shoot at.

Hartzell and Gibbons went on to meet Major Berry. They followed the Marines out across a field, taking cover along a wall, dropping down in the tall grass, then running forward doubled over. A burst of machine gun fire from the edge of the wood sent them flat on the ground, where they lay for several minutes. Lucy-le-Bogage was indeed a hot corner. Up ahead the advanced line of Marine helmets started to inch forward through the grass. Major Berry warned: 'Lie still, we're in range.' But Gibbons couldn't see anything with his nose buried in the grass. Slowly he raised his head and looked around. Another sharp rattle of machine gun fire.

Berry called, 'Get down!' but it was too late. One of the bullets had passed through Gibbons's upper arm; another, through his left eye. He remembered the quick, searing flash of the pain and then, for a while, he remembered nothing at all.

Hartzell was all right; both Berry and Gibbons were wounded. There was nothing to do but lie still and wait. It was half an hour before the Marines wormed their way forward far enough to engage the Germans at the edge of the wood. When it seemed safe to move, Hartzell got Gibbons out of the field and back to a dressing station.

An ambulance driven by Patterson McNutt, brother of the *Colliers' Weekly* correspondent William Slavens McNutt, arrived at the dressing station. He was persuaded to take Gibbons out of the military zone, direct to the American Hospital at Neuilly, on the northwestern edge of Paris. There the Chicago correspondent received prompt attention and such good care that less than a month later he was back at the front with the Marines at Belleau Wood.

In an effort to keep a closer check on the accredited correspondents, Colonel Sweeney issued a memorandum at Chaumont on June 1. One of its provisions read:

Accredited correspondents must live permanently with the Army. This is interpreted to mean at one of the three press centers—Neufchâteau, Beauvais or Fressin [near Hesdin, behind the British line].

As for those correspondents who wished to visit Paris, they would obtain permission from the local press officer, notifying him of the date of departure and the number of days they desired to remain in that city.

Before these new regulations could be posted on the bulletin boards, they were a dead letter. Paris had become press headquarters, Beauvais was closed down, Neufchâteau no longer counted. And before G-2-D could get out new regulations governing the Paris set-up, the French said politely but firmly that the correspondents knew too much and must be moved out of town. On June 7, the American press office was moved out of Paris to Meaux.

Meaux was just about halfway between Paris and Château-Thierry, on a main line railroad. The correspondents had a comfortable lodging at the Sirène, an old hotel built around a court-yard, and just up the street and across the cathedral square was a very good restaurant, one of the best in that part of France. Meaux was convenient; the battle scene was less than an hour away. Communications were good. There were frequent trains to Paris. In spite of a few bons vivants who mourned the boulevards and cafés of the capital, the move to Meaux made sense.

The day after the accredited correspondents were installed at Meaux, General Pershing turned his attention to the growing problem of the 'visiting' newspapermen. On June 8 he sent the following cable to Washington:

FOR CHIEF OF STAFF. RAPID DEVELOPMENT IN FRONT LINE SITU-ATION IN WHICH REPORTS OF ACTIONS OF DIVISIONS ARE GREATLY DELAYED IN REACHING HEADQUARTERS RENDERS ADVISABLE A CHANGE IN POLICY LIMITING NUMBER OF NEWSPAPER CORRE-SPONDENTS. TO THIS END IT IS PROPOSED TO ATTACH ACCREDITED CORRESPONDENTS TO DIVISIONS. THE ORGANIZATION FOR SECURING NEWS WILL THEN CONSIST OF A CENTRAL BODY COMPOSED OF NOT MORE THAN 25 ACCREDITED CORRESPONDENTS UNDER DIRECT CHARGE OF OUR PRESS DIVISION WHO WILL BE PROVIDED WITH AUTOMOBILES AND CABLE FACILITIES. IN ADDITION THERE WILL BE ONE ACCREDITED CORRESPONDENT WITH EACH DIVISION. IT WILL BE IMPOSSIBLE TO FURNISH HIM WITH TRANSPORTATION OR CONDUCT-ING OFFICER OR CABLE FACILITIES, NOR WILL HE BE PERMITTED TO CIRCULATE EXCEPT WITHIN HIS OWN DIVISION. IN OTHER WORDS, CORRESPONDENTS WITH DIVISIONS WILL BE MAILSPECIALS ONLY AS CABLE FACILITIES DO NOT PERMIT INCREASING NUMBER. THERE ARE A NUMBER OF CORRESPONDENTS NOW IN FRANCE WHO ARE INTERESTED SOLELY IN PARTICULAR SECTIONS OF THE UNITED STATES. OF THESE EIGHT ARE NOT ACCREDITED AND FOR YOUR IN-FORMATION THESE EIGHT ARE: HAZEN, PORTLAND EVENING TELE-GRAM; HIGGINS, KANSAS CITY TIMES; HUNT, RED CROSS MAGAZINE; KENAMORE, ST. LOUIS POST DISPATCH; SIBLEY, BOSTON GLOBE; TIMMONS, LOS ANGELES EXAMINER; TOMPKINS, BALTIMORE SUN; WILLIAMS, LOS ANGELES TIMES. I RECOMMEND THAT WAR DEPART-MENT SELECT, ACCREDIT AND ASSIGN ONE CORRESPONDENT TO EACH DIVISION; SELECTION OF CORRESPONDENTS REFERENCE PAPER OR COMBINATION OF PAPERS TO BE REPRESENTED BY EACH TO BE MADE UNDER SUCH REGULATIONS AS IT DETERMINES. ADVISE COM-BINATION OF PAPERS FOR NEWS DISTRIBUTION AS WELL AS FOR EXPENSES OF CORRESPONDENTS REPRESENTING TERRITORY FROM

WHICH DIVISION COMES. THESE CORRESPONDENTS TO BE PLACED
UNDER BOND, GIVEN SAME STATUS AS OTHER ACCREDITED CORRE-
SPONDENTS, BUT TO UNDERSTAND THOROUGHLY AND SIGN AGREE-
MENT IN ACCORDANCE WITH CONDITIONS OUTLINED HEREIN.

PERSHING

This represented a change in basic policy. The previous August
the Commander-in-Chief had turned down the *Boston Globe*'s
application because 'such assignments [to divisional units] would
cause undesirable rivalry between correspondents and make it
difficult to maintain uniform policy throughout the Army.' Furthermore, 'newspaper praise of individual officers and local units would
be detrimental to discipline.'

Now those bogies were dispelled. Pershing was learning; six
U.S. divisions were now in the front line, all the way from the
British sector, Montdidier, to Lorraine, and it was obviously impossible to follow them all from one headquarters. He was also
beginning to understand that the daily lives of American troops in
France held continuing interest for their folks and neighbors at
home, whether they were fighting battles in the front line or hunting rabbits in the rear.

The result was that more newspapermen came over, and G-2-D
tried to make rules to deal with them. They still were herded in a
separate group and classified as 'visiting' correspondents. Before
the June 8 memorandum, 'visiting' correspondents received white
passes for their trips out of Paris and were required to report back
to 10 rue Ste. Anne and surrender them on their return. In Paris
between trips often they had no correspondents' credentials or
other identifying papers. At first G-2 ruled they could wear uniforms with the Sam Browne belt or not, as they chose. Then came
another ruling:

May 22nd

All visiting correspondents are advised that they are entitled to
wear the uniform only when on a trip and when provided with a
white pass in consequence: that they shall not wear the Sam Browne
belt; and that their brassard shall be *white* with a red 'C.' *Accredited
Correspondents only* shall be entitled to at all times wear the uniform
and they only may wear the Sam Browne belt. They shall wear a
green brassard with a red 'C.' They shall be provided with an identity
card indicating that they are accredited correspondents.

It seems likely that Colonels Nolan, Sweeney, and McCabe were not alone in wanting to preserve the distinction between the two groups of newspapermen. Once Junius Wood growled to Tom Johnson, 'What's the use of being "accredited" if they're going to give the same privileges to every police reporter who gets a letter from his congressman?' Probably the Old Guard—Wood, Johnson, Eyre, Herb Corey, and the wire service men, who had been through the long dry runs at Gondrecourt and Arracourt—protested against the newcomers' right to wear the jaunty belt and ride in the press Cadillacs.

Eventually the problem adjusted itself. Late in June, under the new policy, the visiting correspondents received their division credentials and, like Sibley, joined the outfits with whom they had trained. Clare Kenamore of the *St. Louis Post Dispatch* went with the Thirty-fifth Division, already in the line. Otto Higgins of the *Kansas City Star* joined the Eighty-ninth (he would go with the 135th later); Joe Timmons of the Los Angeles Examiner and Harry A. Williams of the *Los Angeles Times* both went to the Ninety-first; Ray Tompkins of the *Baltimore Sun* to the Twenty-ninth.

Slowly, the news coverage of the American Expeditionary Forces developed and grew. The journalistic Old Guard at Meaux handled the big battle stories, the daily cables, and urgent flashes. From the training camps and the quiet sectors came the mail stories, simple homely feature stuff, certainly harmless so far as military information was concerned, but immensely comforting to the people in the United States.

XX

TURNING POINT AND CROIX DE GUERRE

Château-Thierry and Belleau Wood were in the headlines all through June. As the Second Division kept up pressure across the Marne, Americans read about Triangle Farm, Boursches, Hill 204, Vaux, Torcy, and Lucy-le-Bogage—names on a map, obscure small places suddenly important because American soldiers were proving themselves there. The correspondents rode over from Meaux each day and learned every crossroad, every clump of trees. Day by day they followed the fighting; it took more than three weeks to get the last of the enemy out of Belleau Wood. But by July 4 they were able to report that the veteran American division had taken 1,200 prisoners and captured large numbers of machine guns, meinenwerfers and other matériel.

The pace was increasing. In addition to the dramatic thrust of the Second Division northwest of Château-Thierry, the correspondents had to keep track of what was happening to the First Division in Picardy, the Third on the Marne, the Twenty-six northwest of Toul and the Forty-second and the Thirty-second elsewhere in the line.

Melville Stone, the elderly general manager of the Associated Press, arrived in France and had a long session with General Pershing at Chaumont. Mr. Stone had a report of some length on instances where his organization had been beaten by other news services, and he wanted to know why the Associated Press wasn't getting a fair shake from censorship and why so many of its reports trailed half an hour to two hours behind the others. Lieutenant Colonel Palmer, original head of the Press Section under Colonel Nolan, and now one of General Pershing's confidential assistants, sat in the conference.

There was, for instance, the Archibald Roosevelt affair. Mr. Stone had a report on the case which indicated that the A.P. story had been killed, the U.P. story passed. Now for the first time (Colonel Palmer sent for the G-2-D files on the case), he learned the distinction between Captain Roosevelt wounded and Captain Roosevelt decorated with the Croix de Guerre. The explanation did not quite convince him.

Palmer then asked about the Douglas MacArthur case. That officer, too, had been wounded, also decorated, and both wire services had filed almost identical stories at the same time. Yet the A.P. story had trailed U.P. into New York by about two hours. It took somewhat longer to check MacArthur; finally G-2-D found the answer. Draper had filed the story at ordinary press rate; Ferguson had sent it urgent. Stone had a considerable record of stories filed from Paris and Neufchâteau where there was an unexplained lag between the A.P. and the U.P. The A.P. seemed always to get the slowest service and Stone thought there might be discrimination somewhere along the line.

What Mr. Stone did not know, and neither did General Pershing, was that the United Press had made a quiet deal with a French newspaper to take over its leased wire between Paris and Bordeaux, an arrangement which got U.P. copy out of Paris and on the cables faster than any other route.

The conference resulted in the Associated Press gaining one additional accredited correspondent. General Pershing turned down Mr. Stone's request for an automobile for A.P.'s exclusive use at its own expense, but promised to increase the Army cars assigned to press duty to meet the increasing need. The problem of the leased wire and U.P.'s swifter transmission remained undiscovered and, of course, unsolved.

Not long after the conference, an exclusive U.P. story about a new type of gas mask brought fresh trouble to G-2-D. This was an innocent mistake, but again the U.P. scored a minor victory over its rival. On the train from Meaux to Paris Lowell Mellet, one of the U.P.'s pinch-hitting correspondents, got in conversation with a young Army officer who was enthusiastic about a new gas mask just being distributed through the A.E.F. He was happy to give the U.P. man details. The new mask permitted natural breathing through the nose, was light and comfortable, didn't fog the vision area from the wearer's breath, and did away with the awkward box on the chest and the uncomfortable clip on the nose. Mellett, remembering the faulty gas masks that had almost asphyxiated the First Division staff the previous August, knew he had a very good story. The young officer had one of the masks with him. While Mellett tried it on, his informant told him it provided protection against the nine most potent gases, and named all nine.

Mellett intended to take his notes back to Meaux the next day and write the story there, submitting it to censorship in the usual way. But a hurried change in assignments came while he was in Paris. Another U.P. correspondent—Henry Wood—was being shifted from the French front to Italy, and Mellett was reassigned to French G.H.Q. at Chantilly to take his place. With only an hour in Paris, Mellett used the short time to turn out a piece about the new gas masks, not forgetting to list all nine poisonous gases (including mustard and phosgene) which it rendered harmless for its wearers. Mellett turned it over to Webb Miller in triplicate, with one copy for Ed Keen in London and another for Hawkins in New York. Miller agreed that it was a very good story and sent it on its way by mail. The difficulty was that Mellett's piece had not been submitted to censorship.

Published in the United States some ten days later, the gas mask story attracted the attention of eagle-eyed Army men in Washington. The War Department was sensitive on the subject of gas masks, having turned out such an inadequate and cumbersome type in 1917. Its particular complaint was that Mellett's story listed all nine gases which it was designed to thwart. With that information, they complained, German chemists would immediately produce a tenth gas and so render the new masks obsolete.

The complaint from Washington was formidable, and Mellett was called upon for a detailed explanation. His record was good; the circumstances made it apparent that no willful violation of censorship had occurred. The United Press had only told the American people what the Germans learned as soon as they took the first prisoner wearing one of the new masks.

Ten days later the Associated Press became involved in a more serious difficulty with high military authority. A new Associated

Press man, Charles S. Kloeber, accredited in July after Melville Stone's conference with General Pershing, ran across an interesting item in Paris and put it down in his notebook.

Two congressmen, Representatives Ernest Lundeen of Minnesota and C. H. Dillon of South Dakota, had arrived in France to tour the camps and trenches. On the steamship these Middle Western statesmen had aired their pacifist views on deck and in the dining saloon. War was a stupid mistake, they believed, and the whole costly, bloody business ought to be stopped. Being congressmen, they enjoyed a certain immunity from military discipline—or so they fancied; but some of their fellow passengers, irritated by the outspoken pacifism and defeatism, reported their conversations to Military Intelligence (G-2) in Paris. Shortly afterward the two congressmen applied for permission to visit the British front, and the British War Office, in accordance with custom, asked G-2 to endorse the applications. When the American report on their pacifist views reached London, the British promptly turned the two congressmen down. At Paris and Chaumont, Lundeen and Dillon encountered a certain coolness. Their sightseeing was limited to the supply system behind the lines; no opportunity was given them to discuss their views with the troops in the front lines or with the wounded in hospital. Their conducting officer from G-2-D was polite but watchful.

Kloeber picked all this up in Paris, verified it on talking to the two congressmen, and wrote a short, objective piece about it. Mark Watson, one of Colonel Nolan's most experienced and ablest censors, read it thoughtfully and passed it. Its publication in the United States press did not provoke unusual comment, although the Representatives' colleagues in Washington must have been amused. But when the Germans got hold of it and broadcast the item in French, with appropriate comment, from the Nauen radio station, a startled British Intelligence picked it up:

American Congressmen in Europe say people at home want war stopped. Strong pacifist sentiment sweeping U.S.; but Representatives are muzzled by British and American militarists.

The British compiled a report on the affair and protested strongly to General Pershing. There was the inevitable investigation; Captain Francis Wickes (G-2-D) handled the preliminary phase of the inquiry, complaining to Colonel Nolan that apparently a bad lapse of censorship was involved. However, Mark Watson assumed full responsibility for passing the story. Kloeber and the A.P. were exonerated and eventually the case was closed, with an apology to the British.

No one could have foreseen what effective use the Germans would make of the affair on the Nauen radio. However, the information would have been available to the enemy anyway as soon as Representatives Dillon and Lundeen returned home and expressed their indignation to the press. Although at the time the British protest seemed to have merit, and G-2-D took it seriously, the case demonstrated again the futility of an attempt by military authority to conceal its own stupidities and blunders by censorship.

At the time the two congressmen arrived in Europe, the turning point of the war (July 18-19) had passed and German defeat was inevitable. Nothing the two pacifists could see or say along the British battlefront—or elsewhere in France—could have affected the result.

On July 15 the Germans launched a general attack all the way from Reims to the Argonne. It was preceded by heavy artillery fire and gas; then a massed assault with tanks and infantry. The French and Americans in the long line met the blow without giving way, containing the most violent of the enemy's thrusts and blunting his advance.

On July 18 Foch counterattacked in the center. Again Château-Thierry was the focal point of the battle and again the Second Division was called upon to lead the assault. As in the prelude to battle the month before, the Second was thrust into line after a long, exhausting journey in which its components were dispersed and supply system disorganized. It had a new commanding officer, too: General Harbord, who had taken over the Marine Brigade in May, now had been raised to command the division, relieving General Bundy.

On the morning of July 18 Webb Miller was awakened in Paris by a great thunder of guns northeast of the city. For several days the enemy had been attacking all along the center of the line and this ominous rumble might herald the breakthrough. Miller hurried to the U.P. office. Weeks before, Miller, Mellett, Ferguson, and Frank Taylor had worked out a plan for handling U.P. affairs in case the Germans overran the city, and now Miller began to pack the office files and arrange emergency transportation. The morning advanced, the thunder died away to a low growl, and no evidences of panic developed in the city. Maybe the German drive had been stopped.

In mid-afternoon all the correspondents in Paris were summoned to French press headquarters on the Quai d'Orsay. As they crowded in, some of the veteran newspapermen could remember the anxious days in August and September, 1914, when they had waited in the anteroom for the official communiqué. Four years ago tension filled the room and they communicated in low voices. The officials were evasive. Now the atmosphere was changed. There was a cheerful buzzing of voices as the communiqué was handed around.

Foch had delivered the counterthrust through the heart of the German attack, and American divisions were spearheading the drive. That night the communiqué from Chaumont, where Pershing studied the maps, told the story:

> July 18: American troops, cooperating with the French in an attack on the enemy's positions between the Aisne and the Marne, penetrated his lines to a depth of several miles, capturing many prisoners and guns.

That night Miller unpacked the U.P. files and tore up the carefully prepared advance cable describing the German occupation of Paris.

Later, during the Battle of the Ourcq, in which Americans played a leading part, Miller quit the Paris office to fill in for Fred Ferguson for a day or two. It was a novel experience, leaving the telephones and typewriters and the office routine for the great amphitheater of war.

> It should have given me a supreme thrill [Miller wrote about the experience later] actually it was dust and ashes. I felt like a gnat on a huge whirling flywheel. The war took place on such a tremendous scale that when you were close up to it, your mind refused to grasp it. I felt bewildered and obsessed by a sense of futility.

Not long after the counteroffensive of July 18-20, in which the Second Division under General Harbord had achieved solid success, Harbord was summoned to Chaumont by General Pershing and given a new assignment.

A statement announcing the shift was issued by Colonel McCabe for the information of the newspapermen. Major General Francis J. Kernan was being transferred to another duty; his post as chief of the vast Services of Supply was being taken over, on appointment by the Commander-in-Chief, by Major General James G. Harbord. The memorandum to the correspondents bore a footnote:

There is to be no speculation about the causes.

E. R. W. McCabe

The correspondents could not say what many editorial writers in America would be saying in a day or two: General Pershing was so concerned about the supply problems of the A.E.F. that he was taking one of his most successful commanders of troops in the field to reorganize and speed up the laggard services of supply.

The French sent to Chaumont by an officer carrying a dispatch case a number of official envelopes bearing the seal of France and the signatures of high dignitaries. As the war advanced, there were more and more of these, and they were scanned with interest at Chaumont, read aloud at staff meetings, posted on the bulletin boards. On this occasion one envelope bore the name of Floyd Gibbons of the *Chicago Tribune*.

Monsieur Floyd Gibbons, war correspondent of the *Chicago Tribune,* has given on several occasions proof of courage and bravery in going to obtain information in most exposed positions. On June 5, 1918, accompanying a regiment of Marine riflemen who were attacking a wood, he was very seriously wounded by three machine gun bullets while going to the aid of an American wounded officer nearby, thus giving proof in this episode of the finest devotion. Rescued several hours later and carried to a dressing station, he insisted on not being cared for before the wounded who had arrived before him.

Pétain

Monsieur Gibbons had been decorated with the Croix de Guerre, with palm.

Copies of the citation were sent, with a brief announcement, to press headquarters at Meaux and Neufchâteau and to the Paris office at 10 rue Ste. Anne. A messenger carried an official copy to the *Chicago Tribune* office at 420 rue St. Honore. The place was closed for the night. Gibbons was not at Neufchâteau (did anyone remember to inquire at the brewery?) and he had not been seen at Meaux.

The wire services all carried a brief item about the first war correspondent to be decorated for bravery under fire, but neither the *Chicago Tribune* nor its intrepid reporter learned about the honor until the next day.

Gibbons had recovered from his wounds and was back in circulation again. On the night of July 18, he had arrived at General Harbord's Second Division headquarters with Frederick Palmer. The two distinguished figures had a late snack with the general and went over his battle maps. Harbord told about the anxious time he went through the afternoon while aides hunted for Gibbons's corpse. This time, Floyd, the general said, for God's sake keep your head down. Gibbons wore a black triangular patch over his left eye socket, wrote a number of stories about what it feels like to be wounded, and accepted the congratulations of his friends on being alive. Spike Hunt, the *Red Cross Magazine* correspondent, had been hired by the *Chicago Tribune* to take Gibbons's place, as if anyone could, and Gibbons had formally turned over his lodgings in the Neufchâteau brewery to the new man.

There was a party for Gibbons in Paris the night before he sailed for home. Most of the correspondents came in from Meaux, and a number of the 'visiting' group arrived from division headquarters. General Harbord and Nolan, now a brigadier general, made a trip from Chaumont for the occasion. All the principal press officers were there, including Captain Arthur E. Hartzell. There was a very good dinner with champagne, coffee, cigars, and brandy. Fred Ferguson sang 'Nellie and Her Soldier,' a ballad which had enlivened correspondents' affairs at Neufchâteau, Beauvais, and Meaux since April and which was now a minor classic. Gibbons's exploits at Belleau Wood were appropriately set forth in verse. Pershing and Nolan made brief remarks in which sympathy was expressed for the correspondent quitting the good gay life in France for the perils of the U.S. lecture platform. Gibbons replied by giving the group a dress rehearsal of his war lecture, introducing his remarks by saying, 'Now I'm going to show you two-eyed bastards how to make a speech!' The next morning, Gibbons, with his customary good fortune, caught the boat train, and the war was resumed.

XXI

GOOD SHOW AT ST. MIHIEL

On August 16 a group of accredited American correspondents journeyed down from Meaux and called on General Pershing in his new headquarters at Neufchâteau. The general was more relaxed than at previous interviews, and more friendly. As they filed in, the correspondents congratulated Pershing on his new role. He was no longer merely Commander-in-Chief of an amorphous body known as the American Expeditionary Forces in Europe; since August 10 he had been Commanding General, First Army, A.E.F.

Pershing told the newspapermen the critical point of the war had been reached and passed on July 18. Foch's counterstroke, in which the First and Second American Divisions—particularly the Second—had played such a valiant part, had definitely turned the tide in the Allies' favor. From this point on, there could be no shadow of doubt about ultimate victory; the only question was how much longer it would be deferred.

The general called their attention to a curious change in the French attitude since July 18. Up to that date the French communiqués had emphasized every American advance and every American skirmish as an achievement. In June, after the affair at the Marne and northwest of Château-Thierry, Clemenceau had credited the Americans with saving Paris. Earlier, in the Montdidier sector, the French had praised the First Division for repulsing a German attack that never occurred. Partly to bolster their own morale, and also to stimulate the A.E.F. to greater exertions, the French had been lavish in their praise and official appreciation.

On July 19, somewhat abruptly, the French began to minimize the accomplishments of the Americans and shifted emphasis to their own arms. General Pershing did not seem disturbed by the change in French policy, but he thought the newspapermen ought to know about it. He did not expect them to redress the balance by exaggerating U.S. battle achievements and belittling the French. However, he expected the A.E.F. would soon play a larger role in the war, and he did not want its future accomplishments obscured. The important thing was that from now on the Americans would be on their own. He reminded them what he had said at Chaumont a year ago: the line would be broken; soldiers should be trained to climb out of the trenches and use their rifles against the enemy in the open.

For months the newspapermen had looked forward, not so much to spectacular open warfare, as to the time when American forces would take their place in the line as an army. All of them knew about Pershing's long, stubborn fight to retain the integrity of the A.E.F. and prevent its being distributed piecemeal, by brigades or divisions, among the British and French. This was one of the things they respected Pershing for. It made up for a lot of his rigidity, military arrogance, and maladroit handling of the press. He had laid down as a first principle that the Americans should eventually fight as an army, a major unit, and would receive credit or blame for what they did or failed to do. Some of the correspondents realized against what odds he had adhered to that basic policy. Although the British and French had agreed to it soon after the U.S. entered the war, they reopened the question and tried to have it changed at every inter-Allied war conference. When Pershing refused to budge, the British and French worked on President Wilson and Secretary Baker through their ambassadors in Washington and various war missions to the United States. They worked through the State Department. Pétain, Foch, Haig, General Sir Henry Wilson, Lloyd George, Clemenceau—all worked to undermine that policy and none gave up hope.

Events in March gave them temporary ascendancy. When the Germans achieved a temporary breakthrough and a crisis brought unified Allied command under Foch, Pershing had promptly placed the entire U.S. force in France at the marshal's disposal to use where and how he would. It was pursuant to that crisis that American divisions were moved to Picardy, put in to check the enemy's advance into Château-Thierry, shifted to half a dozen sectors in June and July. It was a regiment, not an army, that took Cantigny;

a division, not an army, that drove the Germans out of Belleau Wood; a team of two divisions that counterattacked and broke through at Château-Thierry-Soissons—not an army.

Cantigny, Belleau Wood, Château-Thierry-Soissons, all successes, and all except the last local and limited; all carried out under French generals and in co-operation with French troops. Now in the summer of 1918, the emergency which had placed American forces at Foch's disposal was ended. The time had arrived when American divisions could be welded into an American Army—and that American Army would have its own artillery, tanks, air reconnaissance, planning, intelligence. At last it could be assigned a major objective, not just a few hundred yards of trenches. It could organize, plan, and carry out battle on a grand scale.

What could they write about all this? Not much. However, as they left the general's office, the correspondents knew they would not have much longer to wait. Pershing was putting his Army together, studying maps, shuffling the staff, building up bases. The calendar was edging toward September.

There was another press conference ten days later. The general gave the impression that his plans were maturing. A tentative date had been set, but he would not talk about it except to warn the newspapermen not to set their sights too high.

'Don't win the war on this one,' General Pershing advised.

At Meaux the next day, there was a curious sequel to the general's guarded comment. Captain de Viel Castel, French liaison officer, returned from the French 'Grand Quartier' and told a group of correspondents confidentially that a drive into Alsace by the American First Army was an interesting possibility. A glance at the map showed that such an offensive might capture Mulhouse on German soil, only ten miles from the Rhine. Captain de Viel Castel was enthusiastic about the possibilities: the morale effect would be substantial; Rhine bridges could be destroyed, thus crippling German communications. Choosing his words with care, the French officer suggested that if the correspondents went about it guardedly, not hinting too much, the censors might pass some thinly veiled allusions as to the likelihood of such an offensive. 'Of course,' he added, 'I do not say that the Americans will do that, but it is an interesting possibility, and I am sure Captain Morgan would pass carefully worded dispatches.'

Some of the correspondents swallowed the bait and wrote fuzzy think pieces about Alsace. Those who knew their Civil War history recalled that at Cairo early in 1862, General U. S. Grant's adjutant, Major Rawlins, had called the newspapermen together and announced a great expedition across the river into Kentucky, urging them to write about it. A few recognized the strategem, as in de Viel Castel's case, as an attempt to use the press to mislead the enemy. This raised a puzzling question: should correspondents write speculative stories on future operations, knowing them to be false, to help conceal the Army's real purposes?

At about the same time the newspapermen at Meaux were struggling with this question, a courier with highly secret orders was on the way to General Omar Bundy. General Bundy was at dinner with his staff in Bourbonne-les-Bains. The orders directed him to proceed with his staff to Belfort and take up quarters already reserved at the Grand Hôtel du Tonneau d'Or. There more secret orders awaited. The general was to plan a great offensive through Alsace to Mulhouse and the Rhine.

Because of its location near the Swiss border, Belfort was a favorite rendezvous of spies and a great clearing house for secret information, questionable documents, gossip, rumors. General Bundy began to organize his plan, and the hotel filled up with an odd assortment of tourists, salesmen, sketch artists, Swiss businessmen and other nonchalants. The waiters and chambermaids listened and passed along bits of information. Scraps of paper were retrieved from waste baskets; coins clinked. The word reached German Intelligence: the Americans are going to make a big push in Alsace. The German high command examined the evidence and made dispositions accordingly.

Meanwhile, back at Meaux, the newspapermen, ignorant where the blow was to be struck, suddenly were made aware that the great day was about to dawn. The press officers developed an unusual interest in their movements. What happened to Fred Ferguson probably is typical of the experience of most of the group.

Captain Morgan asked him one evening where he had been that day. Ferguson told him: Along the Vesle, visiting a couple of hospitals, an airfield, a division officers' mess, a Y.M.C.A. hut. Captain Morgan copied the route.

'You will go to the same places every day from now on,' Morgan told him. 'The same roads, the same hospitals; have lunch at the same mess. Do not vary your rounds. The same Y.M.C.A. hut.' Ferguson protested there was no news in the system of following the same route every day. Morgan brushed his objections aside. No matter. All correspondents must do the same. The press at Meaux was believed to be under scrutiny by German Intelligence, the press cars were spotted. The Germans knew that any movement by the correspondents in a new direction probably meant a new offensive. By freezing the pattern of press activity German spies or air reconnaissance would get no clues.

'We must not give them any grounds to suspect that an American offensive is in the works, or, especially, any hint of where it may be,' Morgan said.

Day after day for nearly a week the reporters got in their cars in the morning and followed the same roads, called at the same camps and canteens, like supernumeraries playing small parts in a pageant.

The night of September 10 the correspondents at the Hôtel Sirène in Meaux were advised to pack their gear and get ready for an early morning departure. Aroused before dawn, they were informed at breakfast that the press cars would load and leave the town at twenty-minute intervals. Just at daybreak half a dozen German shells fell on Meaux not far from the Sirène. Some leak, perhaps a concentration of vehicles, had told the enemy that something was up, and the shells, which did no harm, merely served notice that the Germans were keeping a watch on the newspapermen's movements.

There were eight cars in the straggling caravan, three correspondents to a car. The departure from Meaux required nearly three hours. Ahead, almost due east, stretched a journey of 250 kilometers which they made at an unobtrusive pace, with a 2-hour pause for lunch. It was dark when the last of the correspondents' cars drew up before the Hotel Angleterre in Nancy.

Even after the objective of the American First Army's operation had been agreed upon and preliminary dispositions made, the French High Command made one last effort to scrap the plan and distribute the divisions Pershing had assembled among the British and French armies. Foch called on the American general with his new proposal. Presumably that last attempt was urged by the Briton, Sir Henry Wilson, recently promoted to Chief of the Imperial General Staff, who didn't think much of the American capacity to wage war. ('Foch wants us to do all the work. The French are not fighting at all, and the Americans don't know how, so all falls to us.')

There was a stormy scene between Foch and Pershing. Foch asserted his authority as Allied Generalissimo and called on the American to obey his order. Pershing acknowledged Foch's authority as supreme commander but said he could not properly use it to break up the American First Army. He faced the angry Frenchman across the table. Foch stared at him and shrugged his shoulders and walked out. Then he came back and they shook hands, unsmiling. The matter had been decided.

In accordance with the agreement the headquarters of the First Army, A.E.F., were moved up to Ligny-en-Barrois. There the command of the sector which had been assigned was ceremoniously transferred to the Americans. If any low-flying German aviators with powerful binoculars had been in the vicinity they would surely have been mystified at what took place. It was quite formal. The French general and his staff turned out in their peacetime dress uniforms—blue tunics and bright red trousers. There was a ruffle of drums, and colors were massed and saluted with an exchange of courtesies. Everybody shook hands with his opposite number. The French general handed over to General Pershing two bound volumes, each of about 150 pages, one for the defense of the sector, the other for an offensive. General Pershing thanked the French general. The Americans had prepared plans, too, for operations in their new zone, one of eight pages, the other, six.

The name of the sector assigned to the Americans was St. Mihiel.

A map of St. Mihiel was pinned on the wall of General Nolan's corner room on an upper floor of the Hotel Angleterre, as the twenty-five American correspondents were ushered in after dinner. They sat on beds, on the floor, on the edge of a table, on the window sill. The air was heavy with tobacco. There was some ten·sion, too. The newspapermen had waited a long time for this.

General Nolan took some of the edge off the occasion by emphasizing the fact that this was a strictly limited operation, more of a sharp jab than a knockout blow. Nevertheless, the reduction of the St. Mihiel salient presented an interesting opportunity. St. Mihiel was a formidable, wooded projection which the Germans had held since early in the war. Thrust out into the surrounding country, it gave the enemy useful artillery positions and enabled him to observe Allied activities over a wide area. The French had tried several times to dislodge the Germans from the elevated perch, but the attempts had fallen short.

The American First Army's attack, General Nolan explained, was to be in two parts, following the artillery preparation, with U.S. forces driving in from the south and west, converging on Vigneulles. With luck they might achieve their goal in a couple of days and bag some German prisoners and matériel. They hoped to take the enemy by surprise.

The brigadier warned the newspapermen not to attach too much significance to the operation, reminding them what Pershing had said two weeks before: 'Don't win the war on this one.' No nonsense about pushing on to Metz or achieving a breakthrough. For background, he reminded them again that this was an all-American show. Americans had planned it, drawn up the schedules, and organized the supply and support timetable. American artillery would prepare the way. Pershing was in direct command, and Secretary Baker had arrived for the occasion. He and Pershing would watch the rolling barrage and the jump-off from old Fort Gironville on a height to the south.

A special telegraph wire had been strung by the Signal Corps from Nancy to Paris. This would be available for the transmission of press messages. In addition, there would be the regular telegraph facilities from the Nancy post office. The barrage would begin between 3:30 and 4:00 A.M. and it might be possible to see something of it from the roof of the Angleterre.

This was the first time the correspondents had been taken so fully into the Army's confidence. Some of them must have been a little dazed, others nervously elated, as they left General Nolan's room around midnight to seek their separate quarters.

For the two new Associated Press men this was an anxious occasion. James P. Howe, son of the famous Sage of Atchison,

Kansas, Ed Howe, and Burge McFall got along better with the other correspondents than 'Ninety Million' Draper, whom they had replaced in July, but they lacked experience. The Associated Press had suffered another competitive lapse at the time of the great German offensive July 14-16, and Draper, who had asserted the senior Press Association's prerogatives so vigorously and tactlessly, finally departed. The new men had come in cold, breaking in in the desultory fighting alone the Vesle in August. As they left Nolan's briefing, the young A.P. correspondents realized that this was bigger than anything yet, and they were up against some very tough competition. How tough it was the next few hours would disclose.

Fred Ferguson went to his room and began writing. The brigadier's talk and his map had told the U.P. man all he needed to know. This was a big thing indeed, in spite of Nolan's warning about 'limited objective.' The old pro in him surveyed the scene and went to work. The old rivalry with the Associated Press, privileged plutocrat of the wire services, gave him zest as he arranged carbon paper in books and rolled the first take into his typewriter. A paragraph bulletin to launch the attack as soon as the barrage lifted. Then another paragraph putting the attack in motion, storming the enemy's positions. In short takes, each one summarizing the main theme, Ferguson projected the story of St. Mihiel through the first day. Each page emphasized that it was the first full-scale attack by an all-American Army, directed by General Pershing. Each page was so constructed that if the others were lost or delayed and only one got through, it would tell the story. He timed each take, marking on it the hour when he thought it might safely be released, according to the timetable. Written entirely before the fact, it was made up of probabilities, but if Nolan knew what he was talking about and the divisions moved in as they should, this was what would happen.

It was about 2:30 in the morning when Ferguson rapped on Gerald Morgan's door. The chief censor was asleep but Ferguson got him out of bed. Together they went over the typed pages. The United Press man explained he wasn't trying to beat the gun and didn't want to send anything, even a flash, until Morgan gave the word. But he explained how he had projected the story through the day and asked Morgan to censor the copy in advance and then release it when the facts were established. Morgan agreed that this seemed legitimate procedure on such an important story and, after carefully reading all of Ferguson's short paragraphs, stamped them 'approved,' marked them hold for release, and signed his initials. It was agreed that Morgan would turn them over to one of his assistant press officers, who would file them when reports from the front justified.

Ferguson marked his messages 'urgent,' specifying the highest rate for cable transmission; he also sent them 'P.Q.,' ordinary telegraph from the Nancy post office, rather than the special Signal Corps wire to Paris. He had a hunch that the special wire would either get jammed up with a lot of other press messages or break down. Finally, Fergie sent four copies, each by a different route— one via London; a second via Bordeaux; a third via Buenos Aires; a fourth via Malta, Singapore, and Pacific cable to San Francisco. He had a couple of hours' sleep and just before dawn joined his fellow correspondents on the hotel roof. They watched the flashes on the northwest horizon and listened to the low growl and rumble of the guns.

At breakfast, the talk was all about getting up to the front. All the wire servicemen, including Howe and McFall, had filed brief flashes with the censors to be held, like Ferguson's copy, for release. Major A. L. James, Jr., who had taken Colonel McCabe's place as Chief Field Press Officer, invited Ferguson to ride up to the front in his car. The U.P. man said thanks, he'd like to, but only on condition his own U.P. car trailed behind. The major said that was all right with him, but Fergie needn't worry. No worry at all, Ferguson said, but I'm responsible for the car and I like to keep an eye on it. Besides, it just might come in handy later in the day. Suit yourself, the major said.

As they started out, James asked the two A.P. men, Howe and McFall, to ride along with them. When they learned Ferguson was going, the A.P. team said 'Sure.' This was a good thing. They would all go together and could keep an eye on him. Off they started on the twenty-five-mile drive, Major James, the two A.P. men and Fred Ferguson; and trailing behind, empty except for its driver, the U.P. car, under instructions to stay close and keep within hail.

It was a drizzly, foggy day with a cold wind blowing, but they were warmed by expectation. Excitement mounted as they approached the great wooded slope. St. Mihiel was smoldering and smoking and spluttering, and the din of battle came across the fields through the drizzle. They reached the scene of the jump-off in mid-morning and followed the thrust of the tanks and infantry, watched files of German prisoners being marched to the rear, and talked to some of the wounded. An hour before noon, they heard from the attack on the other side of the salient. That, too, was going well. Everything was on schedule, the Germans making only token resistance; American casualties were light. At a luncheon stop, eating cold infantry rations, the A.P. talked about getting back to Nancy. Major James had disappeared, summoned to First Army headquarters. Ferguson's car was waiting nearby, but he wasn't ready to go back yet. Howe and McFall tried to get a ride elsewhere, but all vehicles heading back to Nancy were crowded or the cars were headed somewhere else. In mid-afternoon, they found themselves dependent on their chief rival for transportation, and Ferguson, heedless of their pleas, stayed on at the edge of the battle scene. He was sure his early stuff would tell the whole story; his rivals probably had sent only a brief flash. So he dawdled and delayed the return until almost six. It was seven when they walked into the crowded press office on the Place Stanislaus in Nancy.

A cheerful cry greeted Ferguson. 'Hey, Fergie! Here's a wire from New York.'

The message said: CONGRATULATIONS ON YOUR GREATEST BEAT. HOWARD. The other newspapermen crowded around. 'Well, Fergie, you've done it again!'

In three days at St. Mihiel the American First Army recovered 150 square miles from the Germans and took 15,000 prisoners. The two thrusts from opposite sides of the salient came together, pinching off thousands of the enemy, capturing guns and supplies.

Progress was so rapid that the advance schedules were surpassed. Metz seemed easily attainable; the early pace would have enabled the Army to reach it in less than ten days. Some of the newspapermen couldn't understand why the plan wasn't revised to take advantage of the demoralized enemy and the Army's momentum. A bold follow-up might win the war, the optimists thought. But none of this could be put on paper. The censors were particularly careful to eliminate any mention of Metz. General Pershing didn't want the American people to expect the capture of that city and then be disappointed. On the other hand, the Army planners didn't want the Germans to know for sure that the advance would be halted short of Metz. So the newspapermen made what they could of the day-by-day progress and avoided any speculation about the future.

St. Mihiel was Fred Ferguson's biggest beat: the high point of the U.P.'s war coverage. He had been right about the special wire to Paris; it was jammed with an overload of messages and it did break down. Other transmission troubles developed further along the line. Ferguson's elaborate and costly cable directions, using four routes, sped his copy to the United States ahead of all others. To most of the reading public a few hours more or less in the publication of war news didn't make a great deal of difference; the fierce rivalry between newspapers and press associations must have seemed silly. But to those in the business, speed was the essence of news gathering, and the difference of a few minutes meant getting an extra on the street ahead of a rival. The U.P.'s lead over the other news services gave its subscribers both circulation and prestige in the race for street-corner sales.

Fergie was in his element at St. Mihiel. A veteran of five months with the Army, he had made friends in most of the divisions engaged there, from generals to privates. He had learned where to go and whom to talk to, how much the censors would pass, when he could identify an officer or a regiment and when he couldn't. His two A.P. rivals were new and still relatively unfamiliar with the ropes.

For three days Fergie ran them ragged and maintained the lead he had established on the first day. One night, walking along the corridor of the Angleterre, he paused in the doorway of the A.P. room. Howe and McFall were bent over a map of the St. Mihiel salient, trying to trace the latest advance and anticipate what would happen next. They were too absorbed to notice the little man standing in the doorway. He heard one of them say: 'What d'ya suppose that bastard wrote about today?'

'Boys,' Ferguson said, 'the war's over.' They looked up from the map, not fully comprehending. 'From now on,' the U.P. man continued, 'let's call it quits and be friends.' Howe and McFall might have pointed out that Ferguson's gesture came a little late; St. Mihiel was played out. But they took his offer at face value, and all three went down to the bar for a drink. The next day Ferguson took the two younger correspondents out with him, introduced them to many of his friends, and worked with them in developing the day's news. He suggested angles, advised them on censorship, and told them how he planned his work in advance. For several days he traveled with them during the day and fussed over their stories at night. As a result, the A.P. coverage improved and the U.P. didn't get any worse.

The war had reached a stage by mid-September when the correspondents' feuds and rivalries were becoming submerged in greater involvement with battle and in increasing weariness. There was no longer the compulsion nor the energy to scheme and outwit and dissemble. The Army was changing too.

XXII

THE LOST BATTALION

After St. Mihiel (Sept. 12-16), there was no further talk of breaking up the A.E.F. to fight under the French and British. Pershing's First Army had achieved its limited objective on schedule, proving it could plan and fight. The position was consolidated. Corps artillery moved up into the recaptured terrain. Fresh troops came in to relieve the battle veterans, dug in, and fought off counterattacks. The casualties were back in the base hospitals. The show was over. A few of the correspondents drifted back to Paris. Some discovered the flesh pots of Nancy.

Even as the daily communiqués lapsed to static dullness and the newspapermen yawned, there was renewed activity behind the scenes. The last ambulances rolling down the slopes from St. Mihiel toward the base hospitals passed a fresh surge of Army traffic. There was a great movement of troops along the back roads to the West at night. From the sea ports and Harbord's base at Tours, the services of supply moved train loads of weapons and ammunition, gasoline, mountains of food and winter clothing up to advance bases. And in Paris, through the doorway at 10 rue Ste. Anne, lecturers, writers, poets, preachers, teachers, editors, publicists, statesmen, people with letters from George Creel, friends of generals and of Secretary Baker, all moved with their passes and travel orders off to tour the camps and read the famous battle names on roadside signs.

Three months before, on June 21, Mark Watson had written a long memorandum to Colonel McCabe suggesting the formation of an Army news bureau. American troops, he reminded the colonel, were scattered over a wide area. Facilities for keeping track of developments were poor. The correspondents were perpetually dissatisfied, and they demanded more and more transportation. Even if the Army provided each correspondent with his own car, none would be able to cover the whole war scene.

Meanwhile, Watson warned the colonel, the Committee on Public Information wanted to establish its own outfit at G.H.Q. The War Department was taking this seriously. To Captain Watson the proposal seemed unthinkable. Once the Creel camel got its nose in the Chaumont tent, the A.E.F. would have to share control of news and censorship.

The answer to both of these pressing problems, Watson argued, could be found in an Army news bureau, collecting and co-ordinating information from division headquarters, making it available in timely digests to all the correspondents. A press officer with each division would report the division's activities daily, and a special Information Officer at headquarters would collect and evaluate the reports.

Colonel McCabe may have discussed Watson's proposal with Nolan and Sweeney, but at the time nothing much came of it. The West Point mind, as Herb Corey had observed to Henry Suydam some months before, was not receptive to new ideas, and an Army news bureau was clearly foreign to U.S. military tradition. General Nolan may have pointed out that the Army recently had reversed its policy on 'visiting' correspondents, affording newspaper coverage of individual divisions. The number of accredited correspondents had been increased to 25. Besides, a part of General Nolan's organization already was functioning as an Army information service, collecting daily reports for intelligence purposes from all sections of the front where the A.E.F. was engaged and sifting material for the daily official communiqué. (Watson might have argued that this was of little value to the newspapermen because of its reticence and military doubletalk, and a frequent time lag of two or three days.) There was, however, an occasional squawk from officers at headquarters that A.E.F. information facilities were not keeping pace with the growing military giant. Major Thomas Catron complained to G-2-D in July that some news from Second Division headquarters was appearing in the *Paris Herald* before it was received at G.H.Q. This was the work of Don Martin. Major Catron had no objection to the news items, except for the use of some names, but he resented the fact that they got into print in Paris before the information reached official channels at Chaumont.

Watson's suggestion was rejected at the time, but one step was taken which would lead to its fulfillment. That was the appointment of Captain Arthur E. Hartzell as Information Officer, G-2-D. This new post was created primarily to gather news for the old press headquarters at Neufchâteau. The wire services still maintained correspondents there, for it was handy to Chaumont and was the center of important staging operations. However, it was too far from the front lines to serve as a main base for correspondents. It had been overlooked in the rush of events around Château-Thierry early in June, and the wire service men complained bitterly at the lapse. The new Information Office was to make sure that Neufchâteau was not ignored again. He soon outgrew the original concept of his job.

At St. Mihiel for the first time Captain Hartzell collected information from division and corps headquarters and posted daily digests on the bulletin board at Nancy. Correspondents found the service useful. Press service teams divided up; one man rode out to the front each morning, the other remaining behind in the press headquarters on Stanislaus Place to wait for Hartzell's daily round-up. The information bulletins also were telephoned to Neufchâteau and Chaumont.

The service begun under Hartzell's direction at St. Mihiel was now extended and strengthened. Newly arriving divisions were combed for officers and men with newspaper experience. Press officers were given brief training and assigned to division or brigade headquarters. Communication methods were discussed with the Signal Corps. As the First Army regrouped and refitted for its next operation, the Army News Bureau suggested by Mark Watson in June was taking shape.

On September 25, the official communiqué said: 'The day passed quietly in the sectors occupied by our troops,' giving no clue to what was in the wind. In the afternoon, the newspapermen left the Hotel Angleterre in Nancy and rode westward, retracing about a third of the distance back to Meaux. Their destination, known only to a few, was Bar-le-Duc. That night they assembled in their new press headquarters, a small store up a cobbled side street. Blackout blankets hung at doors and windows. The only illumination came from oil lamps and candles.

There may have been as many as fifty newsmen crowded in the small room. Many were new. Major James had been succeeded as Chief Field Press Officer by a genial, slow-spoken sports writer from the *New York Evening World,* Major Bozeman Bulger. Out of his military experience with the New York National Guard, Bulger had conducted an officers' training school for newspapermen early in 1917 in the old 69th Regiment Armory. Now, after service with the Seventy-seventh Division, he had been transferred to G-2-D and was to carry on, with Gerald Morgan's help, the work begun by Frederick Palmer fifteen months before. Damon Runyon, one of Hearst's sport writers, was there for Universal Service. Newly accredited reporters included Bernard J. O'Donnell of the *Cincinnati Enquirer;* Guy C. Hickok of the *Brooklyn Eagle;* two men from Pittsburgh, George S. Applegarth of *The Post* and Charles J. Doyle of the *Gazette Times.* Among the dozen 'visiting' correspondents (white brassards and red C's) who crowded around the walls were two old-timers, Frank Sibley of the *Boston Globe* and Otto Higgins of the *Kansas City Star.* Walter S. Ball was there for the *Providence Journal.* The 1917 veterans formed a little group apart—Lincoln Eyre, Tom Johnson, Junius Wood, Herb Corey, Ray Carroll, and Wilbur Forrest.

A distinguished guest crowded in among the newspapermen and found a seat on a table, up near the front. He was an English officer, a little bantam rooster of a man with much bounce and with intense hatred of the Germans. Lloyd George's personal observer on the American front, he had passed the day touring the forward area and now was on hand for the jump-off briefing.

Major General Fox Connor stood up before the big map—it covered the whole front wall—and began to talk about the sector where the First Army would attack the next morning, and how it fitted into Foch's grand strategy. The American troops were going to strike—General Connor pointed with his pencil—between the River Meuse and the Argonne forest. The operation was aimed at the hinge of the German line. He pointed out where it headed, his pencil resting on Sedan. If they could cut the railroad there, the Germans would be finished! But the German high command knew the importance of that position and would undoubtedly fight fiercely to protect it.

The American command, General Connor said, had been given one of the toughest assignments along the whole front. They might have to lose thousands of lives in order to end the war and save tens of thousands. The general thought there might be a good deal of criticism back home if the attack bogged down and the casualties started piling up. He wanted the newspapermen's opinion of what public sentiment might make of the situation.

The War Department and General Pershing had become increasingly sensitive to public opinion in the United States. Critics of the Administration were beginning to point out that the war was costing a lot of money, that the people had given General Pershing everything he asked, ships, guns, planes, millions of men, billions of treasure, and still the war was a bloody stalemate. Another area for criticism lay in the suggestion that the A.E.F. was now being given all the tough and dangerous jobs, while the British and French stayed snug in their trenches.

The correspondents were thoughtful as General Connor developed his theme. Some of them wondered at the touchiness of the military caste. As long as they did their job and won the war, why worry about public opinion? But General Connor wanted some reassurance. The newspapermen were supposed to reflect the views of their editors.

'Well, General,' Junius Wood said after an interval of silence, 'I think the people at home are just beginning to find out there's a war.'

As Junius made this sage observation, there was a clatter and a crash. The little English officer had fallen asleep and rolled off the table onto the floor. The spell was broken. General Connor let public opinion take its course and returned to his map to point out the possibilities and pitfalls of the task the First Army was undertaking.

The terrain ahead was difficult, tougher than St. Mihiel. The enemy had taken advantage of every hill and clump of rocks; he had installed a vast complex of trenches and support positions, machine gun nests, pill boxes, tank traps, acres of barbed wire. A network of roads and narrow-gauge railways reinforced the German position. Behind the American lines, only two good north and south roads afforded access for supplies and ammunition. All this went into the correspondents' notebooks in the dim, smoky press headquarters in Bar-le-Duc. And one thing more. This time there was to be no limited objective; this was battle to the finish.

At daybreak most of the correspondents climbed in their cars and made their way northward from Bar-le-Duc to see the surge of American forces into the battle that might decide the war. It was a long, exhausting day. By noon they knew that the German front line had broken and the attack was gaining momentum. They also were aware that the operation was too big for personal experience. There was not much they could see that made sense. About all they could do was to record scenes in the confused rear areas; prisoners straggling back, ambulances and Army trucks crawling along the roads, artillery moving up. Nearly all the newspapermen encountered some significant portents of the battle raging up ahead, but none had it in perspective. They were glad to get back to Bar-le-Duc late in the afternoon to find out what had happened.

September 26: This morning northwest of Verdun the First Army attacked the enemy on a front of 20 miles and penetrated his lines to an average depth of seven miles.

Pennsylvania, Kansas and Missouri troops serving in Major General Hunter Liggett's corps stormed Varennes, Montblainville, Vauquois and Cheppy after stubborn resistance. Troops of other corps, crossing the Forges Brook, captured the Bois de Forges and wrestled from the enemy the towns of Malancourt, Bethincourt, Montfaucon, Cuisy, Nantillois, Septsarges, Dannevoux and Gercourt-et-Drillancourt. The prisoners thus far reported number over 5,000.

By the time the communiqué was issued at 9 P.M. and the first bulletins ready for filing, the good news was dampened by a call from Paris. The French had issued their own communiqué hours before; the correspondents at Chantilly had it, and it had been given out at the Bureau de la Presse in Paris:

At five o'clock this morning the French troops attacked in the Champagne in conjunction with the American Army further to the east.

Again the American correspondents had been beaten on their own story. First news of the combined operation, with emphasis on the French gains in the Champagne, was already on the cables to

America. Some of the edge had been taken off of it, but the breakthrough by the American First Army was still the great development of an eventful day. The correspondents at Bar-le-Duc worked on it until long after midnight.

The next few days demonstrated the value of the Army's new information service. As the Meuse-Argonne attack developed, reports poured in to Captain Hartzell by motorcycle couriers and Signal Corps wires. Almost as promptly as front line changes were disclosed to Pershing at First Army headquarters, the gains and counterattacks were reported to Bar-le-Duc and posted on the bulletin board. Now, almost for the first time, Army and newspapermen worked as a team. A few of the correspondents still rode to the forward areas in press cars and went on foot to the edge of the fighting, but such trips usually provided only adventures in confusion—color, not news. One of the Pittsburgh correspondents, convinced of the futility of trying to cover the battle at first hand, established himself at the bar of the 'Metz et Commerce' in Bar-le-Duc and announced to each newly arrived group: 'I'll buy a drink for anybody here from Pittsburgh.' Occasionally a fellow Pennsylvanian drifted in, accepted the offer, and traded what little he knew for the correspondent's hospitality. Most of the newspapermen, particularly the wire service men—Fred Ferguson, Howe and McFall, and Archie Parke—stayed at press headquarters and watched the shifting pins on the map and Hartzell's bulletins.

The attack slowed down. As General Connor had predicted, the enemy defense stiffened. In four days, the American offensive had ground to a halt. Meanwhile, a report came in from Lieutenant Kidder Mead, press officer of I Corps. The advance of the Seventy-seventh Division in the Argonne Forest had left a gap in the line and enemy squads had begun to filter in behind the New Yorkers. Mead, a Southerner who had worked for the *New York World,* studied the terrain map and realized that in a day or two the battalion commanded by Major Whittlesey would be cut off from the rest of the division. He knew a human interest situation when he saw one. The correspondents at Bar-le-Duc got Mead's first bulletin on Sept. 29. The real story unfolded four days later. On October 3 the battalion was finally cut off, isolated, completely surrounded by the enemy. That night in the smoke-filled tension of Bar-le-Duc press headquarters, the Lost Battalion was born. Mead

continued, twice a day, to report the situation from corps headquarters, and many of the newspapermen journeyed over to the
Seventy-seventh Division to learn the latest news from Whittlesey.
Suspense built up: the battalion had been called on to surrender.
The men had run out of food. Nearly all their ammunition was
gone. One or two messengers managed to crawl through enemy
pickets at night to report the desperate plight of the Americans.
Surrender? The newspapermen, banking on Whittlesey, framed an
appropriate reply to the German commander: 'Go to hell!' By
October 7, when the tired Lost Battalion finally was relieved, all
America was following the perilous adventure in the Argonne
Forest.

Bozeman Bulger and Damon Runyon rode over to Seventy-
seventh Division headquarters that morning and then visited the
hospital where Captain McMurty and others had been taken. They
rounded up the details: how the men had fought and dug in, sleepless, hungry, thirsty, somehow keeping together, sharing their last
rounds of ammunition. Those first hand accounts were carried
back to Bar-le-Duc that night and given to the rest of the correspondents.

General Alexander protested to the censors that the Lost Battalion never was really lost, that the story was grossly overplayed.
Major Whittlesey wasn't happy to find himself a national hero.

Except for overemphasis on the Lost Battalion story, the correspondents did a first rate job on the Meuse-Argonne offensive. In
its official report to the War Department, G-2-D made special
mention of the newspapermen's work on the culminating American
offensive:

The Meuse-Argonne story was a very hard one to write and the
correspondents wrote it remarkably well. At a time when unfriendly
critics were sharpening their knives and getting ready to call the
A.E.F. a failure the twenty-five accredited correspondents were pounding away at the facts. They pointed out day by day that the American
Army was up against the principle [sic] hinge of the German line, which
the Germans had to hold at all costs, with the most and the best troops,
no matter what defeats they suffered elsewhere. The correspondents
pointed out over and over again why the Germans had to fight to the
death in this sector. They pointed out that the terrain was more difficult than anywhere else on the whole front and described that terrain

first hand. They pointed out the difficulties of communication over only two north and south roads. They kept pounding away at facts, facts, facts. They did a good American piece of work and had the United States forces not broken through before the Armistice and silenced detractors that way, they would have been the principal witnesses in a not too easy defense. Between September 26 and November 11 they justified all the confidence which had heretofore been placed in them, and their work was worthy of all praise.

Driving back to Bar-le-Duc one afternoon one of the press chauffeurs tried to pass an Army truck on a narrow road. Three correspondents in the car had warned him to take it easy, but the driver was a speed demon and anxious to prove it. Halfway past the truck, unable to see the traffic ahead, he smashed into another heavy vehicle coming the other way.

Fred Ferguson, who stood up in the rear seat at the moment of impact, was catapulted over the windshield. Herb Corey and Henry Wales, a new I.N.S. man, were thrown violently against the dashboard. First aid arrived in a few minutes. Somebody pointed to Ferguson's recumbent figure lying at the roadside and said, 'No use doing anything for him—he's dead,' so the medical corps man opened his kit and started to patch up the bruised, bleeding Corey and Wales. This took some time. Next they looked around for Ferguson. He was gone. A search revealed him walking along the road a quarter of a mile away. When they overtook him, Ferguson did not know where he was or recall what had happened. But he did know that he had to get to Bar-le-Duc and write a story. He seemed to have a headache.

A day or two later in Paris, Ferguson was at 10 rue Ste. Anne, trying to write an 'anniversary' story for the U.P. to show what the A.E.F. had accomplished in its first year in France. It was an important job, but Fergie was having trouble locating the right typewriter keys, and even more trouble remembering his theme. Mark Watson saw that he was not well and sent for an A.E.F. doctor. He looked Ferguson over, took his temperature and pulse, and looked into his eyes. Then he sent him to bed. He was walking around with a bad concussion. For the next several days the A.P. breathed easier until Ferguson was on his feet again. The dynamic little U.P. correspondent was more and more becoming a thorn in the side of his opposition.

XXIII

TOO SOON THE GOOD NEWS

On a cold, rainy afternoon in October Captain Gerald Morgan came out of the telegraph room at Bar-le-Duc press headquarters and in a voice trembling with emotion read a bulletin just received from Paris. The Germans proposed an armistice to discuss peace on the basis of President Wilson's Fourteen Points.

Since the collapse of the Bulgarian front on September 29, the newspaper correspondents had been watching for signs of the enemy's disintegration. On the Meuse-Argonne front, resistance seemed as stubborn as ever. The American First Army had to fight for every hill, every crossroads, every ruined village taken in its grinding advance. Yet as October advanced, the German position deteriorated along the whole front from Asia Minor to the North Sea. Following the first American assault in the Meuse-Argonne the British had attacked on the St. Quentin-Cambrai front; then a Belgian army with Allied support struck toward Ghent. Foch was co-ordinating all the Allied forces in a series of hammer blows. On the Piave, an Italian offensive had split the Austrian armies; weakened by internal decay, Austria had lost the will to fight and on October 30 asked for an armistice. General Allenby's advance through Palestine and Syria reached Damascus, and Turkey was finished. Now Germany wanted an armistice. Victory was in the air. It was November, 1918.

Fred Ferguson, summoned to Paris for a conference with Roy Howard and W. Philip Simms, left Webb Miller at Bar-le-Duc to cover the Meuse-Argonne offensive launched November 1 for the United Press. The new offensive provided stirring news for the correspondents at Bar-le-Duc. At last American forces broke out and began to drive through the retreating enemy's lines in open warfare. Miller, suspecting that the end was not far away, worked out a plan for covering the armistice. He arranged with a U.S. Air Force squadron to make a flight over the whole battle front as soon as a definite hour had been set for the cessation of hostilities. Flying low, the United Press reporter hoped to observe the first reactions to peace as Allied and enemy soldiers laid down their arms and streamed into the open.

Meanwhile the American Army's swift pace created a dilemma for the correspondents: whether to move ahead with the advancing infantry and see the last great push, or remain behind at Bar-le-Duc, where communications were established, and write from Hartzell's reports.

Wilbur Forrest, following the infantry's advance, found himself on the evening of November 2 at Buzancy, northwest of Verdun and more than halfway to historic Sedan. The *Tribune* correspondent had outdistanced censors, press officers, and communications. At nightfall, after hitchhiking on an Army truck, he was thirteen miles by foot and thirty more by automobile from the main correspondents' headquarters at Bar-le-Duc. During the day he had been swept along in the greatest advance of any American force in the war; but he had no typewriter, no paper, no censor or courier to get his copy out. Hopeless as the situation seemed, Forrest decided to give it the old college try. In a roadside tavern he wrote down on the back of an envelope a summary of the situation, based on his observations, and then found a squad of Signal Corps men stringing wires in the dusk. They had a portable telephone transmitter, and Forrest read his notes to an unknown Signal Corps man miles in the rear, asking him to forward it to Bar-le-Duc for the *New York Tribune*. Half an hour later the message turned up at Souilly, Army headquarters, where it came to the notice of Captain Grantland Rice, former sports writer, now a press liaison officer. Rice telephoned Forrest's brief report to Major Bozeman Bulger at Bar-le-Duc. Bulger had it typed and put on the Paris wire. It appeared word for word in the *New York Tribune* the next morning:

With the American First Army, Nov. 2 (night): The German resistance is broken. The enemy is in retreat.

Buzancy, an important road center, was captured this morning. This afternoon American troops loaded on scores of motor trucks were going through Buzancy in pursuit of the fleeing enemy.

The enemy appears to be partially demoralized, though prisoners today were not so many. All objectives laid down for today's attack were obtained.

Another correspondent following in the wake of the First Army's drive, Will Irwin of the *Saturday Evening Post,* received a telegram from George Horace Lorimer, the *Post's* editor: DROP MILITARY AFFAIRS AND RUSH COPY ON RECONSTRUCTION. At Kiel German sailors had begun to mutiny, and most of the warships broke out the red flag of socialism. Irwin quit the field and hurried back to Paris.

In a left bank Paris restaurant the night of November 6, Fred Ferguson sat at dinner with Roy W. Howard and Mrs. Howard. Howard had in his pocket a travel order authorizing him to return to the United States on the first transport leaving Brest. He also had Wagon Lits reservations on the 9 P.M. train from Gare Montparnasse.

Earlier in the day the Wolf Agency, the semi-official German news bureau, had carried a dispatch from Berlin stating that German delegates had left for an unnamed destination to discuss armistice terms with an Allied mission. The day's official A.E.F. communiqué reported further important gains by the First Army on both sides of the Meuse.

Absorbed in the realignment of their news service and the shift in their own affairs, the Howards and Ferguson dawdled over brandy and coffee until Ferguson, looking at his watch, warned the Howards they had not quite half an hour to catch their train for Brest. While Howard paid the reckoning and assembled coats and luggage, Ferguson left the restaurant to summon a taxicab. Taxicabs were scarce; it was 8:45 before they found one and were beginning the ride up the Boulevard Montparnasse toward the railway station. Halfway up the hill the taxicab motor wheezed and died. The driver cranked it half-heartedly two or three times, and announced he had run out of petrol.

In later years Roy Howard used to look back on that moment in Paris when his taxicab stopped in the street and it appeared that the train for Brest would pull out without him. If only he had missed the train that night, he would have been spared the great contretemps in American journalism—the false armistice. But the dice were loaded against him. Fergie hopped out and waved his arms in the middle of the boulevard. Another rattletrap cab was flagged down, baggage and passengers shifted, and the journey up Montparnasse resumed. With less than one minute to spare the Howards climbed aboard their train.

At Brest the next morning they were met by a young intelligence officer who had instructions to conduct them to the office of Lieutenant Arthur Hornblow, Jr., chief intelligence officer on the staff of Major General George H. Harries, A.E.F. commandant at Brest.

'Well, it's grand news, isn't it?' the young man remarked as they left the train shed a few minutes after 9 A.M. On Howard's inquiry, 'What news?' their escort said that the report that the armistice had been signed. Nothing official yet; doubtless confirmation would come in the course of the day. Lieutenant Hornblow, too, had heard the rumor but lacked verification from official sources. The intelligence officer accompanied Mr. and Mrs. Howard to the Continental Hotel, where accommodations had been reserved. Then he suggested they call on Vice Admiral Henry B. Wilson, but when they reached his office between ten and eleven o'clock, the admiral was out; his aide said he would not return until sometime in the afternoon.

At luncheon with General Harries and Major C. Fred Cook, formerly news editor of the *Washington Star*, the armistice rumor was foremost in the conversation. The general had put in calls to Paris, Tours, and Chaumont, and Lieutenant Hornblow was trying to run it down through intelligence channels. So far, no result.

About the time Roy Howard was finishing his lunch with Harries and Cook at Brest, Will Irwin in Paris met a young woman acquaintance on the rue Scribe near the office of the American Express. Miss Kathleen Burke was a British Army nurse, very smart in her uniform. Irwin had known her in London.

'Heard the good news?' she asked the correspondent.

'What news?' Irwin inquired.

Miss Burke said she had just come from the American Embassy, where it was announced that the armistice had been signed at eleven that morning, to take effect at 3:00 P.M. The bespectacled Irwin beamed: 'No kidding.' 'No kidding,' said Miss Burke, 'they got the news by telephone only twenty minutes ago.'

Irwin kissed the young lady and hurried on. Looking around him as he walked toward that crossroads of Paris, where the Boulevard des Capucines enters the Place de l'Opéra, he observed that French men and women continued to go about their business, oblivious to the momentous news. Little did they know! He overtook an Australian officer and, taking his arm, communicated the great tidings. They shook hands and stepped into the Café de la Paix for a drink at the bar. In accordance with an old custom for great occasions, they exchanged hats. From the Café de la Paix they went to Ciro's and, after a brief pause to pass the word there, on to Harry's New York bar in the rue Danou. The war's over! Everybody have a drink! Half a dozen men in assorted uniforms and two Red Cross girls joined up. From 'Pack Up Your Troubles in Your Old Kit Bag,' the singing progressed to 'Madamoiselle from Armentieres—Parley Voo.' Toasts were exchanged. The Red Cross girls exchanged hats with a lieutenant and a corporal, A.E.F. Somehow the celebration seemed curiously localized for so great an event. Outside people went about their business as before and Paris remained calm.

Irwin called the American Embassy on the telephone to ask about the armistice. The embassy answered and said the announcement of the armistice was all a mistake. Somebody did telephone the embassy pretending to be a high French official at the Foreign Office, but it turned out to be phony.

Sadly Irwin hung up the telephone and rejoined his friends at the bar. He had to tell them the armistice was a false alarm. To make amends he bought one more round. He and his Australian friend changed back to their own hats and went their separate ways.

Was it a German agent or a practical joker who called the American Embassy in Paris some time between 1:30 and 2:00 P.M. November 7, 1918, and announced the end of the war? The desperate German military machine, already in massive retreat toward the Rhine, might benefit if Allied pressure at the front was relaxed by a few hours of confusion and uncertainty. A well-timed monkey wrench tossed into Allied councils in Paris could set military and political minds at cross purposes and might give the Germans a breathing space. If such was the purpose of the unknown caller, results were meager. If the hoax was a practical joke, product of some barroom impulse, the results were extraordinary.

When it appeared that the war's end was approaching, Admiral Wilson had asked Captain Jackson, naval attaché at Paris, to notify him immediately at Brest when the armistice was signed. For official and personal reasons he wanted the intelligence promptly, and he knew several hours might elapse before the military and political heads saw fit to make an official announcement. The admiral was not in his office when the message came from Paris, but he had no reason to question the facts in the brief memorandum which he found on his desk in mid-afternoon.

Shortly after 4:00 P.M. Major Cook and Roy Howard climbed the stairs again to Admiral Wilson's administrative headquarters. Ensign James Sellards ushered them into the admiral's private office. The admiral seemed elated and greeted them warmly.

'By God, Major,' he said, 'this is news, isn't it?'

There was no doubt in anybody's mind what news he meant. Admiral Wilson had some papers in his hand, carbon copies of a typewritten paragraph. He called Ensign Sellards and directed him to have an orderly take one copy to the editor of the Brest newspaper *La Dépêche,* another to the bandmaster to read in both English and French to the crowd assembled for a Navy band concert. On each sheet of paper was the brief announcement that an armistice had been signed that morning at eleven o'clock and all hostilities had ceased at two in the afternoon.

Since his arrival at Brest Howard had weighed the chance of speeding the momentous news, if it could be verified, to the United Press in New York. Here was the Atlantic cable-head; a message filed in Brest would go direct to the United States without relay or office delays. It was now so long after the morning's first rumor that Howard doubted that any time advantage remained. However, it was possible the censors were holding up the official announcement in Paris until the heads of government at London and Washington and Rome had been notified. It was also possible that a sudden flood of messages would temporarily paralyze wire facilities out of Paris and produce similar congestion at the cable-head. At

Brest, Howard enjoyed a distinct communications advantage. It was now only 11:15 A.M. in New York.

Major Cook asked: 'Is it official?'

'Official? Hell, I should say it is official! I just received this over my direct wire from the embassy.'

Howard broke in to inquire, since he had announced the news to the naval base and sent it to *La Dépêche* for publication, if the admiral had any objection if Howard put it on the cable for the United Press in New York.

The admiral had no objection. He repeated that it was 'official,' signed by Captain Jackson. Ensign Sellards was assigned to accompany Howard to the cable office. Sellards was fluent in French and known to the cable personnel. As they hurried down the four flights of stairs they heard a roar from the crowd in the Place du President Wilson; then the band began to play 'There'll Be a Hot Time in the Old Town Tonight.'

Howard and Sellards stopped off at the newspaper *La Dépêche*. The United Press used the Brest newspaper's leased wire from Paris to transmit messages during certain hours of the day. Howard wanted to learn if any additional news had come through from Paris, but there was nothing. Also he wanted to retype the statement Admiral Wilson had given him. He found he could not use the French typewriter. The operator who handled the leased wire typed the message on tape and pasted it on a cable blank so that it resembled all other United Press dispatches relayed through Brest. Howard told the operator to add 'Simms' to his own name on the bottom of the dispatch, for William Philip Simms was the only U.P. executive authorized to send collect cable messages via Brest. At the time, the retyping of the bulletin on tape and the addition of Simms's name seemed minor details, but they were to have much greater significance a few hours later.

By the time they reached the cable office it was about 4:45 and the celebration touched off by the bandmaster's announcement was gaining momentum. The censors' room was empty; all the censors had laid down their pencils and joined the throng in the streets. Sellards suggested Howard wait in the outer office while he took the message to the operations room. At this point the brief bulletin passed out of Howard's control, but he assumed that before it was put on the cable to New York, some responsible member of the

French censoring staff would scrutinize it and, if the facts were in doubt, refer it back to Paris. Ensign Sellards, unconcerned about censorship, handed the message to an operator. To the operator its form was familiar; he had transmitted scores of United Press messages sent from Paris over the leased wire, all on tape pasted on a cable blank. Ordinarily, these messages were all approved by censorship before they left Paris, so he had no reason to hold it up for a local censor's stamp. Unaware that it originated in Brest, the operator added a 'Paris' date line and sent it on its way to New York.

The brief message arrived at the Western Union Cable office at 16 Broad Street, New York City, at 11:56 A.M. Eastern Standard time. It was passed by the New York censor at 11:59. One minute later, on the stroke of noon, the relay brought it on the telegraph line to the United Press office on the third floor of the Pulitzer Building on Park Row.

This is what the U.P. editors read:

PARIS 20

UNIPRESS NEWYORK

URGENT ARMISTICE ALLIES GERMANY SIGNED ELEVEN SMORNING
HOSTILITIES CEASED TWO SAFTERNOON SEDAN TAKEN SMORNING
BY AMERICANS

HOWARD SIMMS

There was no reason to pause and reflect. The message bore the names of the president of the United Press and its chief European correspondent. Presumably it had been scrutinized by French censors. The news was the biggest since the start of the century. In a few seconds, the dispatch was fanning out over the United Press wires to Chicago and the Middle West, the Pacific Coast, the South.

The historic bulletin set bells ringing, automobile horns blowing, caused a feverish clatter of typewriters in half the nation's newspaper offices, started the presses of hundreds of extras, brought business to a standstill, filled saloons, disrupted the stock market, demoralized schools and colleges, snarled traffic, filled the air of downtown New York and Chicago with a ticker-tape and torn paper snow storm, jammed telephone wires, brought hundreds of thousands capering in the streets and led some men and women into churches to fall on their knees and weep. No other newspaper dispatch ever touched off such a gigantic explosion.

The Associated Press, worried lest its rambunctious young rival had scored again, anxiously queried its bureau heads in Paris, London, and Washington. All through that November afternoon, as the saturnalia swept the nation, the A.P. denied that an armistice had been signed. It insisted that the war was still going on and advised its clients not to be misled by unconfirmed rumor.

At the United Press office, one supplementary dispatch had been received after the original bulletin—a short message from Howard telling of the celebration in Brest following the armistice announcement. This was corroboration in a minor sense, but it was not confirmation. The jubilation over what at first appeared to be the U.P.'s greatest 'beat' slowly drained away. Anxiety and doubt succeeded elation, as the U.P. editors waited for the telegraph clatter which would spell official verification of their news. But the cable was silent. In the streets, the celebration roared on. Boisterous merrymakers, annoyed that some newspapers ignored the good tidings, snatched thousands of copies of the doubting press off the news stands, tore them up, trampled them underfoot or burned them in the street.

In Brest, meanwhile, Howard waited confidently for further confirmation of the news which Admiral Wilson proclaimed was 'official.' He and Ensign Sellards had to plough through a surging throng of shouting, singing Frenchmen on their way back to Admiral Wilson's office. The admiral was out; there was no further news.

Shortly after 6:00 P.M., Mr. and Mrs. Howard arrived at the La Brassière de la Marine, Brest's liveliest restaurant, where they were to dine with Major Cook and Lieutenant Hornblow. The place was gay and noisy; they had not yet ordered dinner when a member of the Army intelligence staff arrived. He said the French Army intelligence in Brest, having presumably queried Paris, were now saying that the armistice news was not confirmed. This was disquieting. Howard immediately left the dinner table and went to Admiral Wilson's office. The office was closed. The United Press executive located the admiral dining with the French admiral in command at Brest.

Admiral Wilson told Howard that he had received later word from Paris that the earlier report was 'unconfirmable.' He had tried to send that word to Howard, at the Continental, but he had already left the hotel. However, Admiral Wilson did not seem disturbed by the lack of confirmation; he assured Howard he still believed the news was true.

The United Press executive hurried to the cable office and sent an urgent message to New York, saying the report of the signing of the armistice was unconfirmable. This one should have arrived at the United Press office on Park Row shortly after 2:00 P.M., in time for the editors to warn afternoon newspapers to qualify the earlier report. But the Navy censor in New York sent the dispatch instead to the office of the Secretary of the Navy in Washington.

Meanwhile, before returning to his dinner at La Brassière de la Marine, Howard sent a message to the United Press in Paris, asking for confirmation of the armistice report. Ferguson and Simms, already disturbed by anxious queries from New York, turned to the most authentic official sources. Ferguson got in touch with Colonel Edward M. House, President Wilson's personal representative, who had arrived in Paris for top level Allied conferences. The result was negative, and a wire went promptly to Howard at Brest:

RIGHT BOWER [U.P. code for House] SAYS YOU'RE WRONG.

The next morning it was clear that Admiral Wilson's 'official' message from the naval attaché in Paris was based on a mysterious telephone call to the American Embassy, which could not be traced to any authentic source, although reported to have come over a direct line from the French Foreign Office.

For the fourth time Howard climbed the four flights of stairs to Admiral Wilson's office, and the two faced each other in what must have been an awkward, if not painful, review of their predicament. A stenographer was summoned and the admiral dictated a brief 'To Whom It May Concern':

The statement of the United Press relative to the signing of the armistice was made public from my office on the basis of what appeared to be official and authoritative information. I am in a position to know that the United Press and its representative acted in perfect good faith and the premature announcement was the result of an error for which the agency was in no wise responsible.

HENRY B. WILSON

When Roy Howard sailed from Brest on the Army transport *SS Great Northern* on November 10, men were still fighting and dying along the Western Front. The United Press executive clung to the faint hope that an armistice actually had been signed on the morning of November 7 but had not been carried out for reasons known only to the high command. It was suggested that this first armistice had been signed by representatives bearing credentials from the Imperial German Government, and when Marshal Foch learned that government no longer existed, he demanded the German delegates be accredited by the new regime; hence a four-day delay. This hypothesis was found to be without foundation.

Official records disclosed the telegraphic correspondence between Marshal von Hindenburg and Marshal Foch relative to a meeting to arrange an armistice began at 12:20 A.M. on November 7. Replying to the German request for such a meeting, Foch directed the enemy delegates to present themselves to French outposts by the Chimay-Fourmies-La Capelle-Guise road. The German high command replied that their delegates would leave Spa about noon and expected to arrive at the French lines about 5:00 P.M.—the hour when Howard's dispatch was delivered to the United Press office in New York. The German delegates were delayed, however, and did not cross the outpost line at Haudroy, two kilometers northeast of La Capelle, until about 10:00 P.M.

Subsequently, after a long circuitous tour by motor cars, they were conducted to a railway train which had been prepared for them on a siding in the forest of Compiègne, where on the morning of November 8 Marshal Foch received them in his private train with the curt query: *'Qu'est çe que vous désirez, messieurs?'*

Nearly three days were occupied in study by the German representatives of Marshal Foch's conditions and in their requests for some modification of the harsh terms. The French would neither discuss the conditions nor ameliorate them. Under German protest, the armistice was finally signed at 5:00 o'clock Monday morning, November 11. Hostilities were to cease six hours later.

As Marshal Foch insisted that every detail of the meeting should be conducted in absolute privacy, there was not present at the historic occasion a single representative of the press.

XXIV

RUNAWAY CORRESPONDENTS

Alas for Webb Miller's plan to fly over the battle lines on Armistice morning and watch the joyful arrival of Peace from the air! A heavy curtain of mist descended over the Western Front that November dawn. Most airplanes were grounded. The United Press man rode to the front, like the rest of the correspondents, in an automobile.

As 11:00 o'clock approached—the hour when the guns were to fall silent—press cars loaded with newspapermen and conducting officers crawled over the rutted roads through the mist toward the foremost battle lines. As usual they kept up a lively banter to ease the tension. Would they all lose their jobs, now that the war was over, or go back to being police reporters? Some talked of getting to Paris that night for the big celebration. Inwardly they must have been sobered by the task immediately ahead. How does a great war come to an end? What would those first few minutes of peace be like? How could they find words to convey its impact and its meaning to the people at home?

The correspondents differed on what happened when the hour struck. There was no universal theme in their stories, no single clear note; nothing dramatic or moving—except silence. For some, the war slowed down during the morning hours to occasional desultory rounds of artillery fire and routine patrols. One reporter said awaiting the eleventh hour was like awaiting the arrival of a new year. In other sectors correspondents reported the infantry attacking behind a creeping barrage, meeting strong enemy resistance, fighting and dying right up to the last few minutes. All along the line, and in the artillery positions behind it, officers looked at their watches. In one artillery outfit at 10:59 the men joined hands in a long line behind the gun; as the captain dropped his arm they all pulled in unison, so each could say he had fired the last shell.

A correspondent with the Second Army, A.E.F., east of the Meuse described the scene as the fighting came to an end:

> Against the sky-line figures were suddenly silhouetted. They appeared cautiously at first but soon, growing bolder all along the line, they stood upright. These were Germans.
>
> The Americans were not so cautious. As the barrage died, ending in a final husky rumble ... runners went springing [sprinting] along the firing line. Instantly comprehending, the whole line of doughboys leaped from the trenches, fox holes and shell craters, splitting the unaccustomed silence with a shrill cheer. The roar of voices was like an outburst at some great college contest in America. ... The defeated enemy joined vociferously in the cheering.

Then:

> The rolling plain was alive with cheering, shouting men, friend and enemy alike. Germans and Americans were coming along the narrow stretch of ground so fiercely fought over, some shyly and awkwardly, like embarrassed schoolboys ...

For another correspondent the armistice hour was a letdown, a nothing. He watched the artillery send its last shells aimlessly into the air, saw the officers looking through field glasses at the ruined landscape ahead. Then 11:00 o'clock and silence. Nothing much happened, except that men who had been crouching stood upright and some looked at the sky. Officers looked at their watches. A few shook hands. Maybe they were thinking: Well, I got through it. Some got on the telephone to report to division headquarters. American flags were hoisted, and a special detail went along the front pounding stakes in the ground to mark the furthest line of advance. Men looked at each other and lit cigarettes and made small talk.

The correspondents asked the usual questions. Captain, who fired the last shot? Did you take any prisoners this morning? Who was the last man in your outfit to be wounded? Are you glad it's over, or would you rather have chased them across the Rhine?

By noon most of the press cars were headed back, threading

their way through roads still jammed with military trucks. A few returned to Bar-le-Duc; most of the correspondents took the road to Paris. There was sure to be laughter and singing in the cafés, women to embrace, dancing in the streets. Paris would be the place to share the great experience. The boulevards would be lighted again. The hour of glory had arrived.

Perhaps this was the most difficult day of all for the newspaper correspondents. The world was so hungry for the news of peace that every scrap of detail and incident about the war's end would be read and cherished. They knew modern history had come to another crossroads, and it was their task to keep reasonably clear-headed and tell about it. Not tomorrow or next week, but tonight.

The armistice terms had been made known earlier in the day, but what had happened in the railway cars in the Forest of Compiègne from the arrival of the German delegates Thursday night to the signing at 5:00 o'clock Monday morning? Who would describe the scene and fill in the dialogue? That was an essential part of the story, but they could only guess and write sketchily about it.

Each correspondent had observed for himself one small segment of the front as the armistice hour arrived. What about the rest of the long battle line from Switzerland to the North Sea? Had it all ended so quietly, with so little drama? How many men had been killed and wounded on that last day of the war?

Was it true that three newspapermen, led by an Associated Press correspondent, had 'captured' the town of Stenay just as the Armistice was about to be signed? According to the report at 10 rue Ste. Anne, the three had motored into Stenay ahead of the army, finding the Germans already gone, and had later turned it over with ceremony to an American sergeant.

A few correspondents had been in the Chamber of Deputies when Clemanceau arose to announce the signing of the Armistice and read its terms. The French Premier had been received with the wildest enthusiasm; yet his speech had been dry, almost formal in tone, free from the bitterness and sarcasm that usually marked his oratory.

In Paris the newspapermen noted a curious transition. Everyone knew early in the day that an armistice had been signed and the war would surely end at eleven. The great city remained calm.

Until it had been announced officially, until the fighting actually ceased, Parisians went about their affairs and conducted themselves with good sense and restraint. Then at eleven, the great fact established, Paris threw her chapeau in the air, became alive with color, began to sing and dance.

All this had to be rounded up and worked over, pounded out on the typewriter and put on the telegraph wires. Never was there such a night in newspaper history. As the Paris celebration surged through the streets from the Arc de Triomphe to the Place de l'Opéra, overflowed the Montmartre and filled the cafés of Montparnasse with song, the Associated Press office in the Place de la Bourse, the United Press in the rue Rossini, the A.E.F. Press Headquarters in the rue Ste. Anne, the *Paris Herald* office in the rue de Louvre and the *Chicago Tribune*'s office in the rue Royale were scenes of feverish activity.

On a summer night four years and three months before, Wythe Williams and Walter Duranty had stood at the windows of the *New York Times* bureau and listened to the deep-throated roar of Paris street crowds yelling for war against Germany, crying, 'On to Berlin!' Now another roar filled the streets, and thoughtful newspapermen, bent over their typewriters, might have reflected that wars began and ended with much the same unreasoning clamor.

The show was over. Tension built up over months of danger and continuous excitement suddenly eased off. The newspapermen began to relax and unwind. Frank Sibley bought a canary bird on the Ile de la Cité; thereafter in its small cage it accompanied him in hotels, restaurants, bars and trains. Webb Miller climbed a utility pole in the Place de la Concorde and proved it was practical to light his cigarette from a gas street lamp. The correspondent from Pittsburgh established his headquarters at Harry's New York Bar, where he renewed his offer to buy a drink for any soldier from Pittsburgh. Otto Higgins started for Nice to see something of life on the Riviera, but stopped off at an officers' club at Commercy, lost $1500 in a dice game, and had to return to Paris, where he sold his typewriter. Tall, dignified Walter S. Ball of the *Providence Journal* would deposit his cane on the sidewalk of the Champs Elysées, Opéra, or other well-traveled thoroughfares, caper around it several times, and then leap over it.

The correspondents had little consideration for outsiders who tried to edge into their fraternity. A group of veteran journalists in a hotel sitting room, arguing whether the Paris skyline was superior to the soaring towers of Manhattan, resented the intrusion of a California songwriter wearing the uniform of the Red Cross. The Californian took advantage of a lull in the conversation to produce a gold cigarette case. He explained it had been presented to him by Mary Pickford. The correspondents passed it around and resumed their argument. Presently the cigarette case was missing and when the songwriter demanded its return, the newspapermen affected to know nothing about it, saying it was probably brass and who was Mary Pickford? Greatly disturbed, the Californian made one more request for his missing case and then stalked out the door, saying he was going to jump in the river. The newspapermen were sobered to learn later in the day that he had gone directly from the hotel to the Seine and committed suicide by drowning.

On Saturday, November 16, five days after the Armistice, G-2-D moved press headquarters from Bar-le-Duc to Verdun. A mobile mess was organized; newspapermen accompanying the Army of Occupation into the Rhineland would have to be fed, and the food situation in Germany was precarious. Five days at Verdun; then G-2-D packed up again and moved up to Luxembourg. The liberation of Metz after long years of German occupation made a colorful news story, but the correspondents were forbidden by censorship to report that a French airplane had crashed in a Metz street, killing a number of school children gathered for the celebration and injuring more than a score.

Some of the American newspapermen were growing restive under the continuing restraints of censorship and military control. The war was over; why not unshackle the press and let the news flow freely again? A story of great significance was unfolding just across the border in Germany. The Kaiser had abdicated; a new government was trying to function in the defeated Fatherland. What was happening, orderly transition or chaos? Nobody knew for sure. Meanwhile the restless journalists were told to confine their news-gathering to the old battlefields and newly liberated areas of northern France.

On the morning of November 21 two Army Cadillacs bearing five veteran American correspondents and two military chauffeurs traveled east from the capital of Luxembourg and approached the German border. At Grevenmacher on the Moselle one of the chauffeurs, Sergeant Jack Corper, expressed doubt at the route they were following and suggested they turn back. He reminded the correspondents that they were not to go beyond the Army lines. The newspapermen held consultation over their road maps. Lincoln Eyre, in the leading car, told Corper to continue across the river. They were on the right road. He would be responsible if they lost their way.

Besides Eyre, the correspondents were Herbert Corey, Cal Lyon, Fred E. Smith, and George Seldes. Under Eyre's leadership they had decided that morning to make a break for Germany. It would have been foolhardy for one correspondent to try it alone, but with five representing such powerful newspaper organizations as the *New York World* (Eyre), the *Chicago Tribune* (Smith), Associated Newspapers (Corey), Newspaper Enterprise Association (Lyon), and Marshall Syndicate (Seldes), they might get away with it.

Reassured by Eyre, the chauffeurs drove on, and the correspondents soon found themselves on German soil. At Borg the two Cadillacs became involved with a column of retreating German soldiers, and an angry colonel, finding their presence highly irregular, threatened to arrest them. Just as it appeared that their adventure was ended, a German sailor jumped on the running board of one of the cars. He said he had an uncle in Cincinnati, and welcomed the correspondents on behalf of the Workers' and Soldiers' Council of Borg.

Lincoln Eyre, whose command of German was more fluent than the others, told the sailor the five had come to Germany to look into the food situation, to see for themselves whether it was as desperate as had been reported, and to report back to the people of the United States. Eyre indicated that theirs was a friendly mission, and they were sympathetic to the new regime in Germany. The sailor was impressed. Provided with credentials from the Workers' and Soldiers' Council, they fared on. At Trier (Trèves) they were received as the American Food Mission; friendly officials entertained them at dinner, gave them safe conduct papers, and offered to provide transportation. The newspapermen sent the worried Army chauffeurs back to Luxembourg with a note:

> *Trier, Germany*
> *November 21*

DEAR MAJOR BULGER:

Opportunity has been afforded us to visit the interior of Germany and we are availing ourselves of it, considering this of the greatest importance at the present time.

For that reason we are sending back to you the two Press automobiles that have been used by us during the last few days.

We expect to rejoin Press Division Headquarters in a few days.

> Very truly yours,
> LINCOLN EYRE
> FREDERICK A. SMITH
> C. C. LYON
> HERBERT COREY
> GEORGE SELDES

Thus the adventure of the Runaway Correspondents was fairly launched. It was now too late to turn back. They had renounced their subservience to G-2-D and burned their bridges. For a time their affairs prospered.

At Frankfort they were officially greeted by the newly formed government and entertained at what might almost be described as a civic banquet. An important story awaited them at Cassel. There Marshal Hindenburg was supervising demobilization of the German armies. At first Hindenburg refused to see them, but on orders of the local *Arbeiten und Soldatenrat* leader he reluctantly agreed to receive the American correspondents. Presenting themselves at the castle which served as demobilization headquarters, the five newspapermen first encountered the Field Marshal's chief of staff, General Groener. The general's head was bandaged. Eyre, as usual spokesman for the correspondents, made solicitous inquiry: 'Herr General has not been wounded, I hope?' Upon hearing Groener's reply, Eyre turned and gave a free translation to his comrades: 'The General has not been wounded; he has just lost a World War and has a headache.'

Hindenburg was frostily correct as he faced the journalists across the table. Their names and newspaper affiliations meant nothing to the grim Field Marshal; the proceeding was irregular. He replied perfunctorily and in monosyllables to Eyre's first question. Presently he seemed to thaw a little and made a few gruff comments. Herbert Corey and Cal Lyon, who understood no German, came away with the impression that Hindenburg had said nothing worth quoting. Smith found the interview disappointing, too. But Eyre and Seldes insisted that on one point, 'What was chiefly responsible for Germany's defeat?' the Field Marshal had made a responsive answer. The Americans, the numerical strength of the American Armies and their fighting zest, had tipped the scale for the Allies. It seems likely the general may have made some such comment, for it was true and it was what the American journalists wanted to hear. At all events, whatever he had said or left unsaid, they had seen and talked to the great Hindenburg, and the encounter surely would make front page headlines.

They remained three days at Cassel. Seldes' funds were running low. The last one of the party to be taken into Eyre's confidence, he did not have time to send back to Paris for money. None of the others would finance him. For emergency Seldes had a U.S. twenty-dollar gold piece sewn in the lining of his jacket. Now he had to draw on this reserve for his hotel bill. The rascally landlord, pretending ignorance of the coin's value, returned so little in Germany's doubtful currency that Seldes could no longer pay his way.

The five had agreed informally to stick together, but now the group fell apart. Fred Smith, without taking the others in his confidence, caught a plane ride to Berlin. Eyre, Corey, and Lyon continued by train to the German capital. Seldes turned back. Most of the traffic was north and east out of the Rhineland, and Seldes' journey was against the tide, but some trains were running back toward the border. Hitch-hiking, sharing rations with friendly German soldiers, he managed in four days to get back to Luxembourg. He was very much relieved when, across the border, he encountered an American corporal of the Provost Marshal's guard. Pointing to his green arm band, he said he was George Seldes and had just come back from Germany. He asked to be taken to press headquarters.

In the ten days since the five correspondents had ridden off in the two Army Cadillacs their escapade had become a post-war *cause celebre*. The note Sergeant Corper brought back from Trier —a little too cool, a little uppity—had inflamed rather than softened official wrath. Major Bulger had discussed the affair with Captain Morgan. Copies of the note (in quadruplicate) had been forwarded to Colonel Nolan at G.H.Q., and some hint of it reached General Pershing. It was astonishing, it was irregular, it was outrageous that these newspapermen should go into Germany ahead of the Army of Occupation and gather news without military supervision. An alarmed, or at least indignant, officialdom suggested that these newspapermen might unwittingly convey a lot of information to the German high command, information about the disposition of Allied troops, guns, matériel, morale; information which might cause the Germans suddenly to denounce the Armistice and resume the war.

The other correspondents were of two minds. One group denounced the Runaway Five, demanding that their stories be suppressed and their credentials canceled. But most of them took a more moderate view. The war was over; the affair was a natural reaction against the Army's continuation of censorship. This argument must have carried considerable weight, for during this period censorship restrictions were greatly relaxed. There was, however, no relenting in the Army's attitude toward the missing five.

Descriptions of the runaway correspondents were forwarded to all provost marshals' posts as the Army of Occupation moved up in the Rhineland. Through the apparatus set up to deal with the Germans during the armistice period, the same information was sent to Berlin. All cable offices were notified not to accept any messages from the Runaway Five. Belgium and the Netherlands were asked to keep an eye out for them. Channel ports were warned to arrest them should any attempt to cross to England.

Seldes, the first to return, was placed under parole by G-2-D and sent to G.H.Q. for questioning. The others were apprehended in Berlin and returned to Trier, where press headquarters was moved on December 3. Eventually all five faced a long court martial interrogation by the Judge Advocate General and Colonel Nolan.

The wrangle continued through the waning weeks of 1918. The Judge Advocate, unable to find any precedent in his law books, believed nevertheless that the five runaway correspondents were guilty of violating their oaths, the rules of war, and regulations governing Correspondents and Photographers with the United

States Army, as amended and approved September 10, 1918, particularly Part 1, Section 8:

Discipline—No correspondent shall leave the Army to which he is attached, either to go home or *for any other purpose,* except by permission of the commanding general of the Army in the field or the expeditionary forces concerned . . . In extreme cases of offense, where the commanding general thinks it justified, the correspondent may be sent to the rear and held under arrest until such time as the instructions of the Secretary of War in his case have been received.

At a critical moment in the hearing, Eyre produced a letter signed by Colonel Edward M. House, President Wilson's representative and adviser.

The letter assured the *World* correspondent that, although without authority to authorize such an undertaking, he believed that an investigation of conditions in Germany by American newspapermen at this time (immediately after the Armistice) would prove of great value and interest to the people of the United States. Colonel House's endorsement of the project, and the previous good records of the five correspondents, at length tempered official wrath. The Judge Advocate's first intention to confine the offenders to a military prison for six months was shelved; by the end of December they were restored to good standing and permitted to resubmit for censorship the material gained on their expedition. By this time other correspondents had traveled through Germany, and more recent news of the defeated nation and its people were available to the press. The last skirmish between military authority and the newspaperman thus might be said to have ended in a draw.

On December 8, the Press Division with its mobile mess moved to Coblenz on the Rhine, permanent headquarters of the American Army of Occupation. In the month since the war ended, public interest had shifted to President Wilson's triumphant visit to Europe and preparations for the forthcoming Peace Conference. The map of Europe was to be redrawn. The Army of Occupation made little news, and some doubt was expressed about its function.

General Pershing called the newspaper correspondents to a conference at Coblenz. The job of the American Expeditionary

Forces, he said, was not yet finished. Conditions in Russia were disturbing; the moderate Kerensky government had been displaced by a ruthless Communist dictatorship, and now Germany too, was in danger of becoming Bolshevized. He suggested that the news-papermen inform the American people of the dangers inherent in the post-war vacuum, and of the necessity of keeping a strong military force in the Rhineland in order to resist the spread of Bolshevism and help Europe return to peace and order.

Floyd Gibbons, back in Paris, took charge of the *Chicago Tribune*'s Army edition. Gibbons had had a long talk with Colonel McCormick on post-war world affairs, and they were agreed that the United States should go home and steer clear of European involvement.

This was a popular view among the restless, homesick troops. It had been planned to discontinue the *Chicago Tribune*'s European edition promptly at the end of the War, but now Gibbons an-nounced it would be continued as long as American troops were in Europe. Gibbons ran a banner line on the front page every day:

GET THE BOYS HOME TOOT SWEET!

The pattern of the future was beginning to take shape in the news.

APPENDIX

(*From the official report of G-2-D at Chaumont, Haute Marne, May 1, 1919.*)

CORRESPONDENTS WITH THE ARMY

The following is a list of the newspaper correspondents accredited to the American army, arranged according to their length of service. The dates in each case are the dates of their accreditation.

NAME	ACCREDITATION	ORGANIZATION
Raymond G. Carroll	July 9, 1917	*Philadelphia Public Ledger*
Junius B. Wood	July 9, 1917	*Chicago Daily News*
Herbert Corey	July 24, 1917	Associated Newspapers
Floyd Gibbons	October 9, 1917	*Chicago Tribune*
Thomas M. Johnson	October 9, 1917	*New York Sun*
Lincoln Eyre	October 14, 1917	*New York World*
C. C. Lyon	October 15, 1917	Newspaper Enterprise Assn.
Edwin L. James	March 11, 1918	*New York Times*
Naboth Hedin	March 1918	*Brooklyn Eagle*
Wilbur S. Forrest	March 22, 1918	*New York Tribune*
Dennis B. Ford	March 31, 1918	International News Service
Fred S. Ferguson	April 8, 1918	United Press
Newton C. Parke	April 8, 1918	International News Service
James Hopper	April 11, 1918	*Collier's Weekly*
George H. Seldes	May 12, 1918	Marshall Syndicate
Frank G. Taylor	May 12, 1918	United Press
Charles S. Kloeber	July 27, 1918	Associated Press
Bernard J. O'Donnell	August 23, 1918	*Cincinnati Enquirer*
Guy C. Hickok	September 1918	*Brooklyn Eagle*
Burr Price	October 19, 1918	*New York Herald*
George S. Applegarth	October 14, 1918	*Pittsburgh Post*
Charles J. Doyle	October 1918	*Pittsburgh Gazette Times*
Damon Runyon	October 1918	Universal Service
Edwin A. Roberts	November 11, 1918	*Cleveland Plain Dealer*
Webb Miller	November 19, 1918	United Press
John T. McCutcheon	November 19, 1918	*Chicago Tribune*
Maximilian Foster	November 1918	Committee on Public Information
Ward Greene	December 1918	*Atlanta Journal*
Cyril Brown	December 1918	*New York World*
Parke Brown	December 1918	*Chicago Tribune*
Don Martin (deceased)	May 1918	*New York Herald*

CORRESPONDENTS SERVING AS ACCREDITED CORRESPONDENTS

NAME	ORGANIZATION
Clair Kenamore	*St. Louis Post-Dispatch*
James P. Howe	Associated Press
Burge McFall	Associated Press
Philip M. Powers	Associated Press
Lowell Mellett	United Press
Henry G. Wales	International News Service
Fred A. Smith	*Chicago Tribune*
Cameron Mackenzie	*London Chronicle*
Herbert R. Bailey	*London Daily Mail*
H. Noble Hall	*London Times*
H. Warner Allen	*London Morning Post*
H. Prevost Battersby	Reuters Agency

VISITING CORRESPONDENTS OF LONGEST SERVICE

NAME	ORGANIZATION
Frank P. Sibley	*Boston Globe*
Charles H. Grasty	*New York Times*
Walter S. Ball	*Providence Journal*
George Pattullo	*Saturday Evening Post*
W. S. McNutt	*Collier's Weekly*
Arthur Ruhl	*Collier's Weekly*
Otto P. Higgins	*Kansas City Star*
Frazier Hunt	*Chicago Tribune*
Raymond S. Tompkins	*Baltimore Sun*
Casper Whitney	*New York Tribune*
Adam Breede	*Hastings Daily Tribune*
Elizabeth Frazier	*Saturday Evening Post*
Cecile Dorian	*Newark Evening News*
Harry A. Williams	*Los Angeles Times*
Joseph Timmons	*Los Angeles Examiner*
David W. Hazen	*Portland Oregonian*

CORRESPONDENTS WITH SUSPENDED ACCREDITATION

Wythe Williams, *New York Times* and *Collier's Weekly*, accredited July 10, 1917; suspended February 26, 1918

Heywood Broun, *New York Tribune*, accredited July 10, 1917; suspended February 27, 1918

Reginald Wright Kaufman, *Philadelphia North American*, accredited September 21, 1917; suspended April 28, 1918

Norman Draper, Associated Press, accredited October 28, 1917; departed
July 1918

John T. Parkerson, Associated Press, accredited March 30, 1918; departed
in July 1918

AUTHOR'S NOTE: This list is incomplete; it omits J. Westbrook Pegler,
although G-2-D files leave no doubt that he was a fully accredited correspondent from July 1917 to March 1918. It also fails to include the name
of Burnet Hershey, a *New York Times* reporter, who was accredited in 1918.
The circumstances under which two A.P. correspondents, Draper and
Parkerson, ended their service with the A.E.F. in July, 1918 are obscure.
The statement that they 'departed' is obviously a military circumlocution.

BIBLIOGRAPHY

BOOKS BY CORRESPONDENTS

Ashmead-Bartlett, Ellis, *Some of My Experiences in the Great War:* London, 1918, George Newnes, 187 pp.

Ashton, Harold, *First From the Front:* London, 1914, C. A. Pearson, 167 pp.

Barnard, Chester Inman, *Paris War Days:* Boston, 1914, Little, Brown, 227 pp.

Bartlett, Vernon, *Mud and Khaki:* London, 1917, Simpkin, Marshall, Hamilton, Kent & Co., 187 pp.

Broun, Heywood, *The A.E.F.: With General Pershing and the American Forces:* New York, 1918, D. Appleton, 297 pp.

Cobb, Irvin S., *Europe Revised:* New York, 1914, George H. Doran, 467 pp.

————— *Paths of Glory:* New York, 1915, George H. Doran, 414 pp.

————— *Speaking of Prussians:* New York, 1917, George H. Doran, 80 pp.

————— *The Glory of the Coming:* New York, 1918, George H. Doran, 463 pp.

Davis, Richard Harding, *With the Allies:* New York, 1914, Scribners, 241 pp.

————— *With the French in France and Salonika:* New York, 1916, Scribners, 275 pp.

Dunn, Robert, *Five Fronts:* New York, 1915, Dodd, Mead, 308 pp.

Forrest, Wilbur, *Behind the Front Page:* New York, 1935, Appleton-Century, 350 pp.

Fortescue, Granville R., *At the Front with Three Armies:* London, 1914, Andrew Melrose, 271 pp.

————— *Front Line and Deadline:* New York, 1937, Putnam, 310 pp.

Fyffe, Hamilton, *My Seven Selves:* London, Allen & Unwin, 316 pp.

Gibbons, Floyd, *And They Thought We Wouldn't Fight:* New York, 1918, George H. Doran, 410 pp.

Gibbs, Sir Philip Hamilton, *The Battles of the Somme:* London, 1917, Heinemann, 336 pp.

————— *From Bapaume to Passchendaele:* New York, 1918, George H. Doran, 462 pp.

————— *Now It Can Be Told:* New York and London, 1920, Harper, 558 pp.

————— *More That Must Be Told:* New York and London, 1921, Harper, 407 pp.

————— *Adventures in Journalism:* New York and London, 1923, Harper, 363 pp.

————— *Life's Adventures:* Sydney, 1957, Angus & Robertson, 208 pp.

Grasty, Charles H., *Flashes From the Front:* New York, 1918, Century, 306 pp.

Hunt, Frazier, *One American and His Attempt at Education:* New York, 1938, Simon & Schuster, 400 pp.

Irwin, Will (William Henry), *The Splendid Story of the Battle of Ypres:* London, 1915, reprinted from *The Daily Mail* Mar. 4, 1915.

—————— *Men, Women and War:* London, 1915, Constable, 192 pp.

—————— *The Latin at War:* New York, 1917, D. Appleton, 295 pp.

—————— *A Reporter at Armageddon:* New York and London, 1918, D. Appleton, 354 pp.

—————— *Propaganda and the News:* New York and London, 1936, Whittlesey House, McGraw-Hill, 325 pp.

—————— *The Making of a Reporter:* New York, 1942, Putnam, 440 pp.

Jeffries, J. M. N., *Front Everywhere:* London, 1935, Hutchinson, 288 pp.

Johnson, Thomas M., *Without Censor:* Indianapolis, 1928, Bobbs-Merrill, 395 pp.

—————— with Fletcher Pratt, *The Lost Battalion:* Indianapolis, 1938, Bobbs-Merrill, 338 pp.

McCutcheon, John T., *Drawn from Memory:* Indianapolis, 1950, Bobbs-Merrill, 460 pp.

Miller, Webb, *I Found No Peace:* New York, 1936, Simon & Schuster, 332 pp.

Mowrer, Paul Scott, *The House of Europe:* Boston, 1945, Houghton Mifflin, 647 pp.

Palmer, Frederick, *My Year of the Great War:* New York, 1915, Dodd, Mead, 464 pp.

—————— *My Second Year of the War:* New York, 1917, Dodd, Mead, 404 pp.

—————— *Our Greatest Battle:* New York, 1919, Dodd, Mead, 629 pp.

—————— *With My Own Eyes:* Indianapolis, 1933, Bobbs-Merrill, 396 pp.

—————— *With Our Faces in the Light:* New York, 1917, Dodd, Mead, 123 pp.

Ruhl, Arthur, *Antwerp to Gallipoli:* New York, 1916, Scribners, 304 pp.

Seldes, George, *You Can't Print That: The Truth Behind the News, 1918-1928:* 1929, Garden City, N. Y., Garden City Publishing Co., 465 pp.

—————— *Tell the Truth and Run:* New York, 1953, Greenberg, 293 pp.

Shepherd, William G., *Confessions of a War Correspondent:* New York, 1917, Harper, 211 pp.

Sibley, Frank Palmer, *With the Yankee Division in France:* Boston, 1919, Little, Brown, 365 pp.

Thomas, W. Beach, *A Traveller in News:* London, 1925, Chapman & Hall, 306 pp.

Wile, Frederick William, *News Is Where You Find It:* Indianapolis, 1939, Bobbs-Merrill, 505 pp.

William, Wythe, *Passed by the Censor:* New York, 1916, E. P. Dutton, 271 pp.

Young, Geoffrey, *From the Trenches: Louvain to the Aisne:* London, 1914, T. Fisher Unwin, 318 pp.

BOOKS BY NON-CORRESPONDENTS

Austin, Walter, *A War Zone Gadabout:* Boston, 1917, R. H. Hinkley, 156 pp.

Baehr, Harry W., Jr., *The New York Tribune since the Civil War:* New York, 1936, Dodd, Mead, 420 pp.

Callwell, Maj. Gen. Sir Charles E., *Life and Diaries of Field Marshal Sir Henry Wilson,* New York, 1927, Scribners, 2 vols.

Cook, Sir Edward, K. B. E., edited by A. M. Cook, *The Press in War Time:* London, 1920, Macmillan & Co., Ltd., 200 pp.

Gibson, Hugh, *A Journal from Our Legation in Belgium:* Garden City, N. Y., 1917, Doubleday, Page, 360 pp.

Gleaves, Vice Adm. Albert, *A History of the Transport Service:* New York, 1921, George H. Doran, 284 pp.

Gramling, Oliver, *A.P.: The Story of News:* New York and Toronto, 1940, Farrar & Rinehart, 506 pp.

Harbord, Lt. Gen. James G., *Leaves from a War Diary:* New York, 1925, Dodd, Mead, 407 pp.

————— *The A.E.F. in France:* Boston, 1936, Little, Brown, 632 pp.

Hoover, Herbert C., *Memoirs: Years of Adventure:* New York, 1952, Macmillan, vol. 1.

Lytton, Neville Stephen, *The Press and the General Staff:* London, 1921, Collins, 222 p.

March, Maj. Gen. Peyton C., *The Nation at War:* New York, 1932, Doubleday, Doran, 376 pp.

Morison, Stanley, and others, *The History of* The Times: London, 1952, *The Times,* vol. 4, pt. 1, 534 pp.

Morris, Joe Alex, *Deadline Every Minute:* Story of the United Press: Garden City, N. Y., 1957, Doubleday, 356 pp.

Mowrer, Lillian T., *Journalist's Wife:* New York, 1937, William Morrow, 414 pp.

Pershing, General John Joseph, *My Experiences in the World War:* New York, 1931, Frederick A. Stokes, 2 vols.

Read, J. M., *Atrocity Propaganda:* New Haven, 1941, Yale University Press, 319 pp.

Repington, Col. Charles à Court, *The First World War:* Boston, 1920; Houghton Mifflin, vol. 1, 621 pp.; vol. 2, 579 pp.

Riddell, George A., *Lord Riddell's War Diary:* London, 1933, Ivor Nicholson & Watson, 380 pp.

Simonds, Frank A., *Three Years of the Great War:* New York, 1917, I. Goldmann, 58 pp.

Stone, Melleville E., *Fifty Years a Journalist:* London, 1922, Heinemann, 371 pp.

Swinton, Maj. Gen. Sir Ernest D., *Eyewitness:* London, 1932, Hodder & Stoughton, 318 pp.

Source Records of the Great War: edited by Charles F. Horne and Walter F. Austin, Indianapolis, 1930, The American Legion, 7 vols.

World War History: Daily Records and Comments as Appeared in American and Foreign Newspapers, 1914-1926: compiled by Otto Spangler, New-York Historical Society, 400 vols.

The United States Army in the World War, 1917-1919, *Reports of Commander-in-Chief, A.E.F. Staff Sections & Services.* United States Government Printing Office, vol. 12, part II.

INDEX

Gary, Judge Elbert H., helps stranded Americans, 57; motors to Le Havre, 64, 65

Geyer, Lt., credentials for U.S. correspondents at Brussels, 43

Gibbons, Floyd, *Chicago Tribune* correspondent, sails on *Laconia,* 119; torpedoed, sends story from Queenstown, 120; at St. Nazaire, 131; bored at Neufchâteau, 146, 147; First Division story, 166, 167; room in brewery, 188; signs petition, 197; wife to Dijon, 201; at Belleau Wood, 222; wounded, 223; Croix de Guerre, 233; farewell dinner, 234, 235; 'get the boys home,' 278; mentioned, 124, 136, 149, 160, 163, 187

Gibbs, Sir Philip, *London Chronicle* correspondent, seeks credentials, 55, 56, 65; early adventures, 66; at Ypres, 91; joins Red Cross, 98; at the front at last, 104; rarely saw actual fighting, 114; mentioned, 120

Gibson, Hugh, U.S. Legation Secretary at Brussels, 9, 22, 26, 27, 28, 43

Gleaves, Rear Admiral Albert, convoy commandant, 130, 131; mentioned, 132, 135, 137

Glynn, Elinor, 205

Godwin, Harold, 204

Grasty, Charles H., *N.Y. Times* correspondent, sails on *Baltic,* 123; at St. Nazaire, 131, 134

Great Northern, SS, 267

Green, Lt. Joseph C., assigned to G-2-D, 127; censorship understanding with the French, 136; dearth of news at G.H.Q., 148; organizes motor tour, 157; prefers charges, 158; report on Ashmead-Bartlett, 193, 194; mentioned, 135, 163

Groener, Gen., post-war headache, 274

Haig, Gen. Sir Douglas, 237

Hall, Capt. Reginald, confirms *Lusitania* rumor, 107

Hamilton, Sir Ian, report on Ashmead-Bartlett, 193; mentioned, 116

Hansen, Harry, *Chicago Daily News* correspondent, arrives in Brussels, 32; statement on atrocities, 41, 42; follows German advance, 46, 47; detained by Germans, 50

Hapgood, Hutchins, 177

Harbord, Maj. Gen. James G., press recommendation, 126; at Neufchâteau, 145; on First Division move, 164; supply shortage, 181; ruling on division correspondents, 184; ruling on casualties, 197; accompanies Baker on tour, 199; at Montreuil-aux-Lions, 214; commands Second Division, 231; appointed chief of S.O.S., 233; at Gibbons's farewell, 234; mentioned, 248

Harden, Lt. D. H., first American wounded, 169

Harmsworth, Alfred, *see* Northcliffe, Lord

Harries, Maj. Gen. George H., 260

Hartford Courant, 187

Hartzell, Lt. Arthur, at Belleau Wood, 222; rescues Gibbons, 223; at Gibbons's farewell dinner, 234; appointed Information Officer, 250; Meuse-Argonne news service, 254; mentioned, 258

Harvey, George, administration critic, 177; mentioned, 192

Hastings, Daily Tribune, correspondent in Europe, 202, 203

Hawley, Lt. 'Boz,' on *Stars and Stripes,* 187

Hazen, David W., *Portland Oregonian* and *Portland Evening Telegram,* 224

Hearst Newspaper Organization shares news with *Daily Telegraph,* 22; mentioned, 10; *see also* International News Service

Hedin, Naboth, *Brooklyn Eagle* correspondent, 188, 189

Herrick, Myron T., U.S. Ambassador, 55, 62, 75, 84, 87

Hershey, Burnet, x, 281

Higgins, Otto P., *Kansas City Star* correspondent, viii, ix; arrives in

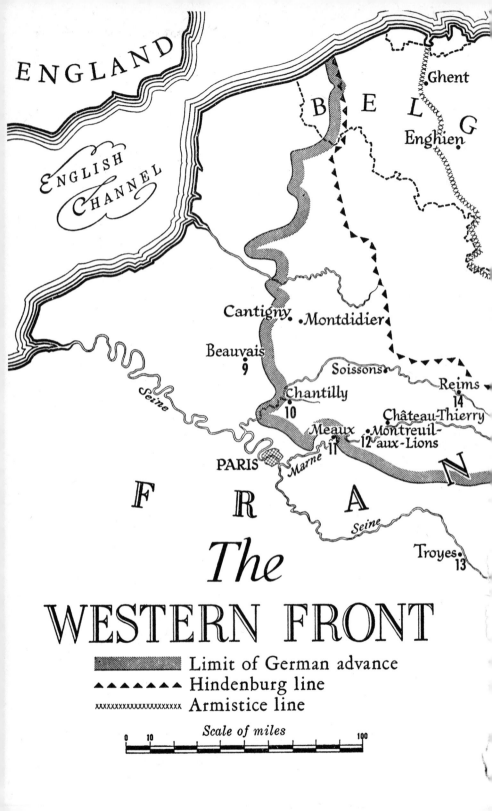

ENGLAND

ENGLISH CHANNEL

BELG

Ghent

Enghien

Cantigny • Montdidier

Beauvais
9

Seine

Soissons

Reims
14

Chantilly
10

Château-Thierry

Meaux
11

Montreuil-
12 aux-Lions

PARIS

Marne

F R A N

Seine

Troyes
13

The

WESTERN FRONT

▨▨▨▨ Limit of German advance
▲▲▲▲▲▲▲ Hindenburg line
xxxxxxxxxxxxxxxxx Armistice line

Scale of miles
0 10   100